Contemporary Brar

For Tamiko.

—JKJ

For Adam, Bryn, and Cindy.

—KAC

Contemporary Brand Management

Johny K. Johansson
Kurt A. Carlson
Georgetown University,
McDonough School of Business

Los Angeles | London | New Delhi
Singapore | Washington DC

Los Angeles | London | New Delhi
Singapore | Washington DC

FOR INFORMATION:

SAGE Publications, Inc.
2455 Teller Road
Thousand Oaks, California 91320
E-mail: order@sagepub.com

SAGE Publications Ltd.
1 Oliver's Yard
55 City Road
London EC1Y 1SP
United Kingdom

SAGE Publications India Pvt. Ltd.
B 1/I 1 Mohan Cooperative Industrial Area
Mathura Road, New Delhi 110 044
India

SAGE Publications Asia-Pacific Pte. Ltd.
3 Church Street
#10-04 Samsung Hub
Singapore 049483

Acquisitions Editor: Patricia Quinlin
Associate Editor: Maggie Stanley
Assistant Editor: Megan Koraly
Editorial Assistant: Katie Guarino
Production Editor: Libby Larson
Copy Editor: Megan Markanich
Typesetter: C&M Digitals (P) Ltd.
Proofreader: Wendy Jo Dymond
Indexer: Sheila Bodell
Cover Designer: Anupama Krishnan
Marketing Manager: Liz Thornton

Printed in the United States of America

Library of Congress Cataloging-in-Publication Data

Johansson, Johny K.

Contemporary brand management / Johny K. Johansson, Georgetown University, McDonough School of Business, Kurt A. Carlson, Georgetown University, McDonough School of Business.

pages cm
Includes bibliographical references and index.

ISBN 978-1-4522-4287-3 (pbk.) — ISBN 978-1-4833-1196-8 (web pdf)

1. Branding (Marketing)–Management.
2. Strategic planning. I. Title.

HF5415.1255J64 2014
658.8'27—dc23   2013034507

This book is printed on acid-free paper.

14 15 16 17 18 10 9 8 7 6 5 4 3 2 1

Contents

Preface

The *Contemporary Brand Management* text is a branding book with a simple, concise but still comprehensive framework for teaching and learning about how to create and manage brands. Although there are many books on branding, what has long been missing is a text with a clear structure and comprehensive managerial approach. This has made branding courses difficult to teach and has limited student takeaways. We hope this text will help solve this problem.

The text's compact nine chapters are structured along the main managerial issues in branding, making for a natural flow of the course material. The first two chapters deal with branding basics, including brand equity. The next two chapters focus on creating new brands, positioning, and building the new brand. The remaining chapters deal with managing and leveraging established brands, including brand extensions and global branding.

The text is intended for the kind of module-length or full-length branding courses that are now increasingly common in business schools, both upper-level undergraduate courses and MBA-level electives. We would also expect it to be useful for the short-term executive courses found today. We visualize that the text will be supplemented with cases and suggest several options for each chapter. For a semester-long course, we have also suggested team class projects for the students.

KEY FEATURES

The simple and logical structure of the text is clearly seen in the table of contents. Most instructors will find it natural, since the chapter headings reflect quite standard marketing concepts. We have selected topics so that each branding issue is distinct from the others but still form a cumulative sequence. We have also simplified the wide variety of branding concepts by carefully analyzing and integrating the available literature. We have included up-to-date material on social media (especially in Chapter 3), but you will find digital media material also in other chapters.

Here are the main features and differences with existing branding books:

- *Brand components.* There are three basic brand components: (1) brand identity, (2) brand image, and (3) brand personality. They correlate generally with the time from the building period to the establishing period and the maturing of a brand.

- *Brand functions.* These are the three functions of a brand: (1) functional risk reduction, (2) psychological risk reduction, and (3) self-expression. These functions, in turn, correlate generally with identity, image, and personality.

- *Brand building.* Building a new brand is covered early, to set the stage. Building a brand is a quite distinct managerial task as compared to managing an established brand (Chapter 5).

- *Brand equity.* The brand "equity" pyramid is discussed early on (Chapter 2). The chapter also introduces brand "value" (in dollars), so that bottom-line concerns come early in the course. (Depending on the instructor and the students, this chapter can be shifted toward the end.)

- *Brands in social media.* Chapters 3 and 4 present new models of how media communications, opinion leadership, and word of mouth have changed with social media. The last chapter has the most recent developments about brand building through social media.

- *Global branding.* With presence on the global Internet, most brands are potentially global from the start. Going international with an established brand is now part and parcel of managing brands (Chapter 7).

- *Brand portfolios.* Portfolio branding issues (Chapter 8) don't arise until the company has several established brands; thus, we can delay issues such as umbrella brands until later in the text.

- *Minicases.* At the end of each chapter there is a minicase focused on the key issues in the chapter. These are short cases on current topics meant to serve as in-class discussion material. The students can also be asked to write short, individual answers to the case questions.

We have tried to make the text readable and easy to understand without compromising rigor. Branding is such a rich and varied—and popular—field that it is difficult to navigate between the various academic concepts, technical terms, and practitioner jargon. The focus on the set of six well-defined basic concepts (three brand components and three brand functions) we think is useful and necessary for effective teaching and student take-aways. The "contemporary" focus of the text should be self-evident. Branding is an area where new ideas crop up continuously. We have designed Chapter 9 to effectively be a chapter where many of the newest developments are captured, but you will find very recent material throughout the text.

The text includes learning objectives at the beginning of each chapter and offers discussion questions at the end of each chapter. It also suggests possible titles for team or individual term projects relevant to each chapter.

ANCILLARIES

For the Instructor

The password-protected Instructor Site at www.sagepub.com/johansson1e gives instructors access to a full complement of resources to support and enhance their courses. The following assets are available on the Instructor Site:

- A test bank with multiple-choice, true/false, and essay questions. The test bank is provided in Word and Respondus formats.

- PowerPoint slides for each chapter, for use in lecture and review. Slides are integrated with the book's distinctive features and incorporates key graphics for visual learning aids.

- Sample syllabi provide example syllabi to build course work and assignments around.

- Chapter synopses serve as great chapter overviews for teaching and lecturing.

- Answers for in-text discussion questions allow for instructors to easily assign questions and review with suggested answers.

- Answers for in-text mini cases allow for further review of the mini-cases.

- Recommended cases provide further reading and research for review.

ACKNOWLEDGMENTS

Our first thanks have to go to the intrepid reviewers who gave advice on two previous drafts. Their help and insights from their own expertise and experience made this a much better text than otherwise. We would like to thank the following:

Lisa M. Cherivtch-Zingaro, Oakton College

Trudy L. Cole, James Madison University, School of Art, Design and Art History

Craig E. Davis, University of Central Oklahoma

Bill Farrar, APR, Virginia Commonwealth University School of Mass Communications

Gary Gray, PhD, Johnson & Wales University

Rebecca W. Hamilton, Robert H. Smith School of Business, University of Maryland

Tammy G. Katz, The Ohio State University Fisher College of Business

Athanasia Panos Schmitt, Gore School of Business, Westminster College

Philip R. Sturm, Averett University

Carlos J. Torelli, Carlson School of Management, University of Minnesota

Tonya Williams Bradford, Mendoza College of Business, University of Notre Dame

We also would like to ask all the brand practitioners and academic colleagues whom we have learned so much from in our past years of working in branding. They include Allen Adamson at Landor, Alan Vandermolen at Edelman, Erich Joachimsthaler at Vivaldi Partners, Dale Tzeng at Ogilvy, Ed Lebar at Young & Rubicam, Erica Parker and Aron Galonsky at Harris Interactive, Simon Anholt of the Anholt-GfK Roper Nation Brands Index, Chris Goodman of KPMG, and Chris Macrae of planetmooc.com.

Among academic colleagues, the writings by Bernd Schmitt at Columbia University, Kevin Keller at Dartmouth, and Rajeev Batra at the University of Michigan have influenced much of the material here, and our former colleague Claudiu Dimofte, now at San Diego State University, was very helpful with insights about global versus local branding.

Our research assistants also provided great support. Thanks are due to Katrina Plummer, Brata Yudha, Roger Tseng, and Henry Sung, who provided data, ideas, and articles, and to Amy Mengyang Tian, Wilbert Hidalgo, and Sharon Chen Shen for graphics. The funding and release time provided by the McCrane/Shaker chair to the first author is gratefully acknowledged.

Last but not least, we want to thank our collaborators at SAGE, acquisitions editor Patricia Quinlin, editorial assistant Katie Guarino, copyeditor Megan Markanich, production editor Libby Larson, supplements editor Megan Koraly and Judith Newlin in Permissions. They worked patiently and diligently with us to help bring this text to fruition.

There's no going back . . . Right or wrong, it's a brand — and a brand sticks.

—Alan Ladd in "Shane" (1952)

PART I

Branding Fundamentals

1

How Brands Work

A brand's idea must be simple in order for its branding to be powerful and compelling.

—Allen Adamson[1]

LEARNING OBJECTIVES

In this chapter, you will learn the following:

- Why brands have become so important today
- About **brand identity,** image, and personality
- How brands reduce consumers' perceived risks
- When brands are used for self-expressive purposes
- About the competitive advantages of strong brands

In recent years, brands have come to be regarded as many companies' most valuable assets. For luxury brands, this is no surprise. The names of Louis Vuitton and Gucci and Burberry have long been recognized as commanding premium prices because of the cachet of their brands. What is new is that companies with more utilitarian products—companies such as Procter & Gamble (P&G), Coca-Cola, and Zara—now also claim brands as their most valuable asset.

---

[1]Allen P. Adamson is managing director at Landor Associates. The quote is from Adamson (2006, p. 223).

How can this be?

The simple answer is that consumers have learned to trust brands, so they rely on them when buying. Brands reduce risk, simplify decisions, and offer emotional benefits. When faced with a choice where a trusted brand is available, consumers do not need to evaluate in detail all the features and specifications of the product, they need not worry about not liking the product or being dissatisfied, and they need not worry about peer group disapproval. In short, the brand reduces functional and psychological risk, simplifies the decision-making process, and in some cases, provides a vehicle for self-expression. To get these benefits, consumers seek out their favorite brands. As the habit of consuming the brand grows over time, the consumer's trust and reliance on it grows as well.

That is why the brand can be so important for any kind of product—and not just for luxury products. Consumers who rely on the brand can be sure they made the right choice. That assurance is the *brand promise.*

This is why firms that build strong brands have a very valuable asset. Their increasingly loyal customer base lowers customer retention costs and reduces the threat from new entrants. Strong brands also improve the firm's ability to charge a price premium, increase its channel leverage, make it easier to enter new markets, and facilitate product line extensions. These benefits generate the brand's equity and value.

To leverage these benefits, the firm must move consumers from knowing the brand, to trusting it, to being fiercely loyal to it. But getting there takes time and focused effort. The consumer has to move from simple awareness of the brand to knowledge of its benefits, to liking, trust, and ultimate bonding. The most valuable asset designation does not come to brands out of nowhere and does not happen overnight. It comes out of long and focused effort. A strong brand has to establish its credentials by demonstrating that it deserves trust and loyalty. Trust has to be gained one experience at a time. And even when a large number of people are loyal to the brand, the trust has to be reinforced on every occasion that a purchase is made. A strong brand is tested every time a consumer buys and uses the product.

Our view of what makes a good brand and what it can do for consumers and the firm that supports it is summarized by Figure 1.1. The remainder of this chapter delves deeper into each aspect of this figure.

WHAT IS A BRAND?

A brand is a name attached to a product or service. The name and its logo are typically registered and legally protected as trademarks. Thus, in practice brands are trademarks that identify the product maker or service provider.

All products have some identification and are therefore potential brands. When generic products became a watchword in the 1970s, "no-name beer" quickly became its own brand name. The Japanese new age company Muji (which means "no pattern") launched a line of "no-brand" products that equally quickly became a fashionable brand, and now you find Muji boutiques not only in Tokyo's Ginza but in New York's Soho district and many European cities (www.muji.com; see Figure 1.2).

Figure 1.1   How Brands Work

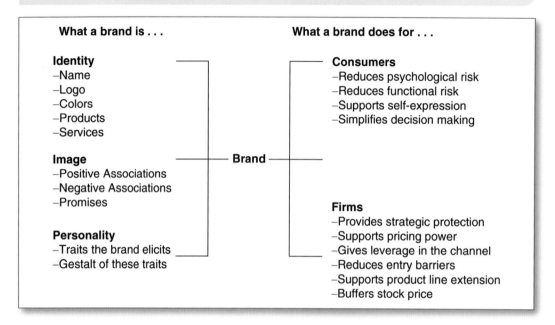

What a brand is . . .

Identity
–Name
–Logo
–Colors
–Products
–Services

Image
–Positive Associations
–Negative Associations
–Promises

Personality
–Traits the brand elicits
–Gestalt of these traits

Brand

What a brand does for . . .

Consumers
–Reduces psychological risk
–Reduces functional risk
–Supports self-expression
–Simplifies decision making

Firms
–Provides strategic protection
–Supports pricing power
–Gives leverage in the channel
–Reduces entry barriers
–Supports product line extension
–Buffers stock price

To be fair, Muji stays close to its original no-brand philosophy, doing little or no advertising for its brand, and does not put its name on the products—which in itself becomes the signifying mark.

Figure 1.2   Speakers From the Muji "No-Brand" Brand

Source: Muji USA Limited. http://www.muji.us/store/art-and-craft/cardboard-speaker-kraft.html

The competitive advantages of a brand derive from the positive associations that customers have with a brand. These advantages can be unique, such as when Bulgari offers the only luxury necklace with antique coins (Vergara, 2012). They can be temporary, such as when the Toyota Prius claims to be the best-selling midsize car in California in 2012 (Hirsch, 2012). The advantages can also be grounded more in perception than reality, such as when Coke loyalists claim Coke tastes better than store brands, yet store brands perform equally well to Coke in blind taste tests. Likewise, competitive disadvantages stem from negative brand associations, such as the reputation BMWs have for being expensive to service (http://forums.bimmerforums.com/forum/showthread.php?211775-Are-BMW-s-more-expensive-to-repair).

A brand is in some ways like a person—it may be born small, is given a name, and may in time grow up to become a well-known name in maturity. The sustainability of a brand advantage comes partly from the legal protection it has against imitation of its name and logo. Competitors may access similar technology and offer equivalent product and service features in their products, but they cannot use the same brand name. Firms with strong global brands have to actively enforce their legal rights internationally against pirates and counterfeits to maintain their reputations. Sustainability also comes from activities that continually regenerate the brand. Such activities, which are discussed at length in this book, include new product introductions, event sponsorships, social media campaigns, and so on.

Since a brand is basically a name, anything with a name can potentially become a brand. This means even a person or a city can be a brand. Figure 1.3 shows some prominent examples that most would recognize.

Figure 1.3 Anything With a Name Can Be Branded

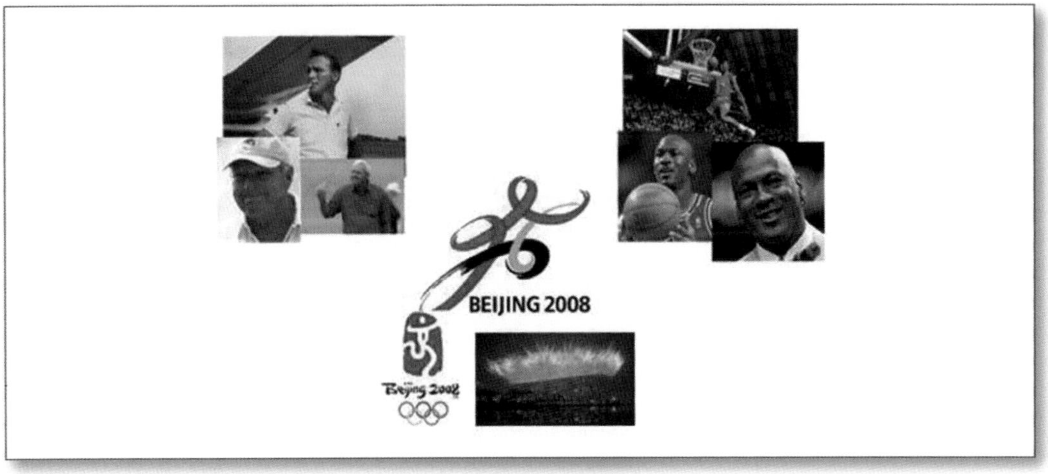

Source: http://commons.wikimedia.org/wiki/File:Jordan_by_Lipofsky_16577.jpg; http://www.rottentomatoes.com/celebrity/michael_jordan/;http://celebgreat.com/Best-awards-winners/Arnold-Palmer.html;http://www.golfdigest.com/magazine/arniesrules;http://blacksportsonline.com/home/2010/03/did-arnold-palmer-punk-ben-roethlisberger/;http://www.boston.com/bigpicture/2008/08/2008_olympics_opening_ceremony.html;http://www.freedomsphoenix.com/Subjects/00218-LAST-olympics-beijing-china-summer-2008.htm;http://sportskenya.blogspot.com/2012/07/road-to-olympics-beijing-2008-olympics.html

It is common now to talk about *personal branding,* but the practice actually is not particularly new. Prominent early examples include sports champions (Arnold Palmer and Michael Jordan), movie stars (Humphrey Bogart is still considered a very strong brand), and sundry celebrities (the Duke of Windsor was an early example; Kim Kardashian is a recent one).

The branding practice has recently been extended to cities. The Beijing 2012 Olympics have been characterized as "branding campaign" (Greyser, 2008), as well as countries (New Zealand has a branding campaign featuring its natural beauty on its website: http://www .newzealand.com/. The activities associated with country and city branding alone have grown rapidly enough to spawn a new industry (Anholt, 2003). Recognized icons such as Egypt's pyramids, Japan's Rising Sun, and Athens' Parthenon actually become brand logos. The functional role of these "different" brands is the same as that of product and service brands: to increase the recognition and attractiveness of the offering to the potential customers—be they sports fans, moviegoers, tourists, or simply gawkers. Chapter 9 discusses these new extensions in more detail.

IDENTITY, IMAGE, AND PERSONALITY

Like a confident and well-known person, a strong brand has a sure identity, a positive image, and a unique personality. These three brand concepts play important roles in brand management, as they support a strong brand and provide strategic leverage to the firm that builds the brand. Our view of how this process occurs over time is represented in Figure 1.4 and is described in detail next.

Brand Identity

To be successful, a brand should have a clear identity. Identity answers the question, "Who are you?" For a person, we might ask for the name, gender, age, photo ID, and what country

Figure 1.4   Evolution of a Strong Brand

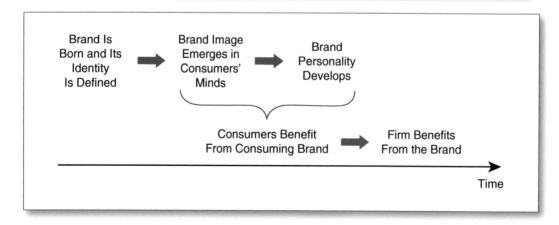

he or she comes from. A brand's identity can be found in its name, a picture of its logo, how old the brand is, what country it comes from, and its product or service category. Identity is the "passport" of the brand—the nationality, the name, birth date, and the product category involved. BMW is a German carmaker, with a blue-and-white circular logo. You may even know that BMW stands for Bayerische Motoren Werke and that its history dates from 1917 when it produced aircraft engines. Today it produces cars, trucks, and motorcycles. Its headquarters are in Munich. By staying close to its heritage of advanced technology and engine production, its identity is a natural foundation on which to build its image as a maker of performance cars—an image that it supports with its slogan, "the ultimate driving machine."

A strong brand has a unique and distinct identity. Consumers know what the brand promises and what the company behind it stands for. BMW has this clear identity (see Figure 1.5). The company gives credibility to the brand when its products fit the expectations that the identity creates. By the same token, when the company ventures outside its traditional range of offerings, the clear identity can become an obstacle. BMW has moved up toward the luxury category of cars—introducing the BMW 7 Series, for example—but only in small steps that still emphasize performance characteristics of the vehicles rather than pure luxury.

Figure 1.5   The BMW Identity

Source: http://wot.motortrend.com/thread-of-the-day-the-best-automaker-slogans-5585.html/image-29276424/#axzz2WEWVXLa4

Brand Image

It is useful to distinguish between brand identity and brand image. Brand identity is what the brand is. Brand image is what the brand seems to be to consumers. The following definition is given by Keller (2013):

> Brand image can be defined as perceptions about a brand as reflected by the brand associations held in consumer memory. . . . Associations come in all forms and may reflect characteristics of the product or aspects independent of the product itself. (p. 44)

While brand identity is based on facts and what managers can control, brand image is determined by the perceptions of customers and outside observers. Brand identity is the foundation on which the image is based. Brand image adds the consumers' perceptions of the product and all the explicit associations that the product conjures among users and nonusers (see Figure 1.6). But the marketer will attempt to mold the brand's image by influencing perceptions of the brand and by formulating a value proposition that emphasizes the brand's strengths.

Figure 1.6   Brand Image

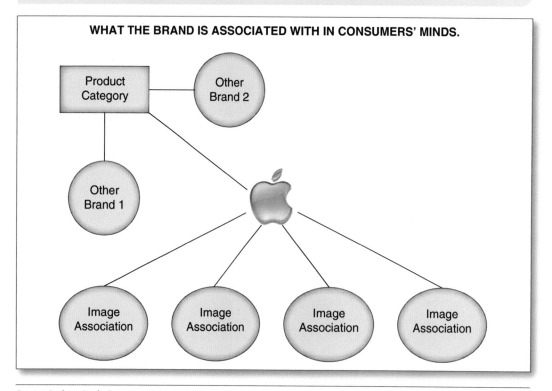

Source: Author; Apple Inc.

As Steve Jobs introduced the various Apple products, he talked about the "insanely great products" that Apple produced. Comparing Apple designs to competitors, he helped create the image of Apple as an outsider company. The "Think Different" mantra was developed. The image of a rebellious but fundamentally creative brand emerged. Later advertising called attention to specific product characteristics to establish competitive advantages—ease of use, slim designs, and so on—but the Apple image was inextricably linked to the Jobs persona.

As people start using the products and word of mouth gets around, the performance attributes of the brand will be recognized and an image of what kind of product an Apple is gets created. Recognition of the brand name and logo will gradually be sufficient to evoke the associations not only of performance but of attributes such as creative, young, and outside of the boring mainstream. A brand asset has been built. Much more about creating a positive image will be discussed throughout in this book.

Brand Personality

The brand personality emerges gradually from all the interactions that consumers have with the brand, as they see the brand in stores, are exposed to its advertising, observe it in use by others, and start to recognize the typical user (Plummer, 1984). The personality of a brand is tied to the identity and the image but goes further in two ways. First, the personality of a brand is the subset of image associations that are personality traits or characteristics. In other words, it is the personification elements of the image. The second way it goes further is that it is strongly influenced by the personality traits of the "typical" user's personality. There will be Apple users and PC users. As Apple's advertising tries to show, PC users are serious, unimaginative, and subservient while Apple users are independent, creative, and rebellious. Gradually, the personality profile of the typical user will be cemented quite firmly in people's perceptions, and these personality traits attach themselves to the brands.

While brand identity answers the question, "Who is Apple?" and brand image answers the question, "What comes to mind when you think of Apple?" the brand personality is what consumers recall when asked, "What kind of personality is Apple?" Brand personality transcends the specific product and service and involves more general traits. One study found that five basic traits (each with several subtraits) could be used to classify brand personalities in the United States—(1) sincerity, (2) excitement, (3) competence, (4) sophistication, and (5) ruggedness (Aaker, 1997).

In practice, the outward expression of the brand personality is sometimes called the brand style. It is the way the "brand walks, talks and dresses" (Schwartz McDonald, 1990). Is the brand "arrogant" (Diesel jeans) or "traditional" (Levi's jeans)? Is the brand "young and active" (Bud Light beer) or "mature and reflective" (Dos Equis beer)? Is it a "warm" inclusive brand (Volkswagen) or a "colder" selective brand (Audi)?

Initially, spokespersons and user personalities drive brand personalities, but gradually the influence goes the other way. When an established brand has a certain personality, consumers use them to express their own personality and style. Users of Apple products probably describe themselves as very creative, not in the mainstream, rebellious but not violent, technologically savvy, smart and young, sensitive and uniquely appreciative of beautiful designs, naïve, and sophisticated at the same time. Many might, consciously or

Figure 1.7 The Origins of the Apple Brand Personality

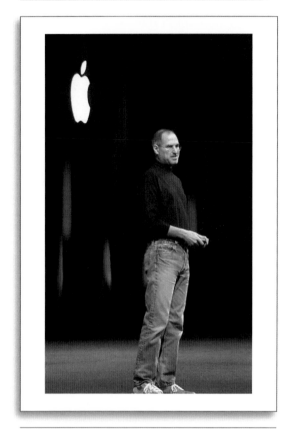

Source: http://upload.wikimedia.org/wikipedia/commons/5/58/Stevejobs_Macworld2005.jpg
Photographer: mylerdude

not, identify with the charismatic Mr. Jobs (see Figure 1.7). In this way, customers of a brand with strong personality tend to use it to display the personality they aspire to. This will also, not incidentally, help cement loyalty to the brand.

Not all brands—not even all strong brands—develop distinct personalities. Brands in many utilitarian product categories do not really develop strong personalities. This is not only because consumers show low involvement with the products. Part of the reason is also that the leading brands do not want to create narrow personalities that appeal only to distinct user profiles. Heinz tomato ketchup, Lipton tea, Pampers diapers, and Colgate toothpaste do well appealing to a large majority of consumers so do not want a confining personality. But other brands can benefit from a distinct brand personality and attempt to create one. Examples of such efforts include not only Apple's contrasting its users against PC users but also Avis ("We try harder"), Nintendo 64 ("Get N or get out"), Dove soap ("Campaign for real beauty"), and Honda ("You meet the nicest people on a Honda").

WHAT BRANDS DO FOR CONSUMERS

At the outset of this chapter, we noted that trusted brands help consumers reduce risk, simplify decisions, and express themselves. In simplest terms, brand names provide a means by which consumers can feel confident even when they shortcut an important decision. This confidence results primarily from a reduction in functional and psychological risk.

Reduce Functional Risk

To economists, the risk-reducing effect of a strong brand is the main role of brands (e.g., Cunningham, 1967; Erdem & Swait, 2001). Customers reduce *search costs* both in terms of having to evaluate all aspects of a product and in terms of looking for alternatives. With a well-known brand, the customer can trust the brand's promise that the product will work and the service will be acceptable. The customer does not need to test the product completely but can rely on the brand name to make a choice. The customer avoids the job of having to examine all features or ask for independent advice from an independent and knowledgeable party. The effort involved in buying is reduced, and there is no need for customers to become instant experts in evaluating automobiles, cell phones, banking services, or over-the-counter drugs. This reduction in uncertainty and search cost is the main economic justification for brands.

Of course, if the consumer is not familiar with a brand, this kind of perceived risk reduction will not happen. Most consumers will have doubts about the functioning of a product whose brand name is new. As an example, the new cars from China will have to prove themselves before their new brand names carry any power. Even if the products are of good quality and get high ratings, the brand name will take time before acquiring the trust and prestige that really matter. In order to help this process along, some new brands try to adapt names and logos of more established brands (see Figure 1.8).

Over time, a brand whose quality is known to be reliable will be relied on by potential customers, simplifying the decision process for customers. In this way, the strength of a brand is tied to the consistency with which its products and services perform. When product performance varies—when some automobiles are "lemons," for example—the brand strength will be diluted. A strong brand might not always have a reputation for high quality, but it should have a predictable quality level—McDonald's is a prime example of such a strong brand, as is IKEA. Their functional predictability lowers perceived risk because customers know what they will get (i.e., customers trust the brand).

Figure 1.8 The Brand Name and Logo for the New Chery From China

Source: http://www.chinacartimes.com/category/chery-automobile/

The brand's promises will set the expectations of a certain level of product performance. The same thing happens not only in goods but also in personal services, as when you go to a restaurant that is rated highly by Zagat or Michelin. Sometimes the actual performance is better—you get happily surprised. Sometimes the actual performance is worse—the brand will be downgraded. The effect is well known to anybody who follows a favorite team in sports (see Figure 1.9).

Reduce Psychological Risk

Marketers have extended the meaning of the brand beyond functional performance. Drawing on insights from social psychology, the risks are extended to include the cognitive dissonance arising from a fear that one has made the "wrong" choice (e.g., Cohen & Houston, 1972; Peter & Ryan, 1976). Even knowledgeable consumers are not always sure they have made the best choice. Should you have paid the price premium for a Sony flat screen TV instead of going with the much cheaper Vizio? As research has found, a lot of the

Figure 1.9   A Strong Brand Delivers on Its Promises

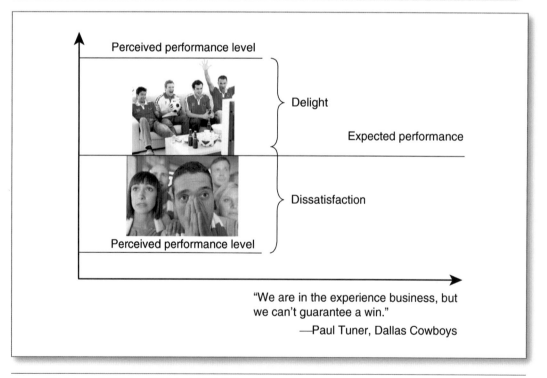

Sources: Thinkstock stk81467cor; Thinkstock 86518367

advertising for a brand is viewed by consumers who have already bought the brand. They want their choice to be supported.

Another social–psychological factor is social disapproval (e.g., Wooten & Reed, 2004). Your spouse or another family member might disapprove of the choice. The choice might not be well accepted by your professional peer groups. Your significant other may offer words in support of your choice ("That's great"), but are they sincere? When faced with a choice between comparable smartphones, the risk is not simply functional but also psychological.

To alleviate social–psychological risk, tangible features and quality are less important than intangibles and brand image. Consider the disaster that was New Coke (Collins, 1995). New Coke was launched to replace the original Coke formula in 1985. Coca-Cola had determined that its taste was superior to the original Coke formula with the help of 190,000 individual blind taste tests. As it happened, the better tasting New Coke was badly received by Coke drinkers. Why? Loyal Coke drinkers insisted that New Coke tasted worse than old Coke. Coca-Cola had built such strong associations with its flagship brand that people did not want to see a new logo. And despite the test results, consumers could not be convinced about the superiority of the New Coke formula (see Figure 1.10).

In commodity-like markets (e.g., industrial products, bank services), the functional risks dominate the social–psychological risks. The brand emphasis is then on convenience and habitual repeat behavior. Gasoline, airlines, hotels, and other service businesses offer frequent user awards to sustain their brands. Strong brands in services can certainly be as powerful as in products. But the service brand is usually sustained by the "stickiness" of usage, created by premium offers for frequency (the carrot) and switching barriers due to network incompatibility, inconvenience, and registration procedures (the stick).

Figure 1.10   The Ill-Fated New Coke

Source: https://en.wikipedia.org/wiki/File:New_Coke_can.jpg; My100cans

Supporting Self-Expression

A strong brand will raise defensive barriers, keeping existing customers loyal and reassuring them that there is no need to evaluate competitive alternatives. However, it is not enough to mitigate functional risk and psychological risk. These functions are important and reflect the reassuring and protective role of a strong brand. But brands also have a more positive and affirmative role in today's markets. The brand is a tool for self-realization, a symbol of aspirations, a sense of

Figure 1.11   The Old College Classic "Must-Have" Jansport Backpack

Source: jansport_superbreak_backpack_hedge_green_1

achievement (e.g., Aaker, 1999; Chernev, Hamilton, & Gal, 2011). Self-expression is not simply an issue for buyers of so-called hedonic products such as luxury watches, sports cars, and designer clothes but affects also more utilitarian choices (Belk, 1988). Not so long ago it seemed almost impossible for a college student to show up on campus with anything other than a JanSport backpack (see Figure 1.11).

The JanSport brand served to define "who you are." In a similar way, acquiring a Mercedes car can foster peer group acceptance and also express a person's identity, an adult who has achieved something and wants to show it. The brand helps express a certain personality, and the brand's character becomes linked to the user. The brand transcends the particular product and service, and becomes a means to an individual's expression of self. They can even take on the mythical aura of icons (see the Iconic Brands box).

Iconic Brands

Figure 1.12   An Iconic Harley-Davidson Tattoo

Source: http://tattoosony.blogspot.com/2011/06/popular-harley-davidson-tattoo.html

The perspective of brands as transcending the product or service has variously been called emotional branding, iconic branding or cultural branding (Holt, 2004; Schmitt, 1999). The common thread in these views is the concept of the brand as an embodiment of a story or myth behind the brand (Zaltman, 2003). It is this myth that allows the brand to become iconic, meaning that they stand for much more than the particular product or service. Apple is more than electronic products. It has the aura of audacity, rebellion, and uniqueness. Corona is more than just a beer; it is a way of breaking away, of pure hedonism, of enjoying life. According to its ads, a Patek Philippe watch tells more than time—it tells of heritage and old family ties, proud achievements long in the making.

It is not surprising to find that these **iconic brands** in their advertising and marketing communications tend to avoid direct references to the product or service and instead focus on users, their dreams and aspirations, and the spiritual uplift that the brand name and logo confer. Consuming a Corona beer is not the point, but feeling the security, the greatness, and the perfection that comes with holding the frosted bottle is the point. "That's me." At the most extreme, consumers become members of the brand "community," sharing a common bond—the Harley-Davidson bikers are a typical example. You will know you have a strong brand when your customers tattoo it on their arms (Figure 1.12).

These kinds of personality *codes* are not new. They originated with luxury brands from Europe, whose main appeal might be with the status cachet that they offer for the user. These brands, called "griffes" by the French (Kapferer, 2004), include names such as Louis Vuitton in trunks and leather goods, Patek Philippe in watches, and Chanel in perfume. They become symbols of a luxurious lifestyle and a perception of high self-worth for the individual user. The concept has gradually been adopted and extended to less exalted products. They even include seemingly mundane names such as Coca-Cola, Corona, Apple, and Starbucks (Holt, 2004). Of course, some brands are not conspicuous enough to stand out. Colgate may not be an iconic brand for this reason. But in the global market place, brands and logos are becoming increasingly overt and explicit. In China, breaking new ground, men's suit labels are sometimes sewn on the sleeves, to make sure the owner's station is duly appreciated.

In a study by one of the authors, sport fans were asked what they wanted to express when wearing the jersey of their favorite team. Figure 1.13 shows some of the most common answers.

The last answer probably reflects the not-so-uncommon reaction to rooting for a team that is a perennial loser.

It is important to understand that the self-expressive effect occurs whether the consumer likes it or not. There is always a risk that the consumer buys a product with a self-expressive effect that is different from that intended. You may think you are expressing a youthful rebelliousness by driving a BMW, but others see your gray beard and dismiss you as a phony. A man may buy a Louis Vuitton bag only to worry afterward that it is basically a woman's brand, even though its ad campaigns have tried to make it more unisex (Chow, 2011). A political candidate getting his outfit from Brooks Brothers will view himself very differently from one with Armani suits—and will in fact be seen differently. "As you are dressed you get judged," as some say.

Simplifying the Decision Process

Because of the reduction of the risks involved in consumer choice, a strong brand can help simplify and shorten the consumer decision process.

Figure 1.13   Self-Expression Via Team Jerseys

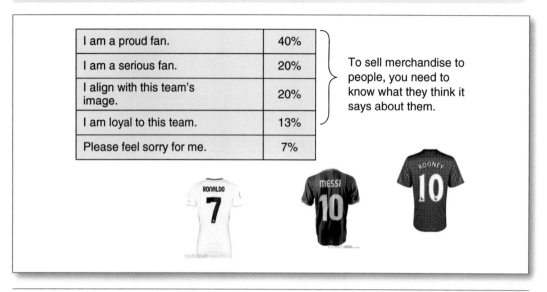

I am a proud fan.	40%
I am a serious fan.	20%
I align with this team's image.	20%
I am loyal to this team.	13%
Please feel sorry for me.	7%

To sell merchandise to people, you need to know what they think it says about them.

Source: http://www.futbolcamiseta.es/ ; soccerpro.com

The consumer decision process is typically seen as a sequence of steps: (1) problem, (2) search, (3) consideration set, (4) evaluation of alternatives, (5) intention, (6) brand choice, and (7) satisfaction (see, e.g., Kotler & Keller, 2012, p. 166). It is well known that in many cases the consumer will not really proceed sequentially through these steps before making a choice (e.g., Dowling & Staelin, 1994). Habitual purchases for many household products and personal care products are common. Impulse buying of low-priced convenience goods happens without much thought or preplanning. Even high ticket items, which usually forces consumers to be more deliberate, do not always follow the sequence of steps. Brand loyalties in cars, computers, and smartphones can make consumers oblivious to competing brands. One reason for the vast number of similar me-too models in these durable goods categories is to offer customers no reason to change brands—all brands have the same features.

It is the risk reduction of strong brands that help assure consumers that even the shortcuts in the decision process are not going to be fatal. Strong brands can offer reassurance to consumers who do not plan every decision. Making choices on the basis of brand strength is a choice strategy that protects against mistakes and frees up consumer time (Bauer, 1960). This is also why there is a lot of research in many countries on the trust of brands among consumers. In the 2013 U.S. rankings by Harris Interactive, the highest trust score was achieved by Amazon.com, followed by Apple and Walt Disney (http://www.harris-interactive.com/Insights/EquiTrendRankings.aspx). In India, the highest trust score in 2012 was reached by Colgate ("Most Trusted," 2012). For emerging markets, the most trusted brands are usually foreign, but in more mature markets they are homegrown. In 2013, the most trusted automobile make in Russia was Toyota, but in Germany it was Volkswagen and in France it was Renault ("Trusted Brands 2013," 2013).

Product Category Differences

Of course, the role of the brand varies across product categories but how is not always obvious. There is surprisingly little research in this area, but research on brand importance has found that brand matters more in categories such as beer, cigarettes, and personal computers and less for paper tissue and headache pills (Fischer, Voelckner, & Sattler, 2010). This suggests that brands matter less in commodity-like products and more in differentiated products.

But whether a product category is commodity-like or not turns out to be partly a matter of promotional effort. Recently, marketers have been able to generate strong brand effects in previously indistinguishable products such as vodka, bottled water, and luggage—as consumers grow ever more sophisticated, even the produce section in grocery stores has become an area of branding importance. Also, somewhat counterintuitive, the brand can be less important as the importance of the choice increases. For example, when products are expensive, the consumer is usually more involved and so will spend more time analyzing specific product pros and cons rather than making a choice on brand alone. Overall, where the risk of disappointment is high, the brand matters more. Also, the brand matters more when consumption is visible to others.

To understand the role of the brand in different categories, it is useful to distinguish between a very rational analysis (this is sometimes called the *think* aspect of a purchase) of the pros and cons of a car, say, and the more emotional involvement (the *feel* aspect) when buying designer clothes, expensive jewelry, and such products (e.g., Claeys, Swinnen, & Vanden Abeele, 1995). In both cases, the brands will support the self-expressive benefits for the customer (see Figure 1.14).

In low-involvement product categories, the brand can also be important but for different reasons. For low-involvement utilitarian think products such as detergent, the brand simply ensures reliability and good functioning. Here is where brand loyalty becomes a strong factor, with habitual purchases of the same brand. The brand may not seem important in a survey, but the consumer simply stays with the trusted choice, with no functional risk taken. In this case, the lack of a well-known brand can be a great obstacle for a newcomer, since no real analysis of pros and cons is undertaken by the consumer.

For low-involvement emotional-based feel products, brands again can serve an important but different role. This situation is a typical "impulse" purchase situation, and exposure to the brand can stimulate a need and desire. Since very little deliberate consideration of the purchase takes place, a well-known brand—as opposed to a lesser brand or a generic—will remove one obstacle for the choice. A famous brand can lower functional risk—you know beforehand what a Snicker's bar tastes like. The psychological risk of guilt feeling may remain even with a strong brand, but advertising tries to find reasons why consumers should indulge. Chocolate brands such as Godiva provide good examples of how brands do matter for sensory pleasures.

Figure 1.14   The Role of the Brand for Different Product Types and Levels of Involvement

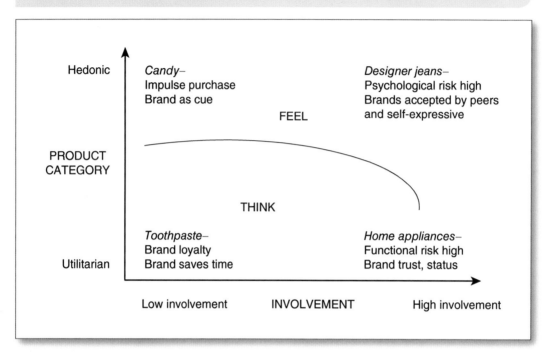

WHAT BRANDS DO FOR FIRMS

Firms that take the time and effort to design and build strong brands can benefit greatly from these investments. The increased consumer preference and loyalty of strong brands are essentially monopolistic advantages that allow the firm pricing advantages and also lead to other benefits.

The firm benefits can be divided into four categories: (1) pricing advantages, (2) channel advantages, (3) entry barrier advantages, and (4) stock market advantages (see Figure 1.15).

Pricing Advantages

Strong brands can collect a price premium from customers over lesser brands. This ability to charge a higher price than competitors will hold even when the products are comparable. A company like Sony used to be able to maintain a 10% premium on its competitors in consumer electronics from Panasonic, Sharp, and others (Nathan, 2001). The recent decline in the Sony brand value has eliminated some of this premium. The strong brand essentially "adds value" to the product, and a weak brand subtracts value.

Figure 1.15   What a Strong Brand Does for Firms

- PRICING ADVANTAGES
- CHANNEL ADVANTAGES
- ENTRY BARRIERS
- STOCK MARKET

- Reduces customer price sensitivity, yields a price premium
- Increases channel leverage, facilitates entry into distribution
- Increases customer loyalty, improves customer retention, lower customer acquisition costs
- Brand equity is a major intangible asset, raises share values

The pricing advantage also relates to price changes. Demand for a product with a strong brand is more inelastic, meaning price increases do not hurt the brand as much as they would a weaker brand. This is the monopolistic effect focused on by economists. In the same way, a strong brand insulates the company from a price war. A firm with a strong brand does not have to respond to a temporary price discount and will try to avoid having consumers become too focused on price. Apple's pricing strategy with the iPhone and iPad offer good illustrations (Farber, 2012). Firms with weaker brands, on the other hand, usually have no choice but to offer price reductions and compete on price.

Channel Advantages

Access to distribution channels is important for very obvious reasons but can also be a real obstacle for market entry. It is common for retailers to charge upfront "slotting" fees for shelf space and ask for shelf stacking, for example, and for wholesalers to require extended credit, high commissions and rebates (Kotler & Keller, 2012, pp. 404–407). A strong brand will facilitate entry in many ways. Retailers like to stock famous brand names, because they attract consumers and can be used as *loss leaders*. A strong brand such as Colgate can negotiate lower fees and avoid extra charges, lowering distribution costs (see Figure 1.15). Some of these advantages play out even stronger in emerging markets where distribution channels are the key to market penetration.

There are other advantages to a strong brand in various distribution channels. In the United States; for example, big brand names contract with universities and other institutions to become the sole provider of certain products. On some campuses you can only find Coca-Cola vending machines, no Pepsi. In other campuses, it is the other way around. Some companies contract for the use of FedEx alone, excluding UPS. More questionable on ethical grounds was the power struggle in the 1990s between filmmakers Kodak and Fuji, where the parties were alleged to have threatened distributors who stocked both brands (http://internationalecon.com/wto/ch2.php). Sometimes even a strong brand is not strong enough to win against another strong brand.

Entry Barrier Advantages

To economists, the consumer's loyalty to a strong brand becomes an *entry barrier*. Because of customer loyalty, a strong brand can defend its market share against encroachment by competitors. Strong brands can also engage in price competition with actual and potential new entrants, lowering market attractiveness and discouraging entry. It might also be able to poach customers from competitors by temporarily offering lower prices. All in all, a firm with a strong brand will have greater pricing power and some monopolistic-like advantages.

A strong brand protects an existing firm from competitive entry because establishing a strong competing brand is expensive. In his classic study of barriers to entry in the United States, J. Bain (1956) pointed to the high advertising costs in America as one major reason for monopolistic advantages. Today, he would likely have stressed the ensuing brand strength of the highly advertised brands even more.

The role of strong brands as entry barriers can be seen most clearly in the difficulty emerging country brands have in penetrating western markets. Because of the practice of outsourcing and the wide diffusion of manufacturing and technology, many firms in emerging countries can produce—and do produce—world-class products and services (as in IT software, for example). But they are unknown, come from a less developed country, and face entrenched strong brands with high loyalty. Such entrants often have to start as subcontractors to better known brand names, and then slowly attempt to grow their own brand. Samsung and LG from Korea took years to grow from original equipment manufacturer (OEM) to world-class brands in electronics and home appliances. Infosys and Wipro from India are now trying to do the same in IT systems, against Accenture, IBM, and others. China's computer-maker Lenovo took a shortcut by buying IBM's ThinkPad, while in automobiles Chinese Geely has bought the Volvo brand and India's Tata has bought Jaguar (Chattopadhyay, Brata, & Özsomer, 2012).

At the same time, strong brands help break down and overcome entry barriers. A company with a strong brand will have an advantage in entering a new or related market. For example, when Unilever extended its Dove soap into the hair care market, it faced a range of strong incumbent brands. By using the Dove brand name, Unilever was able to draw on the existing recognition and strong image of the leading premium Dove soap to establish both shelf space in distribution and mind space among consumers (www.dove.us).

Overcoming entry barriers is also an issue when entering foreign markets. A strong brand's advertising will often spill over country borders, and the brand will be recognized outside its immediate market country. This makes it possible to draw on an existing awareness when entering abroad, helping to overcome the natural resistance of consumers when facing unknown brands, especially if they are loyal to a local brand. The immediate success of strong brands such as McDonald's and Starbucks when entering into some foreign markets has been well documented in the media (Wang, 2012; Weaver, 2012).

Stock Market Advantages

Strong brands offer companies the advantage of higher share prices. Strong brands are recognized in the stock market as very valuable assets, and the effect is a higher share price for the company (e.g., Mizik & Jacobson, 2009; Srinivasan & Hanssens, 2009). The company is more valuable.

Strong brands have also been shown to translate into lower risk for the shares (e.g., Rego, Billett, & Morgan, 2009). This means lower volatility in their shares, and in a stock market downturn, the shares will lose less. The investors recognize that a strong brand will likely have a more loyal following, so the shares are a more secure investment.

Although the brand impact on the share prices usually plays a minor role in brand management, there are cases where branding decisions have been made with an eye on the stock market. The Japanese automobile marque Datsun was changed to the company name Nissan partly in order for Western investors to recognize the Nissan stock ticker (Yip, 2007). Another example was Belgian beer maker InBev deciding to make Stella Artois its one global brand in order to make the corporate global ambition clear to investors in the stock market (Beamish & Goerzen, 2000).

SUMMARY

Brand names and logos have become increasingly important over time as competitive products often share the same functional and design features. Strong brands then become important competitive weapons.

An established brand has a clear brand identity, based on what the company behind the brand stands for. It also has a clear brand image that evokes certain tangible and intangible product characteristics. As it gets more mature and more broadly established, it also can develop a certain personality, transcending the product itself. When these three parts of the brand are diffused in the marketplace, the brand has become an established brand.

The brand can affect consumer decision making at almost every stage of the process from "need" to "purchase" and "satisfaction." There are three basic roles that brands play throughout this process. In the first instance, strong brands serve to reduce functional risk. The brand stands for a promise of acceptable functional performance, and the customer does not need to fully evaluate the effectiveness of the product or service but can accept it on faith.

But customers choosing between competing alternatives also face psychological risk. The perceived risk rises with the amounts at stake but can also consist of the tension involved in choosing between similar alternatives, the chance that the choice is not acceptable to a peer, or simply that the choice affects someone close, as in gift-giving. Again, choosing a well-known brand can help alleviate any cognitive dissonance and reduce psychological risk.

Brands also serve as accessories to an individual user's self-expression. Choosing certain brands can help support a self-image of careless attitude, easygoing personality, and a lively temperament. Other brands can help project oneself as being mature and honorable and having seriousness of purpose. Iconic brands offer images and myths than transcend the particular product or service and become emblematic of the lifestyles and personality of their customers.

How important the brand is in consumer decisions depends partly on the product category. For high-involvement products, brands almost always matter, but even in low-involvement product categories brands can matter as habitual and impulse purchases become more common.

Strong brands also offer clear benefits to companies. These benefits involve monopolistic advantages in pricing and advantages in channel penetration. Strong brands also offer protection via entry barriers for new competitors, and well-known brands can serve to overcome barriers in foreign markets. There is also a more indirect effect of strong brands on a company's share price. Investors and investment analysts tend to favor shares of companies with well-known brands, helping raise the share price of the stock and reduce investor risk.

This text is about brand management. It is a primer on how such a valuable brand is created, built, sustained, and defended. It discusses how to choose a brand name and logo, how to develop an imaginative launch campaign, how to position the brand for maximum effect, how to keep the momentum going as the brand gets established and the initial euphoria starts to fade, and how to manage several brands for synergies in the brand portfolio. The overriding purpose is to help any brand manager define the appropriate strategy for establishing a strong brand, and to show how imaginative management can help avoid the many pitfalls that all strong brands encounter along the way.

KEY TERMS

Brand identity, Brand image, Brand personality, Brand style, Functional risks, Hedonic products, High-involvement products, Iconic brands, Low-involvement product, Psychological risk, Self-expressive benefits, Utilitarian products

DISCUSSION QUESTIONS

1. For a well-known brand of your own choice, try to distinguish between its identity, image, and personality.

2. For what kind of products is functional risk more important than psychological risk? When is the opposite true?

3. Discuss how easy or difficult it is to evaluate an automobile (or some other high-involvement product) without knowing the brand name.

4. Think of examples where your own purchases are based on brand in order to simplify and reduce the time spent. Then explain why this may be a good decision rule.

MINICASE: THE WORLD TRADE CENTER BRAND

For many, a mention of the "World Trade Center" probably brings to mind the terrorist attack in New York City on September 11, 2001. Many might also recognize how that instantaneous mental association is exactly what strong brands also try to kindle. But not many might realize that "World Trade Center" is, in fact, a registered brand name. It belongs to the World Trade Centers Association (WTCA), a nonprofit organization headquartered in New York. The New York Port Authority, which owns the lower Manhattan land where the Twin Towers stood before Sept. 11, 2001, is among more than 300 worldwide members that pay the WTCA a fee to use the words "World Trade Center."

The story of how "World Trade Center" became a registered brand is instructive of the power of branding. After the construction of the Twin Towers was finished in 1973, New York City initiated a branding campaign around the "I ♡ NY" tagline, suggesting a resurgent, global New York. This new brand was registered as a trademark, covering also the use of the heart motif itself. The logo was frequently used by private-sector media and marketing firms, and many firms outside of New York and the United States adapted the motif to their own city of country. Some paid licensing fees, some not. New York City still tries to uphold its trademark by filing objections against unlicensed users and imitators at home and around the world.

As part of the "I ♡ NY" branding campaign, but more as a side effect, the "World Trade Center" became a brand in its own right. In 1986, a retiring official at New York's Port Authority managed to acquire the separate rights to the name "World Trade Center" for the WTCA, where he became president. The WTCA paid a paltry $10 for the name. After the September 11 attack, the name became the most important part of the New York brand, "re-branded" as a patriotic destination. In the most recent years, with New York's resurgence it has again become a symbol of resourcefulness and global ambitions as well. With the wide publicity, it has also become a much more valuable asset.

Of course, today the value of a brand has become more generally recognized. In September 2013, this recognition led to news-reports raising the issue of the unreasonably low price paid for the name. Public officials voiced their concern and particular outrage was directed against the official who had engineered the deal. According to tax documents, he had been paid $575,156 in 2010 and $626,573 in 2011, his last year as president of WTCA (he passed away in February 2013).

The association says its mission is to extend the World Trade Center brand. Its more than 300 members pay the association thousands of dollars every year so they can use the words

(Continued)

(Continued)

"World Trade Center" in their names. WTCA has strict "brand guidelines" that they are supposed to follow, down to the logo and colors for items like letterheads and business cards. The associations Web site states that at headquarters "Focus is on managing and building the WTCA brand, and working with WTCA's intellectual property attorneys to protect our name and service marks around the world . . . also provide support for a variety of member matters" (http://www.wtca.org/cms_wtca/index.php/become-a-wtca/the-wtc-concept).

The association's tax filings indicate that most of its money comes from memberships—$3.3 million in 2011, the last year available. It ended that year with $14.2 million in net assets; it spent $483,573 on conferences, conventions and meetings.

It is clear that WTCA most likely provides a worthwhile service to members and society at large. For example, in 2011 its foundation gave $46,767 to the Japanese Red Cross after the magnitude 8.9 earthquake that struck northern Japan and the tsunami that followed. Nevertheless, as a return on investment, it is clearly difficult to do better than the ROI the WTCA scored on its $10 branding bet.

Discussion Questions

1. The World Trade Center seems such a generic brand name and thus not easy to enforce as a legally protected brand name—what can WTCA claim that makes WTC special?

2. Why do you think the Port Authority let the name go for just $10? What other price makes sense? (Chapter 2 will get into brand valuation more).

3. The public officials in New York are planning to try to claw back some of the earnings of the WTCA President from his relatives—do you think that will work?

4. One learning from this case is that brands can be established from special circumstances for the most generic products—try to think of other similar examples (Hint: Think of branding fried chicken or water).

Sources

Associated Press. (2013, September 18). Port Authority director calls $10 sale of World Trade Center name rights "shameful episode." *The Washington Post.*

Barron, J. (2013, September 18). $10 deal for rights to World Trade Center name draws scrutiny," *The New York Times*, p. A28.

Greenberg, M. (2003, June). The limits of branding: the World Trade Center, fiscal crisis and the marketing of recovery. *International Journal of Urban and Regional Research, 27*(2), 386–416.

SUGGESTED PROJECTS

Brand Identity Exercise: Select three different brands in a category. Write down all the identity elements that are shared and those that are not shared by the three brands. Create a three-circle Venn diagram, with each brand represented by one circle (see Figure 1.16). Write the shared traits in the overlapping regions of the Venn diagram and other traits outside the overlapping regions. If done correctly, brands that share a lot will have a larger region of overlap than those that share less.

Brand Image Exercise: Select a brand of interest (e.g., a university). Get a large piece of poster board, scissors, glue or tape, and several magazines from various different genres. Have a team of two to three people cut and attach pictures and words to the poster board that represent the brand to them. Also allow them to draw or write on the poster board. When finished, ask them to express in one paragraph or less what the brand means to them.

Brand Personality Exercise: Select a brand of interest. Find a sample of 20 people, and give each person the same list of human personality traits. Ask them to circle the three traits that most represent the brand to them personally. Collect the traits from all 20 people, and enter them into a word frequency mapping program (e.g., www .wordle.net/create) to create a brand personality cloud map.

Figure 1.16   Brand Identity Elements

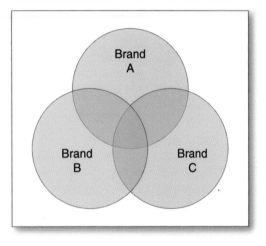

Branding Fundamentals

Brand Equity and Brand Value

Companies must be realistic in what constitutes loyalty: A company is doing well if it receives over 30 % of the purchases made by heavy users in its product category.

—Tom Duncan and Sandra Moriarty[1]

LEARNING OBJECTIVES

In this chapter, you will learn the following:

- About the "pyramid" from brand awareness to **brand loyalty**
- How consumer allegiance to a brand becomes the brand's "equity"
- How the revenues from this equity become the brand "value" to the firm
- How to measure **brand equity** and **brand value**
- About the **lifetime value** of brand loyalty
- About the trade-off between reach and depth

In Chapter 1, we explored some of the benefits of strong brands to consumers and to the firm. But what exactly is a "strong" brand?

---

[1]Tom Duncan and Sandra Moriarty are cofounders of the Integrated Marketing Communications graduate program at the University of Colorado. The quote is from Duncan and Moriarty (1997, p. 42).

In this chapter, we identify what makes a brand strong and lay out a framework for how firms can build strong brands. Generally speaking, strong brands are brands with a high degree of recognition and affinity in at least one significant market segment. That is, there is some depth of affection on the part of the customers for the brand. But the brand also has to have a significant number of such customers. Some brands have a few dedicated fans, sometimes gathered in brand communities, but are also-rans in the market at large. Examples include Saturn, the GM brand discontinued in 2009, and Indian, the old motorcycle brand. Even the infamous car Trabant (see Figure 2.1) from East Germany has a dedicated following (Kelsey, 2010). But these are not strong brands.

Brands with loyal customers and with many customers will be considered strong. They have both high brand equity and high brand value. Brand equity comes primarily from a high level of customer affection and loyalty. It is the "depth" of brand allegiance. Brand value is the dollar value of a brand and depends critically on reaching many customers. It is the "reach" of the brand. Brand value can be seen as the "monetization" of the brand equity across markets. As we will see, the two criteria of depth and reach sometimes go counter to each other. It is easier to kindle affection among few, and reaching out to many customers can weaken the bond with the few. Whether to spend promotional dollars on existing core customers or on attracting new customers is a constant managerial problem.

BRAND EQUITY DEFINED

There are several definitions of brand equity in the branding literature. According to an online business dictionary, brand equity is "the brand's power derived from the goodwill

Figure 2.1 A 1962 Trabant 601, Made in (East) Germany

Source: http://vinson.hagleyblogs.org/2012/09/the-trabant/

and name recognition that it has earned over time, which translates into higher sales volume and higher profit margins against competing brands" (http://www.businessdiction ary.com/definition/brand-equity.html). It can also be thought of as that added value from a brand that makes a customer prefer one product over another product even though the products are otherwise indistinguishable. For example, Keller (2013, p. 41) viewed customer-based brand equity as the differential effect that brand knowledge has on consumer response to the marketing of that brand. The brand provides the tipping point in favor of one product.

In some branding treatments, the concept of brand equity has been used for all the positive associations that a brand name will gradually acquire over time. For example, Aaker (1991, p. 4) defined brand equity as "a set of assets such as name awareness, loyal customers, perceived quality, and associations that are linked to the brand and add value to the product or service being offered." This added value from high brand equity will presumably translate into a competitive advantage.

In this book, brand equity is viewed as a measure of allegiance to the brand from its target segment. A brand with high equity will generally have a deep relationship with its customers, with favorable attitudes and high brand loyalty. The existence of fiercely loyal Coca-Cola drinkers and Apple fans mean that both brands have high brand equity. Of course, some cola drinkers might drink Pepsi when Coke is not available, and some Mac fans may still consider a PC model for work. But on average, brands with high equity can count on the allegiance from its loyal customers.

The equity for a given brand will typically vary across markets. The allegiance to a brand will usually be stronger in its home market than abroad. Lenovo, the Chinese PC maker, is strong in China but less so in the United States and Europe. Acer, the Taiwanese PC brand, is stronger in Europe than in the United States. Even inside countries there are differences. The Corona beer brand has higher equity in the American South and West than in the Northeast. For a brand manager aiming to raise brand equity, one major decision is whether it is better to focus on building increased loyalty in an already strong market segment or try to reach out to improve equity in another segment. This issue will come up later in several places in this book.

BRAND VALUE DEFINED

Brand value is the value of the brand as a business asset. It is based on the equity of the brand in each of the markets where the brand is available. It can be seen as the dollar price that one would pay to acquire the brand name and logo. In some interpretations it is the intangible "goodwill" embodied in the brand, accounting for its value on the balance sheet. In some countries, such as Great Britain, the brand value can be recorded separately as an asset on the balance sheet. In the United States, this happens only when a brand is newly acquired.

When branding professionals declare that the "brand can be a company's most valuable asset," they think of the brand value in monetary terms. Because these values are quite openly quoted and discussed—the Coca-Cola brand is supposedly "worth" close to

$70 billion, for example—corporate management are starting to pay increasing attention the their brand value rankings. For example, when Korean Samsung overtook Japanese Sony in the Interbrand Top 100 Global rankings in 2005, Samsung's corporate management could proclaim that a major goal had been achieved (Quelch & Harrington, 2008). Since brand values tend to rise when the brand is extended across markets, many corporations have been focusing their marketing resources on establishing one or two "flagship" brands with multinational and even global presence (e.g., Johansson, 2012).

Brand equity and brand value are sometimes used interchangeably to identify "strong" brands. In general, this is not a big problem. Many global brands also have a loyal following in many countries—McDonald's, Nike, Apple, and Toyota are examples. These are strong brands. But for managerial purposes, it is important to recognize the difference between equity and value. Brand equity involves customer allegiance, loyalty, affinity, and other emotional ties. Brand value is a matter of dollars (or euros or yuans). A brand can have high loyalty but still not bring in much money. You might "walk a mile for a Camel," as the old slogan went, but this might not be enough to bring in revenue to the brand. Another brand can have relatively low loyalty and still make a lot of money. Many convenience goods, for example, rely more on being easily available at an affordable price than worrying about brand loyalty. Dasani and Aquafina, the water brands from Coca-Cola and Pepsi, respectively, are world leaders but might not score particularly high on loyalty and affinity in any one market.

THE BRAND EQUITY PYRAMID

Managing a brand involves growing brand equity. But to grow brand equity, several stages of consumer acceptance need to be passed through. There is an initial stage when the brand has to create awareness and recognition of its name. Then follows the further development of knowledge and assessment of the brand, which leads into the stage where consumer attitudes and preferences enter. Finally, the brand may reach the stage of loyalty and trust.

The stages of increasing consumer allegiance can be shown as a pyramid with both rational and emotional factors (see Figure 2.2).

Consumer Recognition

A certain level of awareness and familiarity with a brand is necessary before a consumer can use the brand as a cue or information signal. At the most basic level, consumers are aware the brand exists. This level of recognition is not useful, as it does not allow the consumer to consider the brand as a solution to a problem. For this, a higher level of recognition is required. Specifically, consumers must come to recognize the brand as providing a solution for a specific problem. In other words, consumers must recognize the functional risk the brand promises to help remove.

Awareness of this sort can be built through promotional campaigns that create exposure, interest, and attention to the brand as a viable solution for the problem it promises to help

Figure 2.2   The Brand Equity Pyramid

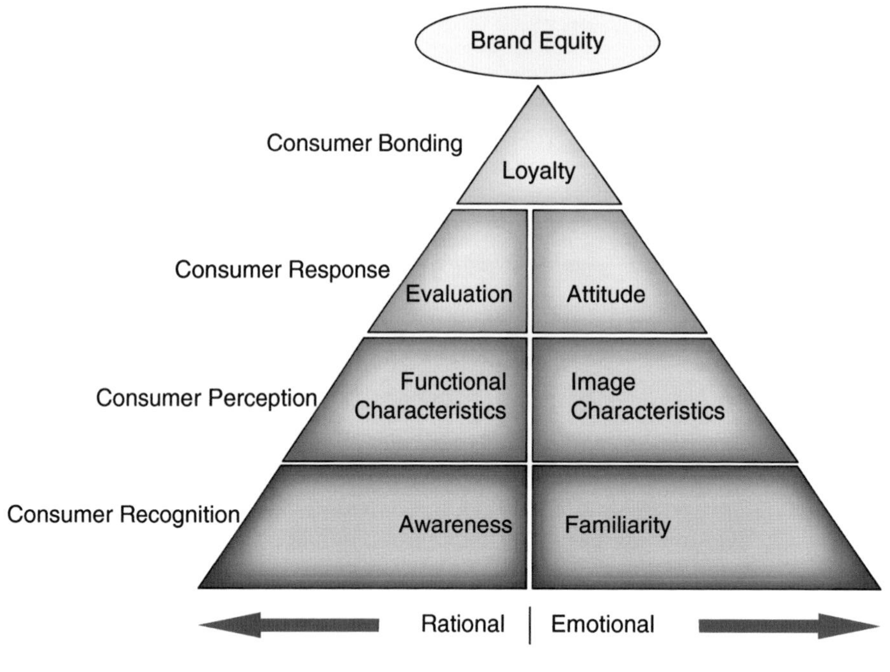

Source: Adapted from Keller (2001); http://www.knowledgenetworks.com/accuracy/fall-winter2010/shutterfly-pharma-fa112010.html

remove. The basic information defining the brand identity drives the promotional messages, aiming to make the brand memorable and accessible in memory. This is the stage where the consumer starts feeling the brand more or less "familiar." Reaching a high level of consumer awareness and familiarity can involve considerable promotional expenditures for a new brand.

Consumer Perception

The next level involves more in-depth knowledge of the product and service behind the brand and also the kind of image that the brand wants to convey. This is where the consumer develops a better understanding of the psychological benefits of selecting the brand. In particular, the consumer comes to believe that selecting this brand will help remove psychological risks associated with choices in the category. Naturally then, the consumer comes to understand what the brand stands for and begins to develop an internal image for the brand. The building blocks of this image are provided by promotional messages and possibly product trials, but now the aim is the presentation of the value proposition of the brand and its positioning. The brand identity is still the basic driver of the perceptions, but gradually the messages attempt to highlight the superiority of certain attributes and points of parity (POP) with competing brands.

Consumer Response

In the next step, the attitudes and preferences of the consumers in the market come strongly into play. The response of the consumer has to be positive in terms of rational evaluation but also in terms of the attitude toward the brand. Creating the right associations and inducing trial and repeat is typically what brand management focuses on. If some of these associations have personality elements, the consumer may start to assign a personality to the brand. Segmentation plays a major role in brand management decisions—it is crucial to choose the right message, the right spokesperson, the right media, for the specific target segment. Tough decisions have to be made about whether the brand should be niche brand or a mainstream brand.

Consumer Bonding

The final step in the pyramid captures the sense that a consumer's allegiance to a brand can become a bonded relationship. When a brand provides functional risk reduction, psychological risk reduction, and opportunity for self-expression, it has all the necessary elements to forge a strong bond with its consumers. Brands that have personalities provide a unique value proposition in that they encourage the consumer to acquire, use, and display the brand to project the elements of the brand's personality onto themselves. Some writers have compared this level of bonding to that of a love relationship. For example, the well-known Hello Kitty brand from Japan's Sanrio company is one that is reputed to inspire some quite impassioned sentiments among its fans (see Figure 2.3). The "charm" is said to lie in the avoidance of giving the character a mouth, which then allows the owner to impute any comforting emotion to the doll (Johansson & Nonaka, 1996, p. 70).

One writer has coined the term *Lovemarks* to transcend the whole idea of a brand (Roberts, 2005). A Lovemark is a product, service, or entity that inspires "loyalty beyond reason" in this version. Not all writers go this far, but it is clear "bonding" in some form can be seen as a "marriage" between the consumer and her brand.

As the pyramid shape in Figure 2.2 suggests, the brand will appeal to an increasingly narrow segment at the highest level of allegiance. Empirically, the final bonding segment tends to be a relatively small part of the total market. The brand with such a fiercely loyal group of customers will also tend to have a strong brand personality, colored by those users. As will be discussed next, the choice between a narrow positioning appealing to a smaller segment with deeply loyal customers or leaving the positioning broader to capture less loyal customers as well is a critical managerial question that has to be decided after careful analysis.

In the pyramid, the brand equity of a strong brand seems to come from the top only, but the fact is that company will also benefit from positive judgments and feelings of a brand even among consumers who are not completely loyal.

Figure 2.3   The Hello Kitty Logo

Source: http://lesleyanneyp.com/2013/02/what-is-the-hello-kitty-story/

Brand management beyond the creation familiarity with the brand name and logo is a steep challenge. The brand manager needs to understand not just the functional strengths and weaknesses of the product behind the brand but also the underlying consumer motivations and attitudes and also how different media can be used to reach and persuade the target consumers. Strong brands have a deeper meaning to consumers far beyond simple awareness and knowledge. The have great presence in the marketplace, and they will usually appeal to more than just a loyal segment.

MEASURING BRAND EQUITY

Because of the importance attached to brand equity and brand value, several independent research agencies are in the business of assessing a brand's relative standing. Although each agency uses its own proprietary method, the equity approaches are generally customer-based and rely on survey responses from representative samples of consumers. Most agencies track many brands and product categories, showing how a brand and its competitors are perceived in different markets at home and abroad. In contrast to brand equity, brand value measurements are typically based on the financial reports with the brand as an intangible asset of the firm. The brand value is then the return the company can expect from the brand asset over time. We will deal with the customer-based equity measurement first.

The basic assumption behind customer-based measures is that the equity of a brand resides in the consumers' attachment to the brand. Brand equity is related to higher perceived quality and lower functional risk but involves also a more emotional attachment to the brand itself. Accordingly, while the respondents to the typical questionnaire may be asked about the quality a brand, the questions attempt to cover questions about attitude and liking; image associations such as trustworthy and competent; semantic opposites such as warm or cold, active or passive; and so on.

These various questions relate to the perceptions a respondent has to each particular brand. The responses are then grouped together using statistical analysis techniques—typically factor analysis—to identify the most basic dimensions that together constitute brand equity.

Brand Asset Valuator Model

One example is the approach used by Young & Rubicam, an advertising agency, to derive its Brand Asset Valuator (BAV) model (Aaker, 1996, pp. 304–309). This model sees brand equity as consisting of brand knowledge and esteem, summarized as brand stature. To arrive at a high level of brand stature, a brand needs to begin by building differentiation and relevance, which together constitute the two dimensions of brand strength. A simplified version of the BAV model is depicted in Figure 2.4.

The BAV "stature" of a brand emerges only over time. Relevance and differentiation are achievable relatively quickly through advertising, promotion and early trials. It takes longer

Figure 2.4 Young & Rubicam's Brand Asset Valuator Model of Brand Equity

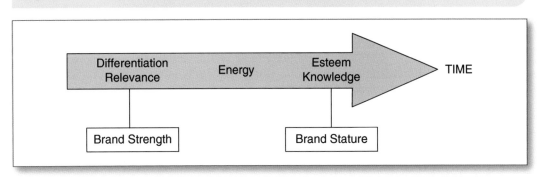

Source: Adapted from Gerzema and Lebar (2008).

to establish a brand's stature, where the brand commands esteem and high familiarity. "Knowledge" here should be interpreted broadly. Knowledge is more than the traditional awareness of a brand, or share of mind. It measures whether there is a true understanding of what a brand stands for, what its products and services are, its positioning, and its values. The "energy" component has recently been added to reflect the momentum that a dynamic brand has. Energy is the dynamism in a brand. It is the consumer perception of motion and direction in a brand.

How to combine the scores on the "pillars" of BAV's brand equity model is not obvious. A brand with high equity will generally have both stature and strength. But one cannot simply sum up the scores on each of the four dimensions. For example, a highly differentiated brand might not be able to score very highly on relevance, since it likely targets only a niche in the market. Therefore, most companies use the BAV model to diagnose on what dimensions the brand is strong and where the brand needs more support (Gerzema & Lebar, 2008, pp. 44–49). A familiar brand scoring high on knowledge might concentrate promotional spending on raising its esteem score, for example.

EquiTrend

An alternative customer-based brand equity measure is the one provided by EquiTrend from Harris Interactive, another research firm. In EquiTrend, the brand equity is computed as a product of three factors: (1) familiarity, (2) quality, and (3) purchase intention (Johansson, Dimofte, & Mazvancheryl, 2012).

To calculate brand equity, the familiarity score is first weighted, giving more weight to the very familiar consumers. The mean of quality and purchase consideration is then multiplied by the weighted familiarity measure. The result is translated into an index from 0 to 100 (Johansson et al., 2012). Table 2.1 shows the top EquiTrend brands and their scores in 2012.

EquiTrend also measures overall relevance by averaging the equity score across all respondents, regardless of familiarity. Similar to the BAV model, EquiTrend also provides measures of a brand's distinctiveness. The EquiTrend data are used by companies to assess not just brand equity but also the degree to which the brand is unique and without direct competitors. This means that for EquiTrend a high score on brand equity can still be found for a brand that is relevant to a relatively small market. For example, Yuengling is a comparatively small brand (mainly distributed on the U.S. East Coast) but has the allegiance of its customers and a favorable ranking in terms of brand equity at 65.60. For comparison, among the larger brands Heineken came in 9th place with a score of 54.48 and Corona in 10th place at 53.93. Bud Light beer, the leading brand in the United States, scored a low 49.43, below the beer category average of 53.91.

MEASURING BRAND VALUE

The financial value of a brand is the amount that a brand is worth in terms of future revenues. The projected revenue stream depends naturally on the level to which the brand

Table 2.1 Top EquiTrend Brands in 2012*

1.	Amazon.com	79.09
2.	Google	76.27
3.	Hallmark	74.51
4.	Craftsman (Sears)	74.47
5.	Microsoft	74.04
6.	Lay's Chips (PepsiCo)	73.95
7.	Subway	73.07
8.	Home Depot	72.81
9.	Coca-Cola	73.30
10.	Rubbermaid	71.80

Source: http://www.harrisinteractive.com/Insights/EquiTrendRankings.aspx

*Not including candy and chocolate brands.

attractiveness and consumer allegiance can be maintained going forward, but at the heart the brand value is the net present value (NPV) of the expected cash flow. When a company is acquired, its brands may be worth more than any other assets.

The specific details of the brand value measures are less transparent than the survey methods. Nevertheless, the main features of the approach can be identified. The objective is to convert the value of the brand into dollars and cents. To do this, the approach attempts to identify how much of a company's revenues and profits are due to the brand itself.

The share of revenues and profits due to the brand requires an assessment of how much the company would make without the brand. This is akin to asking how much a generic brand would make—for example, how much would Coca-Cola make if it were just another cola? The answer is typically derived in two steps. First, for the product category, how important is the brand? Second, how strong is the brand in question? Thus, for the cola example, how important is the brand in the choice of colas? Then, how strong is Coca-Cola relative to competition? Those two factors together are assumed to explain how much the brand is worth.

To get the actual dollar figures, the starting number is often the intangible earnings of the company. The actual computations are complex and are proprietary as well. But for management it is useful to at least have a sense of what is involved. The approach used by Interbrand is instructive (see Calculating a Brand's Financial Value box).

Calculating a Brand's Financial Value

Interbrand's calculation of a brand's value can be broken down into eight distinct steps, as follows (Lindemann, 2004):

Step 1. Identify the separable markets/market segments where the brand is sold.

Step 2. Estimate intangible earnings in each market as brand revenue less operating costs, taxes, and cost of capital employed.

Step 3. Assess the role of the brand in intangible earnings to get a "branding index." First ID the demand drivers (e.g., price, advertising), then the role of the brand in the drivers' effectiveness (e.g., lowering the price elasticity). The closer this index is to 1.0, the more important is the brand for the product category. A value close to zero here means that the brand has no impact for this category.

Step 4. Calculate present earnings due to the brand by multiplying the intangible earnings in Step 2 by the branding index.

Step 5. Estimate the competitiveness of the brand to derive a "brand strength score" that indicates the long-term viability of the brand.

Step 6. Calculate the appropriate discount rate as a function of the brand strength score—stronger brands have lower discount rates.

Step 7. Compute the NPV of the projected future earnings attributable to the brand, using present earnings and the applicable discount rate.

Step 8. The total brand value is the sum of the brand's NPV in each market.

Note that the calculations focus on the intangible earnings, which can be derived from the annual reports. From a branding perspective, the two key steps are Steps 3 and 5. In Step 3, a "branding index" is estimated. This is a measure of the share of intangible earnings due to the brand. In Step 5, the calculation involves how the brand will fare in the future. The brand strength score goes higher (and the discount interest rate lower) if the brand can easily defend itself against newcomers.

The brand strength scores typically vary across segments and markets. Microsoft is a company whose brand strength is very high, since the company has such a dominant share of the market. But what might happen in the future is also important. Apple, for instance, may have a lowered brand strength score because its future will depend very much on how the company will fare after Steve Jobs. A consequently higher discount rate means future sales are less certain.

For the top brands, the resulting brand value rankings for the top brands become a source of "bragging rights" for company CEOs. Interbrand releases its annual "Top 100 Global Brands" in *Business Week* while its main competitor Millward Brown releases its "BrandZ Top 100" report in *The Financial Times*. The brand values reach remarkably high levels. Table 2.2 offers a comparison between the top 10 Interbrand (http://www.interbrand .com/en/best-global-brands/2012/Best-Global-Brands-2012.aspx) and BrandZ from Millward Brown (http://www.millwardbrown.com/BrandZ/Top_100_Global_Brands.aspx).

As can be seen, there is also some disagreement in exactly how valuable some brands are. For example, the large difference in dollars attributed to the Apple is surely a reason for caution. Things may have changed somewhat between May and September but hardly much. The Samsung brand's strong showing in Interbrand rankings with $32.9 billion is not really reflected in BrandZ, where Samsung is worth $14.1 billion, with a rise of 16% but in 55th place. As the agencies readily acknowledge, these numbers do not really reflect brand equity (customer allegiance) but sometimes monopolistic market power (China Mobile), simple reach (Google), and possibly temporary advantages (AT&T and Verizon with the iPhone).

Two things should be pointed out. One, most of these brands are global, with reach into major markets in the world. Second, one might have expected the well-known luxury brands to score higher. They do score well but are still behind more mundane products. In

Table 2.2   Top 10 Global Brands in Value, Interbrand and BrandZ Rankings 2012

Interbrand (September 2012)			Millward Brown's BrandZ (May 2012)		
Brand	Value $M	Change	Brand	Value $M	Change
1. Coca-Cola	77,839	8%	1. Apple	182,951	19%
2. Apple	76,568	129%	2. IBM	115,985	15%
3. IBM	75,532	8%	3. Google	107,857	−3%
4. Google	69,726	26%	4. McDonald's	95,188	17%
5. Microsoft	57,853	−2%	5. Microsoft	76,651	−2%
6. GE	43,682	2%	6. Coca-Cola	74,286	1%
7. McDonald's	40,062	13%	7. Marlboro	73,612	9%
8. Intel	39,385	12%	8. AT&T	68,870	−1%
9. Samsung	32,893	40%	9. Verizon	49,151	15%
10. Toyota	30,280	9%	10. China Mobile	47,041	−18%

Source: Interbrand (www.interbrand.com) and Millward-Brown (www.millwardbrown.com).

the Interbrand rankings, Louis Vuitton comes in at number 17, with a value of $23.6 billion. In BrandZ, Louis Vuitton is also the highest, at number 21 with $25.9 billion. In beer, with many global brands, the highest ranking brand is Budweiser. It comes in at number 31 in the Interbrand list, with $11.9 billion, a decline of 3% from 2011. Corona comes in as number 89 with a worth of $4.1 billion, a rise of 3%. Heineken is at number 92 with $3.9 billion and also a 3% rise. In the BrandZ listing, Budweiser is at number 48, with a value of $15.9 billion—no increase. Of this total, Bud Light is valued at $8.4 billion, rising 17%. Heineken (at $6.1 billion and minus 8%) and Corona (at $5.1 billion and minus 6%) are not ranked among the top 100 brands.

REACH VERSUS DEPTH

As we have seen, a strong brand does not only have deep "vertical" allegiance among consumers but also a wide "horizontal" reach into many markets. The issue of *depth* of consumer attachment versus great *reach* of the brand is particularly critical in measuring the equity and value of global brands. In an effort to rank the most powerful global brands, Forbes decided in 2012 to develop a measure that combines both the value of the brand and its customer equity.

To determine the best global brands, Forbes started with a universe of more than 200 global brands (Badenhausen, 2012). The chosen brands had to have more than a token presence in the United States, which eliminated some big brands like China Mobile, the world's largest mobile phone provider.

First the brands were ranked on financial metrics, and earnings over the past 3 years were averaged. Next, similar to Interbrand, a percentage was used to derive earnings due to the brand based on the role brands play in each industry. Brands were considered crucial for beverages and luxury goods, less for airlines, for example. This resulted in a final sample of 130 brands each valued at more than $2.5 billion. The earnings were indexed so that the top score would equal 100.

To get at the brand equity and consumer allegiance part, a sample of 2,000 global consumers was surveyed on their perceptions of the brands on 13 attributes such as the following: "invests in innovative ideas and research," "positively impacts the everyday lives of its customers," "maintains high standards of quality in its products," and "understands and addressees my unique needs." Ratings were averaged and the scores were added to derive at a sum score for each brand. The sum was indexed so that the top score would equal 100.

Forbes then averaged the two scores to determine the world's most powerful brands. The result is listed in Table 2.3. It is the combination of financial value and positive consumer sentiment, which puts the Apple brand on top of this inaugural list of the most powerful global brands. But the brand value ultimately carried more weight because of the wide disparity in values, which range within the top 100 from Apple at $87.1 billion to Armani at $3.1 billion.

Note that in terms of consumer perceptions, Apple is not at the top of the list, getting beaten by Microsoft, Intel, Google, and BMW. McDonald's in particular seems to receive

Table 2.3 Forbes' 2012 Rankings of the 10 Most Powerful Global Brands

Rank	Brand	Brand Value	Consumer Perception	Revenue ($Bil)	Advertising ($Mil)	Industry
1	Apple	87.1	11	108.2	933	Technology
2	Microsoft	54.7	1	73.7	1,600	Technology
3	Coca Cola	50.2	29	22.8	3,256	Beverages
4	IBM	48.5	20	106.9	1,373	Technology
5	Google	37.6	7	36.5	1,544	Technology
6	Intel	32.3	6	54.0	2,100	Technology
7	McDonald's	37.4	85	85.9	769	Restaurants
8	GE	33.7	49	124.7	-	Diversified
9	BMW	26.3	5	73.7	-	Automotive
10	Cisco	26.3	15	46.1	325	Technology

Source: Badenhausen (2012).

surprisingly low consumer allegiance scores, but this is probably a reflection of its wide reach. The larger the brand is in terms of reaching different consumers, the more difficult it is to maintain a unique consumer allegiance.

Both brand equity and brand value measures have their proponents. Brand equity measures are sometimes seen as "soft" measures since they are based on perceptions and attitudes, not easily translated into revenues and profits. The financial brand value measures by contrast are "hard" measures, clearly identifying the expected revenue streams. But the precision in these dollar figures can also give the misleading impression of accuracy. Managers need to remember that they are just projections into an uncertain future— and the differences in the two listings show the uncertainty of these projections.

There are very few published studies directly comparing customer-based and financially based brand measures. One recent study of global brands in the 2008 financial crisis does shed some light on which measure seems better (Johansson et al., 2012). The study found that the share prices of top value brands (from Interbrand) fell 32.9%—even more than the stock market as a whole (the S&P 500 dropped about 30.3% in the 4-month September-to-December 2008 period). At the same time, the shares of the brands with the highest equity (from EquiTrend) fell significantly less than the market (29.5%). The customer-based equity measure outperformed the financially based brand value measure. The article concluded that in an economic downturn, customer allegiance to the brand is a better predictor of brand strength than a possibly over-optimistic financial projection of future revenues.

Regardless of what measure is used, it is important to track brand equity and brand value over time. According to the BAV model, a strong brand needs "momentum," for example, and rising equity over time is important (Gerzema & Lebar, 2008). A strong brand also needs to best competition, making brand equity a matter of comparative advantage. This means brand equity and brand value measurement needs to be repeated over time and also cover major competitors. Such measurement is expensive. This is why measuring brand equity and value has become an attractive business opportunity for independent research agencies that can syndicate their periodical reports and sell them to all firms in an industry.

LOYALTY AND CUSTOMER LIFETIME VALUE

One hears a lot about the intense devotion of some consumers to their favorite brands. It is perhaps most prominent among Apple users, Harley-Davidson bikers, BMW (and now Audi) drivers, and Coca-Cola loyalists. The brand has to generate excitement, happiness, and involvement and, yes, even love. Instead of attracting many and perhaps new customers, the brand manager should focus on building relationship with existing customers (Reichheld & Sasser, 1990)

The stress on brand loyalty is often couched in terms of the lifetime value of a customer (known as CLV, or customer lifetime value). The CLV is the net present value of a customer over his or her expected life span with the company. Figure 2.5 shows the basic idea of a

Figure 2.5   The Customer Lifetime Value

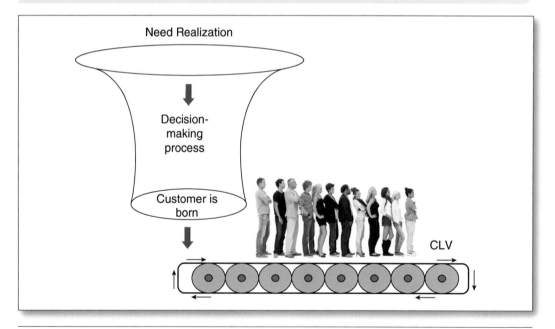

Source: Istockphoto.com/Yuri

Note: CLV = Customer Lifetime Value

customer being "born" and then how that customer generates value for the firm over his or her lifetime.

Studies have demonstrated the advantages of focusing on customers with high CLV (Blattberg & Deighton, 1996; Gupta et al., 2006). One particular case where CLV becomes prominent and obviously beneficial is where brand loyalty is based on "stickiness." Stickiness refers to the case where an initial investment by the consumer necessarily leads to further purchases in complementary products. A typical case is where a consumer opts for an iMac Desktop, for instance. Later purchases of applications and accessories and upgrading will more likely involve other Apple products. The required complementarity makes the brand loyalty a matter of stickiness, convenience, and learning rather than brand allegiance as such. In these kinds of cases, the recruiting of a new customer from a competitor can be exceedingly expensive, justifying the typical CLV argument about the relative cost of attracting new customers (Reichheld & Sasser, 1990).

For many smaller brands, however, sales and profit results are not usually sufficient to allow the company to focus on retaining existing customers. A niche strategy with smaller market share does not have enough customers to support a full branding program. The few loyal customers do not buy enough to justify the spending. Brand management also has to see to it that the brand reaches a larger market and moves into new markets. Empirically, the data show that in many cases marketing resources are better spent on attracting new customers. This alternative strategy becomes increasingly preferable the smaller the brand's market share is.

To grow a small brand, the brand manager should focus more on increasing brand reach than brand depth. Widely known brands reap the benefits of being the "second choice" regardless of loyalty levels. On any one purchase occasion, situational and other factors (brand availability, gift buying, variety seeking are examples) could derail the loyal choice. Then a widely known brand that is not the one the buyer is committed to is often chosen. As data analysis has shown, the probability of a brand being chosen as a "backup" choice is almost proportional to its market share (Sharp, 2010, claims this is one of the few "laws" of marketing).

The fact is that in most product categories, most buyers are only light users. Light users are usually not as bonded and loyal as heavy users. Loyalty programs do not usually attract new customers or light buyers; these customers generally see less value of the programs. In addition, many customers participate in several competing loyalty programs. Empirical data show that even when most brands feature loyalty programs, there is a lot of brand defection (Sharp, 2010). This means that loyalty programs become mainly a necessary defense against losing customers. In addition, the evidence shows that for at least low-involvement products such as most consumer packaged goods (CPG), convenience and availability often dominate any feeling of loyalty.

GROWING A STRONG BRAND

The basic brand strategy suggested by the consumer-based brand equity pyramid model is to move each customer from awareness to positive affect to loyalty. This is useful insofar it goes. Customer relationship marketing and loyalty programs are examples that fit into this strategy framework. But a strong brand grows not only with depth of allegiance but also with reach across a market. A strong brand is one that has both great depth and great reach (see Figure 2.6).

The strategy to increase depth is more readily appreciated. It is the one that refers to the Harley-Davidson aficionados, Apple communities, and Virgin's frequent-flier patrons. It fits well with the so-called customer-based measures of BAV and EquiTrend, and with the awareness-to-bonding pyramid. But a strong brand also involves reaching out to a significant share of the market. This does not mean discounting prices and mass merchandising. Low prices and mass outlets will more likely reduce brand equity without a compensatory rise in brand value, as companies such as Casio, Dell, and Reebok have learned the hard way.

"Reaching out" entails letting many consumers know about the brand and making the brand acceptable, liked, and, if not becoming the first choice, at least to be in the consideration set. It a strategy is to attract the light and more fickle consumers. Such a strategy focuses on making the brand easy to find, safe to choose, and simple to purchase. It is less concerned with exclusive commitment and more concerned with being physically and mentally available.

Figure 2.6   The "Golden Middle" Where Strong Brands Have Both Reach and Depth

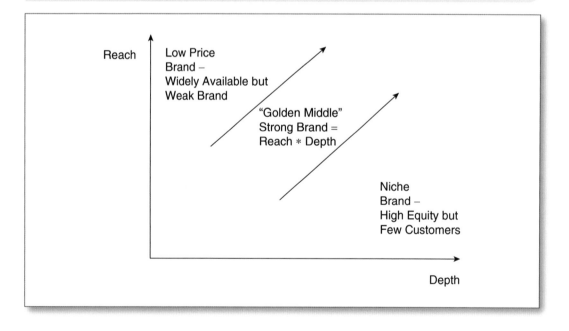

Of course, everything else the same, getting any one consumer to progress from brand awareness and knowledge to affinity and bonding is useful and beneficial for sales. The idea is that loyal brand bonding does the selling job. But courting one customer at a time can be too expensive—the amount of sales generated by one customer is simply too small. This is why some high-end companies like Mercedes-Benz, Giorgio Armani, and Martha Stewart try to introduce slightly lower-end model versions. One might think that among the so-called heavy users the purchase frequency and amounts ought to justify focused marketing expenditures. Again, however, the data show how mistaken this strategy can be. Even in cases where the 20% of "heavy users" account for 80% of total sales—cases in point are colas and beer—there is still a large of number of sales to light users. As research shows, the so-called Pareto share in most categories is only about 50% in a year, meaning just half of the sales come from the top 20% of the customers (Sharp & Romaniuk, 2007). The 50% light users also contribute revenues.

A successful branding strategy should certainly involve making existing customers more loyal. However, the strategy should also aim to make the brand more distinctive, widely available in a cluttered store environment (physical availability) and with easily recognized name, logo, and coloring. The stress should be on distinctiveness; with true product differentiation difficult to maintain, for many categories, the consumer makes decisions quickly and without much premeditation. This is why brand loyalty also still is important; from the consumer's viewpoint, it simplifies the choice, even without necessarily engendering a passionate outburst.

SUMMARY

Customer-based brand equity represents the culmination of the effort to connect the brand into a meaningful relationship with the customer. The new brand moves from awareness and familiarity to positive customer perceptions and attitudes and ultimately bonding. The dollar value of the brand increases with the depth of allegiance for a high equity brand but also rises as the brand expands into many markets. Even if the new customers do not become loyal to the brand, the increased exposure and availability boosts the brand value. The available financial measures of brand value show the highest scores for the largest brands, a reflection of the importance of growing the brand by reaching new markets, making global brands particularly valuable in monetary terms.

Extensive customer relationship programs are useful in raising loyalty scores among existing customers and increasing CLV. However, the expense of loyalty programs is often not justified for smaller brands with few existing customers—partly because even loyal customers may defect for lack of brand availability and other reasons. In addition, many loyalty programs reward customers for purchases they would have made anyway. This is why the manager of a small brand is often better off growing the brand by expanded reach.

For larger brands, by contrast, investing in existing customers via loyalty programs is often a beneficial strategy—especially among heavy users who might be induced to increase the frequency of purchases further.

KEY TERMS

Brand allegiance, Brand Asset Valuator (BAV) model, Brand depth, Brand equity, Brand equity pyramid, Brand loyalty, Brand reach, Brand value, EquiTrend, Interbrand, Lifetime value, Niche brand, Powerful brands

DISCUSSION QUESTIONS

1. Identify a niche brand that has a high level of allegiance among a relatively small part of a market. What would happen to brand loyalty, if anything, if the brand expanded to a larger part of the market?

2. Can you find a large global brand that also seems to have a fiercely loyal following? Define its target segment, in terms of demographics, lifestyle, and customer benefits. Is it a mainstream brand in all markets?

3. Discuss the CLV concept, and try to find a brand example for which retaining a customer really does seem to pay off (hint: look for examples where stickiness explains the loyalty).

4. Discuss how brand equity can suffer when the brand expands its reach. Any examples? Any counterexamples, where extending reach increases equity?

MINICASE: HOW MUCH IS MANCHESTER UNITED'S BRAND WORTH?

In recent years, the valuation of sports teams has become an increasingly important financial topic. Part of the reason is the astronomical salaries that sports stars command. Additionally, some stars become celebrities outside of the arena also, with lucrative sponsorships, extravagant lifestyles, and an icon of the "rich and famous"—David Beckham, the British soccer player is one prominent example. As a personal brand, Beckham was valued by Forbes at $20 million in 2013 (http://www.forbes.com/pictures/mlm45jemm/4-david-beckham/).

Beckham came up with Manchester United, often cited as the world's most valuable soccer club. The Red Devils, as they are called, were bought by the Glazer family from the United States in a leveraged buyout in 2005. To cash in on its brand value and pay down debt, the new owners decided to go public in 2012. The IPO on the New York stock exchange offered shares at $14 apiece, making the capitalized value of the club about $2.3 billion.

The shares did poorly at first but soared in 2013. By end of January the share price stood at just under $17, with Manchester United's stock outperforming the S&P 500. The increase in its stock price pushed up Manchester United's value (equity plus debt) to $3.3 billion, the highest value of any team in the world. But in the ensuing Champions League tournament, Manchester did not perform all that well, and the club was overtaken by competitors.

One was Real Madrid, a perennial foe. The Spanish team posted greater returns in its annual report for 2012–2013, with the highest returns of any team in sports ($650 million during the 2011–2012 season), and revenues up 62% over the last 3 years. Signing superstars Cristiano Ronaldo and, more recently, Gareth Bale has led to increasing income from advertising and sponsorships as well as attendance and television. The club has an equipment supply deal with Adidas worth $42 million a year. It has signed a new sponsorship deal with Emirates Airlines to put its name on the team's shirts, a contract worth $39 million annually for 5 years. As a result, the value of Real Madrid increased to $3.4 billion, narrowly beating out Manchester United.

Real Madrid did better than Manchester United in the Champions League, but was still beaten in the semifinals. In the final, two German teams met. Bayern Munich, a 10-time finalist, defeated Borussia Dortmund by a score of 2–1. As a result, the winning German club vaulted to first place in the soccer team brand ratings, as published by BrandFinance, a brand equity ratings firm headquartered in London that covers brand equity sports ratings. BrandFinance calculates the value of the brand equity in terms of an equivalent royalty rate: if a team would license its name to a third party, how much would it be able to charge. This allows the company to focus only on the brand equity, expressed in terms of dollar value.

The brand equity rankings after the 2013 Champions League final from BrandFinance show the top three teams as follows:

1. Bayern Munich   Brand value: $868 million

2. Manchester United   Brand value: $845 million

3. Real Madrid   Brand value: $627 million.

The estimated value of Bayern Munich using the enterprise value (equity and debt) calculation used for the Manchester United and Real Madrid above is about $1.3–1.5 billion. That is, the enterprise values of the three teams as of late summer 2013 are as follows:

1. Real Madrid   Team value: $3.4 billion

2. Manchester United   Team value: $3.3 billion

3. Bayern Munich   Team value: $1.3–1.5 billion

(Continued)

(Continued)

In fact, Bayern Munich is also beaten by one arch-rival, Barcelona, at $2.6 billion, and is virtually tied by London's Arsenal.

Discussion Questions

1. Why is there a difference between the stock market valuation of a sports team and its brand value?

2. If brand equity represents allegiance to a brand, what would you say determines the brand equity of a soccer team (or any sports team)?

3. What factors would you say determine the value of a soccer team (or any sports team)?

4. Use the difference between your answers in Questions 2 and 3 to explain why Bayern Munich could lead in brand equity but still not be the most valuable team.

Sources

Badenhausen, K. (2013, July 15), Real Madrid tops the world's most valuable sports teams. *Forbes,* Business.

Brand Finance. (2012, May). Brand Finance football brands 2012. Retrieved from http://brandfinance.com/knowledge_centre/reports/brand-finance-football-brands-2012

Nicola, S. (2013, May 28). Bayern ousts Manchester United from soccer brand-value throne. *Bloomberg.* Retrieved from www.bloomberg.com/news/2013–05–28/bayern-ousts-manchester-united-from-soccer-brand-value-throne.htm.

Ozanian, M. (2013, September 7). Real Madrid scores record revenue and team's value increases to $3.4 Billion. *Forbes,* SportsMoney.

SUGGESTED PROJECT

Equity Exercise: Develop and apply a brand equity index to three brands in a particular category. To keep things simple, we recommend building an index with three components, to measure the three things a brand does (i.e., functional risk reduction, psychological risk reduction, and self-expression). For each brand, measure how well it is perceived to accommodate these three purposes. For example, for functional risk reduction, you might ask this question: How well does Brand X deliver on its basic promise to _____? The response scale could be a 101-point scale anchored by 0 = *worse than all other brands in this category;* 50 = *average for brands in this category;* 100 = *better than all other brands.* Have a small sample of people respond to each question, and weight the responses to form an index (Note: A simple averaging of three responses, one for each aspect, assumes equal weighting of the three brand functions.)

Branding Fundamentals

Brand Positioning

Differentiation without relevance is of little value.

—David Aaker[1]

B*rand positioning* is the act of designing a company's brand strategy to occupy a distinctive place in the mind of target consumers to maximize the potential benefit to the firm (Kotler & Keller, 2012, p. 276). A "distinctive place in the mind" does not simply mean that consumers remember the brand. They should also have favorable beliefs and emotions about the brand. Preferably these beliefs and emotions should also be more positive than their feelings about competitor brands (Ries & Trout, 2000). The more a brand dominates

---

[1]David A. Aaker is vice chairman of Prophet Brand Strategy and professor emeritus of marketing at the Haas School of Business, University of California at Berkeley. The quote is from Aaker (2011, p. 302).

the competition in this battle for the consumers' positive beliefs and emotions, the more likely it is that consumers will see the brand as a means to reducing functional and psychological risk and as a means for self-expression. This is why good positioning emphasizes attributes where the brand has relative advantages and deemphasizes attributes where it is relatively weak.

Before deciding on the various attributes to be stressed in positioning, it is important to determine what the intended target segment is and who the competitors are. A strong brand will be recognized far beyond its target segment, but the perceptions that matter most are those of the target segment. Levi's jeans might target the young and restless in all countries, but the brand is stylish in some markets, utilitarian in others. Its positioning and value proposition differ across markets.

POSITIONING ELEMENTS

Positioning Statement

The brand positioning strategy is based on company objectives and represents the way the brand manager would like the brand to be perceived and evaluated. The positioning statement captures the desired brand position (Kotler & Keller, 2012, p. 506). It follows a standard template: our brand is positioned toward *target segment* and offers a *product* that is superior in terms of *points of distinction relative to the competition.*

For example, a possible BMW positioning statement might be worded as follows:

BMW's position is aimed towards the driver who values performance and luxury in a car, and who needs a vehicle whose performance in terms of handling, driving comfort and acceleration is superior to other luxury cars, and whose luxury features are at least comparable to other luxury vehicles in the same class.

As a tool, the positioning statement helps keep everyone in the organization on message when engaging in brand positioning activities.

Positioning activities do not always succeed at creating the intended brand position. What determines the position is ultimately how consumers perceive the brand. The resulting position might be different from the intended position. A well-known example is the boxy Honda Element, a car that was initially positioned as a fun and affordable utility car (high enough to accommodate a bicycle) for college students but ended up positioned more as a practical and inexpensive vehicle for an older generation—still a successful position but not quite what was intended (http://www.askmen.com/cars/car_vs_car/1_car_vs_car.html).

Value Proposition

When done well, brand positioning supports a clear and compelling value proposition for consumers in the target market. The brand's "value proposition" is the unique value it provides customers over competing brands (Aaker, 1996, p. 71). The superior benefits in the proposition should correlate directly with the positive associations and "promises" of the brand. For its target market, BMW might frame a possible value proposition as follows:

> We help our customers who enjoy driving succeed by offering the best handling cars on the road. Unlike other cars, the technology and engineering in a BMW ensure the best handling cars and the most enjoyable drives, as demonstrated by outstanding quality scores and the highest buyer loyalty in the automobile market.

Another example is Levi's jeans. Levi's value proposition has changed over time, although the brand identity has changed little. One version of the value proposition was the "Unbuttoned" campaign in which Levi's stressed a core message of "not pretending, no restraints, freedom of thinking and acting and do your own thing," which helped the brand with a more youthful segment while still staying close to Levi's original strengths in active lifestyles (Insites Consulting, 2009).

Brand Platform

Combining the positioning statement and the value proposition, some companies develop a brand platform formula. Brand platforms tend to be comprehensive statements, moving from company values to brand vision to communication strategy. One representative example is the platform developed by Kirschner, a multinational branding agency hailing from Brazil (see Figure 3.1).

Figure 3.1   Kirschner's Brand Platform Formula

Discover	**Concept**	**Develop strategy**
"We start by learning and understanding your company and values. We research the consumer market, evaluate internal (products, pricing, capabilities etc) and external (gaps, needs, positioning etc) cultural elements of the company. With this information we figure out where the best opportunities are".	"After the research step we develop the structural elements of the brand concept. These are the gaps in the market where the brand can create value and develop. Motivating and touching consumers in different ways".	"In this step we provide the tools and define the vision for the brand to develop and grow. The brand idea and it's purpose is expressed by communication that is the voice that engages the consumer. We can develop the tools that communicate the voice of the brand like website, magazine, music, games, event, POS materials and products".

Source: www.kirschnerbranding.com.br

Slogans and Mantras

The positioning and value proposition are frequently abbreviated into a brand slogan or mantra for easy communication. Slogans are the traditional versions used in advertising. They are usually devised by the creative arm of the ad agencies and may or may not highlight the core of the brand. Examples are "When it rains it pours" for Morton Salt and "We bring good things to life" from General Electric (GE).

Mantras aim to communicate the essence of the brand. In addition to Nike's "Authentic Athletic Performance," there is Disney's "Fun Family Entertainment" and also Apple's "Think different" and Audi's "Vorsprung durch Technik" (Kapoor, 2010). These are short (3 to 5 words) statements that serve to focus the activities of the brand teams and avoid extending the brand too far (Keller, 1999). A Nike brand should be "authentically athletic," for example, steering the brand clear of leisure shoes and casual gear.

The difference between slogans and mantras relate to the intended audience. Slogans are aimed at customers, creating memorable taglines that help anchor the brand in the consumer's mind—sometimes with the help of jingles and a catchy melody (Yalch, 1991). The most successful jingles can become popular and take on a life beyond the commercial, increasing word of mouth exponentially. A famous early example is the "I'd like to buy the world a Coke" TV commercial, which first aired in 1971.

The commercial was set on a hilltop outside Rome, Italy, with about 200 young people from different countries miming the text (see Figure 3.2) as sung by the popular group the

Figure 3.2   The "I'd Like to Buy the World a Coke" Commercial

Source: http://memory.loc.gov/ammem/ccmphtml/colaadv.html

New Seekers. The company spent more than $250,000 for filming, at the time one of the largest budgets ever devoted to a television commercial. When it was released in the United States, the response was immediate and dramatic. Many people even called radio stations and asked them to play the commercial (http://inventors.about.com/od/cstartinventions/a/coca_cola_2.htm).

There is an interesting footnote to this story as well: Since radio disc jockeys refused to play advertising jingles, the song was reworked slightly as "I'd like to teach the world how to sing (in perfect harmony)." The New Seekers release was a bestseller in the United Kingdom (where it reached number 1), the United States, and several other countries (http://en.wikipedia.org/wiki/I'd_Like_to_Teach_the_World_to_Sing_(in_Perfect_Harmony). For many people, the association to Coca-Cola was still probably quite obvious.

Mantras are basically shorthand for the core identity of the brand—something for the internal marketing and production teams to keep in focus when making decisions about promotions and upgraded products. "The customer is always right" is a typical mantra. Mantras are used to remind employees of "what we are about." Mantras may or may not show up in advertising. "Vorsprung durch Technik" and "Think different" are frequently used in ads, while Nike promotions use "Just do it" as the slogan instead of the more cumbersome "Authentic Athletic Performance."

THE POSITIONING MAP

The tool managers use to accomplish the positioning task is a mental map of consumers' minds. This positioning graph or "perceptual map" is usually depicted as a two-dimensional graph (we will show examples next). The graph shows where the various brands are located, based on how the brands are scored by consumers on important attributes. A brand's position can be described by where it is located on all the important attributes (see, e.g., Urban, 1975).

Because a brand's position is determined by consumers' perception of the brand relative to the competition, positioning activities begin by identifying the salient attributes for the product category. This is typically accomplished with the help of focus groups and other marketing research techniques, nowadays often online. The aim is to generate the important choice and buying criteria used by the target customers and to elicit customer perceptions of competing brands. The attributes along with the product are judged to have superiority are candidates for use in identifying the desired positioning and the ensuing brand position. The position should be based on the competitive advantages of the branded product.

The brand attributes should include functional, psychological–emotional, and personality characteristics. The benefit of providing such a spectrum is that the positioning map will thus have the potential to reflect each brand's relative advantage in terms of perceived ability to provide functional risk reduction, psychological risk reduction, and self-expression.

Once the positioning dimensions have been identified, representative survey research and discriminant analysis can be used to establish which of the dimensions are most important for the target market (e.g., Huber & Holbrook, 1979). Since the positioning involves fine-tuning the appeals by which the target segment will be approached, management needs to identify which of the possible positions best reach the intended segment. Attributes that rank high on customer concerns and on which the branded product has superiority are prime candidates to define the positioning. They will typically also be the dimensions along which brand position rests most firmly, since they tend to be most salient. Starbucks may be a coffee house, but it is really the atmosphere that sets it apart.

The results can be portrayed in a positioning graph or a perceptual map where the length of the arrows is proportional to the importance of the attribute (see Figure 3.3).

Positioning also involves competitive advantages and disadvantages. The new brand has to be perceived as offering superior benefits to motivate its introduction. If competition offers superior attributes, the only reason for customers to consider the new product would be price, since the brand is not yet established. A discounted price is rarely the way to build a strong brand. The survey respondents should be asked to rate the competing brands in the market on the important criteria. The results can be displayed directly in the positioning map, by projecting each brand's scores onto the important dimensions (see Figure 3.4).

Figure 3.3   Salient Attributes of Beer Brands

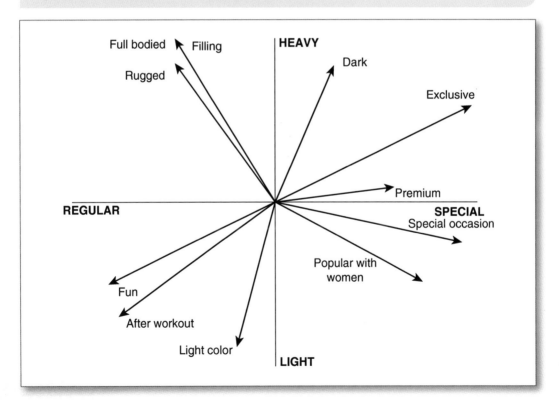

Figure 3.4   Where the Beer Brands Are Positioned

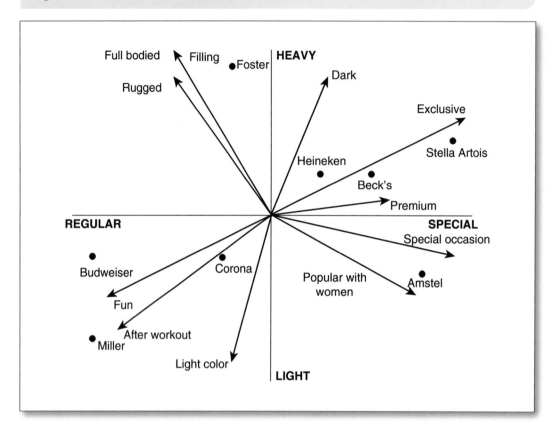

Brands that are closer to each other on the map have closer perceptual positions in consumers' minds. Thus, they are more likely to be co-considered, they are more likely to compete, and they are more likely to be used by consumers as references. Brands that are very different tend to occupy a region of the map by themselves and are perceived by consumers to have a niche position (Sujan & Bettman, 1989).

Survey research can also be used to identify the preferences of the target customers. The survey respondents can be asked to indicate what kind of beer they prefer, regardless of cost and brand. These answers about the "ideal" beer can also be projected into the positioning space. The cluster of respondents in any one location can be represented by a circle, the size proportional to the number of consumers in that market niche. This gives the new brand an overview of the market and where potential customers might be less than well served—an empty part of the space (see Figure 3.5).

Whether a particular product can be competitive or not depends crucially on what position in the product space it selects—and what customers it tries to attract. In this case, it looks as though the most promising positioning would be to introduce the new brand in

Figure 3.5   Different Segments Want Different Beers

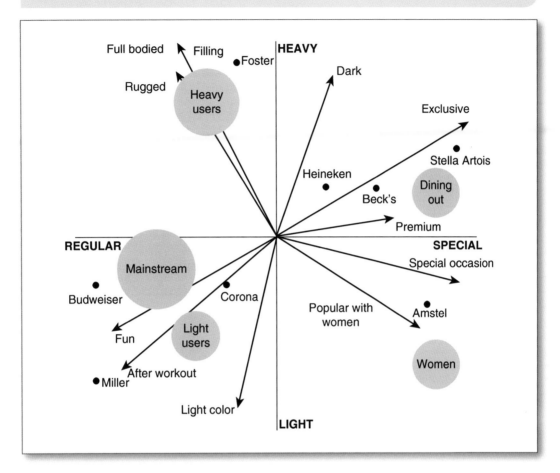

an untapped niche of full-bodied beer where competition is not strong—assuming, that is, that the new product can pass as full-bodied. It may not attract a majority of the market but may be without an immediate competitor.

Positioning is, in fact, a way to identify competitors and market niches, customers with special needs where a new brand can be successful. It is common for new brand strategies to stay away from leading mainstream brands and start in a less competitive part of the brand and product space. This was how the early Japanese brands were introduced in the U.S. market, with Honda Super Cubs entering in an unoccupied part of the U.S. motorcycle market)—although, in all fairness, this was done once Honda's larger bikes had failed in the mainstream bike market (Johansson & Nonaka, 1996, p. 60). It is not, however, the way the Toyota Lexus entered the luxury auto market in America (see Figure 3.6).

Figure 3.6 Positioning of Three Automobile Brands

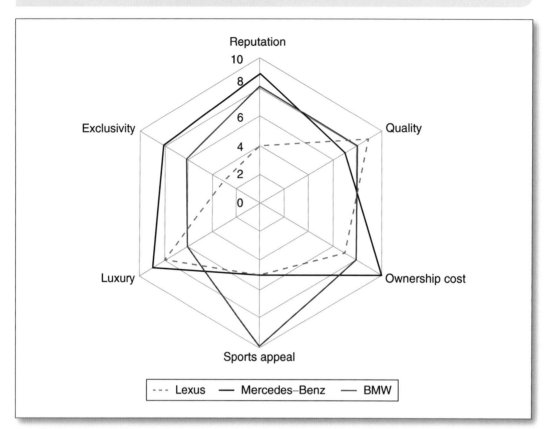

This figure offers an alternative way to demonstrate the competitive positions of brands. As can be seen in the figure, Toyota went head-to-head against established Mercedes-Benz and BMW with its Lexus model, beating them on quality and cost of ownership. It still suffers from less exclusivity and brand reputation but is equal in terms of luxury, although probably not so in Europe where Japanese cars still face an uphill battle (Truong, McColl, & Kitchen, 2009).

IDENTITY, IMAGE, AND POSITION

Identity and Positioning

As we saw in Chapter 1, the *brand identity* defines what the brand stands for. It becomes the platform on which positioning decisions about name, logo, and brand communications can be based. The brand identity both enables and constrains the positioning decision.

The outstanding attributes that the brand identity reflects is the basis for a credible positioning statement. At the same time, the brand identity sets a limit to how far away the positioning can go without jeopardizing the brand.

BMW's and Levi's brand identities can be stated as follows:

BMW: A German-made driving vehicle with superior engineering and outstanding road handling characteristics for customers that demand highest performance

Levi's jeans: Stylish and durable apparel for people with active lifestyles and the pioneering spirit of the original American West

Notice how the identity involves core *product* elements (e.g., superior engineering for BMW, rugged jeans for Levi's) as well as extended identity elements about *origin* (e.g., German-made, American West) and also the kind *customers* targeted (demanding high performance, pioneering spirit).

The Levi's logo is an interesting example of how a seemingly old-fashioned but original trademark can assume a special cachet among its customers. The Levi's logo dates from the company's mid-1800s origin, and harks back to the rough-and-ready days of the gold-digging "49ers" with horses, whips, and riveted pants (see Figure 3.7).

This original trademark for rugged and durable jeans does not suggest "stylish" and would seem to exclude the women's market. But it is still retained and presumably offers loyal customers the assurance of a trusted, reliable, and authentic brand. And for the

Figure 3.7 Levi's Original Trademark and a Modern Version

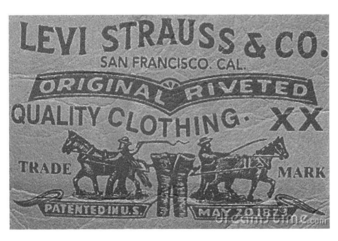

women's market and a slightly more contemporary look, the company has created a less traditional logo for some styles, also shown in the figure.

The explicit statement of the brand identity is particularly useful as a road map for the company employees. A well-developed brand identity makes the employees aware of what the company and its products are about. A clear brand identity will help employee identification with the company, a prerequisite for a strong brand. Brand mantras are in fact shorthand for the core aspect of the brand identity, easily communicated and recalled.

How do firms decide on how to relate positioning to the identity of a brand? The choice is not free—the position has to represent the product or service honestly. If the firm offers a standardized product at a lower price, the brand identity cannot kindle expectations of a "premium" or "best-in-class" offering. Recognizing this, when Toyota decided to launch a luxury car, the company needed another brand and created Lexus for its alliterative association with "luxury." Sometimes, however, a strong brand is used for its power, although the identity may be threatened.

According to reports, Mercedes-Benz's decision to introduce its 190 model in the 1980s stirred serious debate in the company about a position that could potentially "devalue" the Mercedes-Benz nameplate. Engaging in unprecedented prelaunch testing of the new "baby-Benz," company managers were finally convinced of its quality and performance and decided to introduce the smaller and lower priced Mercedes-Benz car (Cammisa, 2013).

By contrast, when Levi's recognized that some of its young loyal customers had grown older and needed less snug fits, the company introduced looser khakis, but used a new name Dockers to avoid hurting the Levi's jeans identity (Carducci, Horikawa, & Montgomery, 1994).

The brand identity is also constrained by the intended user of the product. The Honda Motor Company considers its core identity to be based on engineering excellence and its brand identity to be based on who drives its cars. Its mantra is "Man Maximum, Machine Minimum" (Wood, 2011). Not surprisingly, its highly loyal customers come back not for the status of the brand—as Mercedes-Benz customers might—but for the high reliability, fuel efficiency, and simple pleasure of driving the cars.

Image and Positioning

In practice, brand image and brand position are often used interchangeably. One reason for this is that both the brand image and the brand position are based on consumer perceptions. However, the two concepts are in fact different in an important way.

The image is the aggregate consumer perception of the brand and all the cognitive elements in the consumer's mind that are associated with the brand. Therefore, its support is all the cognitive and affective elements in the consumers' minds and the linkage between the brand and these elements. Some of these associations benefit the brand. These are positive associations. Nike's "Just do it" evokes a certain irreverence that can be a positive in its target market. Others detract from the brand, as negative associations. Toyota's problems with unintended accelerations detracted from its brand value in 2010. Some associations are quite irrelevant associations simply evoked by memorable taglines or mascots. For example, the brand image for the insurance company Geico involves an association with lizards due to its use of a gecko as its mascot and spokesperson. Aflac, another insurance company, uses a quacking duck to make sure potential customers remember its name. Whether positive or negative, these associations at least serve as effective memory triggers.

Whereas the brand image is based on all associations between the brand and the cognitive and affective elements in consumers' minds, the brand position is based on a subset of these associations. The position depends on the associations along which the brands compete. These associations are what determine each brand's relative position in the marketplace. They typically come from the attributes and benefits that the competing brands try to promote for positioning purposes, each brand stressing those where it has a competitive edge.

There is a lot of unavoidable dynamics in the process. What consumers say is important is what companies have said is important—and vice versa. After one brand offers 2-in-1 shampoo with conditioner, some consumers will find this is an important attribute for them. When a cell phone manufacturer offers a camera feature, many consumers find it impossible to even consider a cell phone without a camera. In the United States, German automobiles emphasize their origin ("Das Auto" by Volkswagen and "Vorsprung durch Technik" from Audi), drawing on a favorable heritage association and in the process making country of origin an important attribute. In defense, "Crafted with pride in America" has become an advertising slogan for American automobile manufacturers.

The more general brand image can be retrieved directly by simply asking people—even nonusers—how they view the brand. For example, one of the authors of this book did a survey on what constitutes the image that comes to mind when individuals think about their favorite sports team. The respondents were first instructed to choose their favorite sports team and then think about all the things that spring to mind when they think about this team. Aggregating the responses and analyzing the collages, the results are shown in Figure 3.8.

It is worth noting that athleticism (represented by the factors in the box) is not among the main considerations when one thinks of one's favorite sports team. Most fans see their favorite teams in terms that extend beyond athleticism (e.g., competitive, consistent, excellent).

In general, each individual person has his or her own perception of a particular brand. The way you perceive a car such as an Audi is not exactly the same way as your neighbor. One-to-one marketing exemplifies this variety: Brand image differs across individuals. Still, we probably have more in common in our perceptions of Audi than simply the identity elements of the brand name and logo. The car designs, the advertising, and other promotion we are exposed to and also the kind of Audi drivers we have each seen may be quite similar. So may our information and knowledge about the company itself. Thus, the image of the Audi brand may not differ very much between us—especially if we are in the same market. On the other hand, different cultures and nationalities may have quite different perceptions of the brand. Even if the product is standardized and the promotional messages similar, the reactions and interpretations can be quite different. Add to that the possibility that target segments may differ and it is easy to see why a standardized positioning may require widely different communications. In a sense paradoxically, to maintain the same

Figure 3.8   Image Items Associated With One's Favorite Sports Team

What Does Your Favorite Team Mean to You?

Winners	17%
Competitive	12%
Best	8%
Underdog	7%
Inconsistent	7%
Excellent	7%
Consistent	5%
Fast	5%
Tough	4%
Talented	3%
Strong	3%
Athletic	3%

position, a brand may have to adapt its marketing communications and perhaps even product design in different countries. Conversely, a standardized marketing mix can result in quite different brand image and positioning in culturally different markets.

SELECTING TARGET POSITION

There are basically three major factors to consider when selecting a brand's target position. They involve (1) the target segment, (2) the relevant competitors, and (3) the salient attributes along which to position the brand.

Target Segment

What possible unfilled segment niches exist in the marketplace? Are there customer segments that could be served better (such as IKEA targeting the newly divorced singles)?

Firms tend to discover unfilled niches in the market not so much by market research but by staying close to the customer and observing the situations in which products are being used. Typical examples include the development of the sliding doors in minivans and the development of the hatchback SUV. One author called this approach "hidden in plain sight," stressing the fact that careful observation of how people use a product such as a family car can uncover hidden needs that even the customer is not quite aware of (Joachimsthaler, 2007).

Brand positioning goes hand in glove with market segmentation. It assumes that not all individuals in a given market—for example, the market for bicycles—have the same preferences, needs, and wants. Some riders would like the sportier mountain bikes and others a more comfortable street bike. But even among the customers for mountain bikes there are differences in what attributes are important—weight, number of gears, handlebar design, and so on—and different individuals will have different preferences in terms of the attribute scores.

Selecting a potentially promising target segment usually involves matching the specific product features against the important attributes and preferred ratings on these attributes for different segments. With today's detailed consumer data—for example, the PRIZM zip-code based segmentation system identifies 66 separate segments in the United States (http://www.nielsen.com/us/en/search.html?q = prizm&sortbyScore = false)—this is not as simple as it sounds. It's not just a matter of getting positioned toward the mountain bike segment; it is a matter of demonstrating to one subsegment of the mountain bike customers how the brand is a superior mountain bike on the attributes that matter to them. One should not be surprised that this fine-tuning kind of effort sometimes misses the target. Schwinn's long association with leisure bikes has made it difficult to stretch the brand into the mountain bike market, where the brand has settled for a low-price position (http://www .schwinnbikes.com/bikes/mountain).

Relevant Competitors

Brand positioning is also closely tied to which brands are the closest competitors. In some way, selecting the target position is akin to selecting what competitors the brand will have. The relevant competitors are typically those who occupy a similar positioning. The underlying consumer research for a positioning analysis involves asking target segment respondents to score all the relevant competitors on the salient attributes. It is customary to include a wide range of competitors in this effort (exemplified by the beer brands in the earlier graphs), but the relevant competitors become the ones closest to the chosen position.

Brand positioning can also be used to spot new empty niches where competitors are non-existent and irrelevant. Apple's range of i-branded products attempts to do that. Colgate has introduced a Max Fresh brand where "freshness" is featured as a new important attribute and advertising stresses "liquid crystals" are used to establish superiority over the existing toothpaste brands. In a similar vein, the product market can be reframed so that competition becomes more or less irrelevant. Since coffee houses are fairly easy to establish, Starbucks has raised competitive barriers by focusing on "the experience," not just great coffee. This has helped shore up its brand position and protects the chain against imitators.

Salient Attributes

The competitive position depends on what are called points of difference (POD) and on points of parity (POP). On what attributes does the brand have superiority over competition (positive POD), where is it inferior (negative POD), and where is the brand equal to competition (POP)? Negative POD put downward pressure on the brand while positive POD raise its attractiveness (see Figure 3.9).

Generally speaking, the brand message should stress positive POD, using advertising and other communications to establish a favorable image, and seek to lock in a position through the use of a slogan. One example is Coca-Cola's stress on tradition using old ads with "The pause that refreshes" and its global tagline of "Always." Another is Sony's ad that shows a Vaio computer flying off like a feather in the wind, with the slogan "Lightweight like no other."

The brand message also has to render negative POD less important. Stressing the positives sometimes also suggest less importance for the negatives—stressing cool and refreshing, Coca-Cola avoids having consumers drink it warm and sweet—and lose customers. The comfort and style of a Cadillac helps make the weak mileage seem less important. The small keyboards of cell phones matter less when autofill substitutes "cool" abbreviations.

DISRUPTIVE POSITIONING

The positioning maps show what the market is at present. But when a new brand enters, the map changes. The market can be disrupted in several ways depending on the new product attributes.

Figure 3.9   Making Positive Attributes More Salient

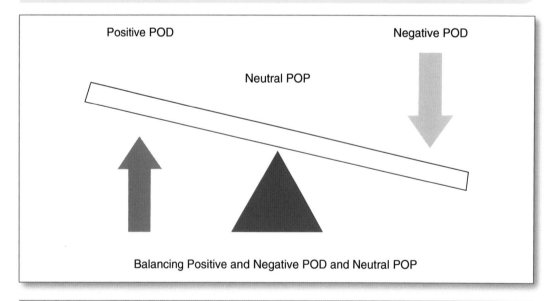

Source: Adapted from www.marketingstudyguide.com.

Note: POD = points of difference; POP = points of parity.

- Offering more of the same will extend the end points of the axes (e.g., more miles per gallon than before).

- Offering a new feature will introduce another salient attribute (e.g., cameras in cell phones).

- Offering new combinations can change the whole space (e.g., Internet on cell phones).

The more the new product offers new features and combinations, the more disruptive it will be. Disruptive innovations change the existing market space. Brand positions will change, consumer preferences will change, and competitors will either change or die.

In recent years, several market strategists have tackled this question. One example is the approach called "blue ocean strategy" (Kim & Mauborgne, 2005). The strategy aims to change existing "red" markets where competitors vie for marginal advantages into new ("blue") markets that the innovator and first entrant "owns." While the traditional structural approach ("red ocean strategy") asks, "What is?" the blue ocean approach asks, "What could be?" Creating a new kind of market (a blue ocean) typically involves satisfying a previously unmet customer need and has the added advantage of eliminating competition. One example is the creation of the new brand "[yellow tail]" wine from Australia. Reducing complexity by offering only two wines, and making wine drinking more "fun and approachable," the wine proved to be a great success in the college market segment.

Aaker (2011) suggested that the inherent conservatism of brand positioning can be resolved by focusing on "brand relevance." The key differentiating features have to be particularly relevant to the target market. This, Aaker suggested, requires innovation, including the kind of blue ocean strategy that involves creating new markets. The implication is that the brand manager will be tasked with creating new market niches, a challenging assignment since this requires innovative products in addition to a strong brand.

As we can see, by slightly reframing the product market, it is sometimes possible to exclude competitors and generate a blue ocean target market where competitors are irrelevant. Starbucks has pretty much accomplished this in the U.S. marketplace. By contrast, if the brand has a clearly superior product over competition, it may well position itself as the new standard, targeting in the mainstream of an existing "red ocean" market. This is the kind of disruptive positioning that the iPhone brought on to a very competitive cell phone market (see The iPhone Disruption box).

The iPhone Disruption

When Steve Jobs of Apple introduced the iPhone in 2007, he used a very simple illustration to show the superiority of the new product. He showed a two-dimensional positioning graph, a "Business

(Continued)

(Continued)

School 101 Graph" as he called it, with two axes, "Smart" and "Easy to Use" (the presentation at Apple's MacWorld event is available on YouTube). The iPhone was positioned far away from competitors, demonstrating how unique it was (see Figure 3.10).

This graph expresses the degree to which the iPhone disrupted and reinvented the cell phone market. The professional segment was interested in smarter phones, and younger users were more concerned with style and extra features. The iPhone showed how you could have both a smarter phone and ease of use. A positioning graph today would look quite different, with the Android system and me-too products from Samsung and other makers crowding the iPhone space.

Figure 3.10   Steve Jobs' iPhone Positioning

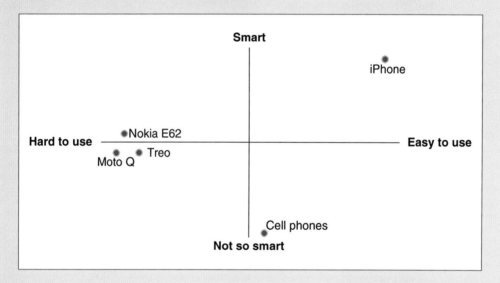

TRADITIONAL AND DIGITAL MEDIA

Positioning a brand naturally requires effective marketing communications. As everyone knows, there has been a virtual explosion in communications media in the last decade or so. With the advent of the Internet and digital communications, consumers now learn about new product and brands not only through television, magazines, newspapers, and other traditional media but more likely through ads and interactions over Facebook, Twitter, mobile phone apps, blogs, and online shopping. This naturally affects communication strategy.

For branding purposes, it is useful to separate positioning communications from more general brand building activities. Positioning involves targeting a segment and presenting the specific combinations of benefits and features that constitute the basic promise of the brand. The positioning involves characteristics such as reliability and durability, ease of use, energy efficiency, organic, no artificial ingredients, and so on. Such specific POD and POP are best communicated through traditional media where the message can be more carefully controlled. Positioning is how management intends the brand to be perceived by the consumer.

Most brand building communications involve a much wider selection of media and messages. Brands, after all, are built not only on rational, cognitive criteria but also include a good deal of the emotions, dreams, and excitement that underlie brand affinity. Traditional media might set the stage, but the "buzz" that adds the affective components comes more likely from word of mouth, Facebook "likes," Twitter followers, and other more interactive media. The problem from a positioning perspective is that such buzz is beyond management control and involves often both positive and negative messages. The position achieved by the carefully orchestrated traditional media campaign will not always be the one intended. A notorious example of how a user segment can affect brand identity negatively is the case of Burberry's famous check pattern on baseball caps that became popular among soccer hooligans in England in the 1990s. Finally, against the notion that "any publicity is good publicity," the company decided in 2004 to withdraw the caps from the market rather than risk further damage (Kelbie, 2004).

Traditional Media

Which traditional mass media to use depends intimately on the image and position to be created and the audience to be reached. Not all advertising media is equally capable of creating a certain brand position and image. Magazines have traditionally been seen as a major image-creating medium, and they still are despite audience shrinkage. Because magazines can be carefully targeted to the intended audience, magazine readers tend to be highly involved, and it is possible to put across more elaborate messages about POD. By contrast, television is less suitable for image creation but very good at quickly spotting the one or two exceptional POD. Some media, like outdoor media and transit ads, are useful for creating awareness, but less useful for the more in-depth impressions necessary to create a "place in the mind" of the customer.

Print media as a whole and especially newspapers have lost ground as people turn toward web-based media. One example is the emergence of image creating vehicles, things such as online video. Firms now spend promotional money on professionally produced story line videos shown on their websites and sometimes repeated on YouTube. L'Oréal's short clips of its main models such as Jennifer Lopez serve not so much to raise their celebrity status but to indirectly demonstrate product features and superiority.

In another shift, many television commercials are produced with an eye to repetition on YouTube, an example of viral marketing. Paying the high media placement cost for a 30-second Super Bowl commercial might be worth it when a strong commercial can count on doubling viewership on the Internet (although, of course, the savvy network executives have also figured that into the price). One example is the Volkswagen 2011 Super Bowl ad called "The Force," which was even released on YouTube before airtime. It registered

12.4 million views, 10,000 comments, and 62,000 likes with 4 hours to go until the game (http://www.huffingtonpost.com/2011/02/06/volkswagen-super-bowl-ad-_n_819297.html).

The positioning effort is mainly cognitive and "left-brain" oriented but also needs to put across more emotional "right-brain" impressions. This part of the image takes some skill to capture in print media. Trying to portray "excitement" with a still magazine photo is not easy, but the common trick of consumers jumping into the air is a tried-and-true effort that sometimes succeeds. Online videos may be good for young audiences, and television commercials can create excitement for more mature targets. Ruggedness can be projected well in many traditional media, using severe settings, large visuals, and big print. It is harder to do in online media, where violent explosions and car crashes are too commonplace and even the most rugged-looking individual seems vulnerable.

Digital Media

Today, with mobile access to the Internet, the consumers as well as companies are always accessible. There are many more *touch points* where a brand meets its customers. In real time, consumers are able to do the following:

- Collect information on brands and firms

- Receive ads, coupons, and other brand promotions

- Easily compare prices of a brand in different outlets

- Tap into social media to share brand opinions with others

- Interact directly with firms, giving more brand feedback over and above satisfaction

- Use the Internet to choose and purchase a brand

Similarly, firm capabilities are also greater. Firms can do the following:

- Reach consumers anywhere

- Send targeted ads, coupons, samples, and brand information to customers

- Change brand prices to reflect variations in supply and demand (dynamic pricing)

- Tap into social media to leverage their brand message

- Increase word-of-mouth brand communication among customers

- Collect competitive brand information about customers and markets

- Use the Internet as a brand sales channel

SOCIAL MEDIA

One particularly intriguing component of digital media is *social media*. The networks of consumers connecting on the various social platforms—Twitter, Facebook, Tumblr,

Google+, Instagram, and others—clearly function quite differently from other media. With the personalized content, often one-to-one, there is an implicit (and sometimes explicit) endorsement of any brand mentioned. There is almost a complete loss of corporate control (which may of course increase the credibility of any messages).

Facts and Rumors

For brand managers, the new capabilities raise several issues (see Figure 3.11). The first question is perhaps what happens when consumers exert control over the brand itself. Word of mouth and consumer empowerment can cut both good and bad ways for a brand. The fact that some brands are explicitly disrespected is not news. Claims that McDonald's hamburgers contain worms date back to 1978 (http://en.wikipedia.org/wiki/McDonald's_urban_legends)

Figure 3.11 Social Media Dos and Don'ts

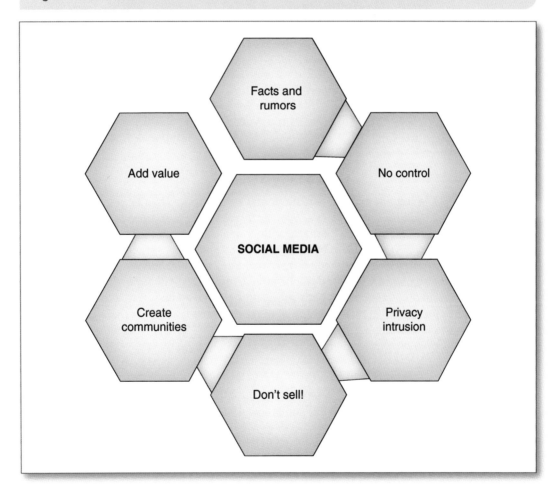

and the notion that the Procter & Gamble (P&G) logo of the man in the moon (the logo discontinued in 1993) is in fact satanic was first heard in 1970s as well (http://www.businessinsider.com/pg-puts-moon-in-new-logo-despite-satanist-accusations-2013–5?op = 1).   To mitigate the spread of such ill-founded rumors, the firms' counterargumentation has to be increasingly subtle and sophisticated. Straight-out denials might only raise the credibility of the false claim. It will be tempting to adopt stealth strategies such as corporate-sponsored bloggers and infiltration of social media and chat rooms. Such efforts are obviously quite subversive, and being "found out" would be devastating for not just the brand image but its identity, redefining "what the brand stands for."

No Control

It is hard to see how companies can stay in control of the brand positioning, image, and personality. The digital possibilities have actually opened up a Pandora's box of pros and cons. Consumers take "ownership" of brands such as Coca-Cola, demanding that the company produce such things as a pink can (www.coca-colablog.com/brands/2-million-facebook-fans-request-pink-coke-cans/). The company response? "As a company, we are already actively involved with two of the leading breast cancer organizations." No pink cans, apparently. Google's fan base also polices the company ("No cluttering up of the home page!"), limiting any changes to variations on the name design. Even the "Michael Jackson" brand has posthumously been usurped by a group calling itself "Michael Jackson's Rapid Response Team to Media Attacks," which protects the brand against what it considers irresponsible and unwarranted media reporting of its hero's life and achievements (Baker, 2012).

Privacy Intrusion

The next important question for the brand manager is how to handle the potential pushback from consumers claiming intrusion of privacy. With continuous access, the temptation to always try to connect with the consumer might be difficult to control. Clearly there are times when the consumer does not want to be approached. Much care and restraints have to be exercised by the marketer so as to make any intrusion relevant to the consumer's specific situation. Receiving a one-to-one targeted price deal or coupon on the way to the store is clearly preferable to suddenly receiving a pop-up ad on the way to the beach. On the upside, precise targeting is going to be more and more possible as the technology progresses. The Tom Cruise experience in the futuristic film *Minority Report* might not yet be completely realized, but we seem to be edging closer every day.

Don't Sell!

The brand manager contemplating using digital media will also want to know if social media generates not only awareness and interest but also higher level brand equity. One might even ask the following: Do social media produce sales? A positive answer should be self-evident—after all, more exposure and awareness should help any brand—but the evidence is not yet clear. Much points to the notion that this is not the time to sell. An IBM study in 2012 suggests that when friends are "hanging out" digitally with their friends, they are not really in a buying mood (Baker, 2013). For example, on Black Friday 2012 (November 23, the day after Thanksgiving Thursday, traditionally the busiest shopping day of the year in the United States) only 0.68% of all online purchases came via Facebook. The traffic from Twitter was so low as to be undetectable. E-commerce as a whole grew to nearly $39 billion during the 2012–2013 holiday season, but social media played apparently a minor role in this. According to data from comScore, in 2012 corporations spent only 14% of their advertising budgets on social media (Baker, 2013; http://www.comscoredatamine.com/).

Create Communities

Still, many companies and brands have taken the plunge and participate actively in the brave new media world. Some steps can be taken to help navigate the waters. Brands such as Harley-Davidson and Saturn have taken the initiative by establishing fan base communities. Other "brand communities" (Apple's Macintosh, for example, and Saab) have emerged more or less spontaneously (Muniz & O'Guinn, 2001). These communities help the brand navigate the new world, in part serving as a testing ground for new ideas and also as a protective force against outside derogation. "Crowdsourcing" ideas for new designs, features, and advertising, allowing consumers to offer advice and insights, are also possible strategies that have been attempted to involve future customers and protect against missteps (Whitla, 2009).

Add Value

In the social media world, the company should not so much send messages but rather try to add value as a member of a community (Scott, 2010). For example, Starbucks uses social media as a positioning tool to portray itself as an inclusive and engaging brand. The company's Facebook page is updated daily with videos and posts about everything from how to grow coffee beans to the latest music. Consumers are invited to learn and be part of the conversation, rather than feeling promoted to. This positioning is perfectly aligned with the brands competitive advantage. Starbucks sells much more than just coffee; its coffee shops provide an environment where customers can hang out, connect with others, and spend time.

There is also the emergence of "branded content." Published on sites such as mashable.com under its "What's Inside" headline, companies sponsor technical articles that cover areas of interest to its target market. Although the articles may be objective and might seem editorial, they are sponsored by brands that want to contribute to the brand community. Sites such as BuzzFeed rely on these contributions to keep their content fresh and up to date. The writers of the articles do not identify or promote specific brands, but the sponsorship by the brand owners is explicitly stated. The Huffington Post, another web publisher, has struck partnership with Johnson & Johnson to help publish articles on women and children (Vega, 2013). The effectiveness of such sponsorship is not clear, but it helps the brand owner to play a constructive role in its brand community and keeps the brand relevant.

Of course, not all efforts in social media are successful. In 2009, Pepsi was losing sales volume, especially in the teenage segment, and falling behind Coca-Cola in market share. The newly hired social media director decided to shift one third of the marketing budget to interactive and social media. The key driver of this experiment would be the Pepsi Refresh Project, a social media campaign that asked consumers to submit "refreshing ideas that change the world." While the campaign was successful in generating social media buzz, it was unsuccessful in capturing market share. Pepsi's mistake was to forget its position as a mass brand. In order to fend off competitors and nurse brand loyalty, Pepsi needed to maintain exposure in traditional media (Poses & Aaker, 2010). Social media and social responsibility were only effective in communicating with a limited market segment.

TRACKING BRANDS IN SOCIAL MEDIA

Tracking consumer brand perceptions for positioning purposes traditionally involves using longitudinal surveys to assess brand positions. Tracking brands via social media is a completely different thing. Since social media data are generated continuously and in real time, they can be used to keep track of the buzz around specific brands continuously and in real time. These advantages have led to a rapid growth in "buzzmetrics" measures that can be used to capture the buzz around brands. And research agencies have established firms that collect and analyze these data, including Nielsen Buzzmetrics, Brandwatch.com, and Pulsar TRAC.

Though continuous and in real time, buzzmetrics tend to focus on relatively simple brand data, such as how often a brand is discussed, whether the mention is positive or negative, and how many people participate. Nevertheless, these tools can provide a very good tool for monitoring consumer brand perceptions. For example, it is easy for anyone to track a brand using www.socialmention.com. This website allows you to type in any brand you wish, and check out the resulting measures of brand buzz. There are four basic dimensions, all referring to social media discussions:

- Strength—the percentage of mentions of the brand in the last 24 hours, relative to all mentions;

- Sentiment—the ratio of positive mentions to negative mentions;

- Passion—the likelihood that any one person repeatedly talks about the brand;

- Reach—the number of unique "authors" relative to the total number of mentions.

"Strength" is really a matter of how "buzz worthy" the brand is at this time. "Sentiment" is the degree of favorability. "Passion" is close to what we termed "depth" of allegiance in chapter 2. Similarly, "Reach" is equivalent to our "reach" concept in Chapter 2.

Many client companies ask that their brands be continuously monitored on the Web. This helps in uncovering sudden shifts due to special promotions but also to unforeseen events, recalls, and the effects of rumors and misinformation. The reports can be extended to include excerpts of the actual mentions and discussions, and such comments can, of course, be revealing. But generally speaking, although the data are definitely up-to-date and reveal consumer responses to current events, they tend to be less informative for how consumers in general view the brand.

For a more systematic tracking of how the brand is perceived, traditional market research must also be done. It is not surprising to note that some of the early pioneers in the field have gradually moved on to what is called "Social Media Analytics," attempting to better understand the psychology and behavior of consumers who engage in social media (Murphy, 2013). Overall, it is quite clear that social media can be very viable as vehicles for brand communications and the effects can be closely monitored. However, for most brand positioning efforts they need to be supplemented by more traditional media and tracking methods.

MEDIA PROS AND CONS

To summarize, the main positioning media, their suitability, and key strengths are indicated in Table 3.1.

Table 3.1 Pros and Cons of Select Branding Media

	Media	Suitability	Key Strengths
Print	Magazines	****	Good at specific POD, visual image
	Newspapers	*	Mostly store information
Broadcast	Radio	*	Mostly sales information
	Network television	***	One or two main characteristics, visuals
	Cable television	****	Can be narrowly targeted,
Outdoor Advertising		0	Useful mainly for brand awareness
Direct Mail		0	Mainly to create trial
Online	Banner and portal ads	0	Mainly awareness creation, sales
	Websites	***	Good for product descriptions
	Videos on websites	***	Good for demos, excitement
Social Media	Facebook	***	Very good for validation of claims
	Twitter	*	Too brief; but creates buzz
	Blogs	***	Good for opinion leadership
	YouTube	***	Interest and excitement, visuals

Note: POD = points of difference. The stars indicate level of applicability.

As the table indicates, the traditional media tend to be better at communicating specific information about the brand (as in positioning), and the new media are more suitable for the emotional brand messages that create affinity and bonding.

SUMMARY

The aim of brand positioning is to establish a unique identity and image of the brand in the consumer's mind. Positioning involves the use of advertising and other communication vehicles to establish consumer perceptions of the brand, which reflect the brand's value proposition. But management is not in complete control of the message. The brand position achieved reflects also other information about the brand, including customers' word of mouth and the "buzz" in social media.

The brand position is typically depicted as a particular point in a positioning map. The positioning map is derived from salient product attributes and the relative ratings of competing brands. The target position for the brand is one with a strong consumer segment without very close competitors. But the product attributes, brand identity, and the value proposition place limits on the degree to which the brand can be placed anywhere in the market space. A typical new brand will offer superior benefits along on or more dimensions of the positioning map, such as offering more speed or lighter weight for PCs. The brand will stress positive POD while matching competitors on other attributes (POP).

Because of the potentially intense competition from similar alternatives, however, the brand manager has to be innovative. One innovative solution is to reimagine the market space and introduce new attributes, such as adding a color screen or a camera to a cell phone. This tends to disrupt the existing positioning map and give at least a temporary advantage. But companies go further. The new product might be disruptive, and the brand might create a whole new market. This happened when the digital cameras were developed, for example, and also when the iPhone came in. In such cases, the market is completely changed, and the positioning maps need to be entirely redrawn.

The choice of positioning media involves a careful analysis of what exactly the value proposition and target position are. Brand positioning is not simply a matter of creating awareness but is a very deliberate effort to create favorable associations and perceptions of superiority. This means simple exposure and audience coverage are not sufficient criteria. The media chosen, whether traditional or digital, will color how the message is interpreted and what the positioning will be. Using digital media will automatically give the brand a "current" aura and also open up a whole new set of interactions with the customer. But there are a number of issues that complicate the management especially with social media, where the brand might be the topic of conversation but largely outside company control. What can be done is to help enhance the conversation and provide incentives for organizing brand communities and special events. But the management has to avoid intrusion of privacy and stay away from outright selling efforts.

KEY TERMS

Brand platform, Disruptive positioning, Mantra, Positioning map, Positioning statement, Slogan, Social media, Value proposition, Word of mouth

DISCUSSION QUESTIONS

1. For a brand of your own choice (pick a favorite brand), try to develop a value proposition and positioning statement.

2. Find the positioning attributes for a product category of your choice by analyzing a few competing brands' advertising. Are some important attributes neglected? Check to see if all the brands have competitive parity on those neglected attributes.

3. Use the iPhone example (or some other example of your own choice) to analyze how a disruptive innovation can change the positioning map of the market. Does the innovation simply add attributes, or does it also render some attributes irrelevant (such as clam shell)?

4. For a brand of your own choice, first define its target market and position. Then find out how its social media effort has developed (When did it join Facebook? Twitter? etc.). See if you can also find the way the brand has integrated its traditional media with social media. Any critique? Evaluation?

MINICASE: RE-POSITIONING THE CATHOLIC CHURCH

For many years the position of the Catholic Church on what is generally called "gay persons" has been quite adamant. It was crystallized with emphasis in the annual Christmas message of then Pope Benedict on December 22, 2012, when he declared that homosexuality destroyed the "essence of the human creature." He claimed that a person's gender identity is God-given and unchangeable. As a result, he sees gay marriage as a "manipulation of nature" (Kuruvilla, 2012).

The ensuing reaction by various groups of the LGBT (lesbian, gay, bi-sexual, transgender) community was quick and vociferous. A protest was staged at St. Peter's Square. "Equally Blessed," a coalition of Catholic organizations in the U.S. that supports gay marriage, repudiated the Pope's claims. In a joint press release, activists said that Benedict's view of gender identity was out of step with reality. Same-sex couples have created happy homes for their kids and transgender people live "healthy, mature, and generous lives."

(Continued)

(Continued)

In late February 2013, Pope Benedict XVI announced that he was resigning. The pope, 85 years of age, said he had come to the certainty "that my strengths, due to an advanced age, are no longer suited to an adequate exercise of the ministry" (Cullinane, 2013). A spokesman stressed that the pope's decision was not because of any external pressure. The last pope to resign was Pope Gregory XII in 1415. He stepped down to end the "Great Western Schism"—during which there were rival claims to the papal throne.

On March 13, 2013, a new pope was selected when thick white smoke billowed out from the Sistine chapel's chimney. Cardinal Jorge Mario Bergoglio, 76, is the first pope elected from Argentina and was the runner up to Pope Benedict XVI in 2005. Bergoglio, now Pope Francis, is revered for being a man of the people and for his continued commitment to social justice. He chose to live in a small apartment, rather than in the luxurious bishop's residence, and can still be seen using public transportation.

Pope Francis did not take long to introduce a new aura in the Papal office. His simplicity and social concern overrode more ideological and philosophical concerns. Acting more as a plain fellow man than a bearer of judgment, Pope Francis aimed for a Catholic Church more open to all kinds of people. In a wide-ranging published interview over three meetings in August 2013, the pope answered critics who wanted him to speak up about gay marriage and the role of women in the church. Significantly, Pope Francis repeated his own sentiment about gays: "Who am I to judge?" He also stated that women must play a key role in church decisions.

The interview was conducted by the Rev. Antonio Spadaro, editor of La Civilta Cattolica, a Jesuit journal based in Rome, in Francis' apartment in Rome. Jesuits from around the world submitted questions to Spadaro, and the pope answered them with the honesty and humility that has come to typify his papacy. The pope approved the transcript in Italian, and advance copies of the interview were provided to several news organizations.

It does not mean Pope Francis is breaking entirely with past dogma. For example, Francis is against women's ordination, a position that disappoints many Catholic liberals. But that doesn't mean the church should consider women secondary or inferior, Francis said. "The feminine genius is needed wherever we make important decisions," he told the interviewer.

Some American Catholics complain that Francis has been largely silent on issues such as abortion and contraception. But the pope claims the church's teachings on those issues are clear. "It is not necessary to talk about these issues all the time," Francis said.

Only false prophets claim to have all the answers, Francis said. "The great leaders of the people of God, like Moses, have always left room for doubt," he said. "You must leave room for the Lord."

Discussion Questions

1. In what respects can this interview be seen as an effort to reposition the Catholic Church, and in what sense does it represent an affirmation of the existing position?

2. Describe what you would imagine the target population to be for the new Pope's message—and how that population differs from the existing one.

3. How would you judge if the Pope has been successful?

4. In your assessment, how likely is he to be successful?

Sources

Antonio Spadaro, S. J. (2013, September 30). , A big heart open to God. *America: The National Catholic Review.*

Cullinane, S. (2013, February 28). Pope Benedict XVI's resignation explained. *CNN.* http://www.cnn.com/2013/02/11/world/europe/pope-resignation-q-and-a/

Collier, M. (2013, March 13). New Pope Francisco elected; Cardinal Jorge Mario Bergoglio of Argentina to lead church. *Christian Post Contributor.*

Kuruvilla, C. (2012, December 22). Pope Benedict denounces gay marriage during his annual Christmas message. *New York Daily News.*

Marrapodi, E., & D. Burke. Pope Francis: Church can't "interfere" with gays. *CNN Belief Blog.* https://www.google.com/#q=Marrapodi%2C+E.%2C+%26+D.+Burke.+Pope+Francis%3A+Church+can%E2%80%99t+%E2%80%9C interfere%E2%80%9D+with+gays.+CNN+Belief+Blog.

SUGGESTED PROJECTS

Position Exercise 1: Select an iconic brand of interest (e.g., Coca-Cola, Apple, Honda). Using materials you can find on the Internet (e.g., slogans over the years, TV commercials, posters), chronicle how the brand's positioning efforts have changed over time. Look for instances where the brand's position has narrowed or become more focused and where it has broadened.

Position Exercise 2: Select a second iconic brand from the category that was given in Position Exercise 1 (e.g., Pepsi, IBM, Chevrolet). Perform the same analysis as Position Exercise 1. Develop two vertical position time lines, one for each brand. Look for interactions in the two brands' positioning activities. Try to determine which brand tends to lead and which tends to follow when it comes to positioning efforts.

Branding Fundamentals

CHAPTER 4

Building a New Brand

Great brands are no accident. They are a result of thoughtful and imaginative planning.

—Kevin Lane Keller[1]

LEARNING OBJECTIVES

In this chapter, you will learn the following:

- How the three brand components are built over time
- How the **brand name, brand logo, brand slogans,** and **spokesperson** fit together
- The launch process for a new brand
- The most effective media choices for the introductory campaign
- How to track the penetration process of the new brand

Strong brands have solid identities, positive images, and desirable personalities. Brand identity is what the company and its products stand for. With the brand identity as the base, the brand image is the representation of the brand in consumers' minds. The image is partly determined by the firm's positioning messages and partly determined by consumers' experiences and word of mouth, the "buzz" in interactive media, and so on. When branding works, the image a brand has in a consumer's mind is aligned with the underlying brand identity the firm has developed for the brand. Over time, strong brands come to embody

---

[1]Kevin Lane Keller is the E. B. Osborn Professor of Marketing at the Tuck School of Business at Dartmouth College. The quote is from Keller (2008, p. 5).

traits that define their personality, the way a BMW might suggest "sporty" while a Mercedes-Benz is "classy."

THE FOUNDATION

These aspects of a brand are hierarchical (see Figure 4.1). The strength of a brand is founded on a complete integration between the three parts. They serve to define the brand's character, uniqueness, and advantage over competitors.

There is a direct connection between these building blocks of a strong brand and the role of brands in the choice process—the brands' primary function. As discussed in Chapter 1, strong brands help consumers reduce functional and psychological risk, and they also facilitate self-expression. There is a natural hierarchy to these functions as well. A brand must first reduce functional risk for the consumer. For a consumer to choose a brand, the consumer must believe the branded product will function as promised and expected. This requires a basic trust in the brand and the firm, engendered by the brand identity and what the firms stands for. The psychological risk involves more of the sense that the choice is socially acceptable and safe. This brings in the image component of the brand—the way the brand is viewed by peers and others. Finally, when the brand is used for self-expressive purposes, as a booster of self-esteem, the brand personality becomes more important. The match of the desired self-perception with that of the brand is what the consumer looks for. The ability of a brand to facilitate such self-expression requires that the brand has also reduced functional and psychological risk.

This is the fundamental relationship between the components of a brand and the primary choice role of a brand. First, for a brand to credibly reduce functional risk

Figure 4.1   Building the Brand Foundation

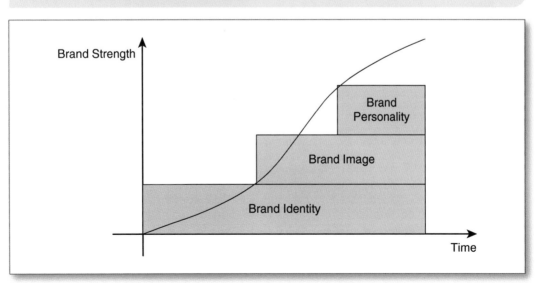

(i.e., to solve a problem), the brand must have a strong enough identity that suggests it is capable of solving the problem. Second, for a brand to reduce psychological risk, consumers must have an image of the brand that suggests that the brand is more—or at least as—acceptable than other brands. Third, for a brand to be able to enhance self-expression, the brand has to be sufficiently established to have its own personality.

As a new brand is built, it will develop an identity, image, and personality (the brand character, for short), and these building blocks will allow the brand to deliver value to consumers in the form of risk reduction and personal expression. As consumers become aware of these benefits and purchase the brand to receive them, the brand's penetration grows. This development is captured in Figure 4.2, which shows how the early stages of a brand's creation are supported by efforts to build the brand and the benefits these efforts have for consumers.

The remainder of this chapter deals with the nuts and bolts of building a brand. It covers activities such as how to find a brand name and logo that fits the desired brand identity, image, and personality; how to launch the new brand; and how to communicate to the new customers, focusing on the pioneers and early adopters that are necessary to help the diffusion process. It is important to note at the outset that this discussion is about a new brand, not about new products and services. The issue in this chapter is establishing a new brand in an already existing market.

In a new market, when the product represents an innovation, the primary task is to educate consumers about the innovation, its uses, and benefits. Then an established brand can certainly help convince the potential customer to try the new product; this is a topic of brand extension, which is covered in Chapter 6.

The natural sequence in the launch of a new brand can be depicted as a process over time. There are decisions to be made before launch, then the launch itself, and then the activities postlaunch. The activities in each stage necessarily overlap—the spokesperson

Figure 4.2   The Brand Foundation and Brand Functions

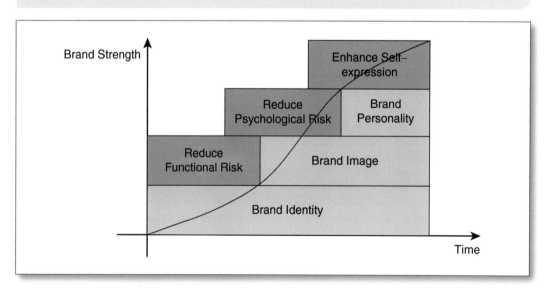

might have to be changed once the choice of media has been made, for example—but basically the main activities involved are as in Figure 4.3.

The chapter discusses these decision tasks in order from prelaunch to postlaunch.

Figure 4.3   The New Brand Launch Process

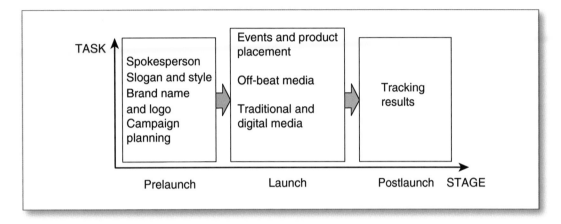

BRAND NAME

New brand building involves first finding a suitable name and logo for the given product. Suitable means a name that evokes the desired associations about the brand's identity, image, and, ultimately, personality. With the increasing importance of branding in recent years, finding a new brand name has grown into a very large business. It used to fall on a company's ad agency to find a new name, but now special agencies such as Interbrand in London and Landor in the United States provide specialized expertise.

One reason is that whereas brand names used to be selected mainly for legal reasons (i.e., representing the firm properly), they are now selected more for their image and global potential. For example, the Postum Cereal Company was established in 1898, and its first product was a cereal-based drink, Postum. As product lines were extended, new names were needed. When breakfast cereals were added to the product line the Postum name was shortened to Post. Another example is General Foods, which was the result of several acquisitions and mergers that predated its conception in 1929. These brand names were reflections of their heritage and the identity of the firm.

Over time, companies have recognized that sometimes the old name must go to make progress in building a strong brand. For example, in 1985 General Foods was acquired by Philip Morris, the tobacco company, which dropped the General Foods brand in favor of a stronger subbrand, Kraft, and then changed its own name to Altria. The later move was precipitated by a desire to distance its products from the negative associations consumers had with Philip Morris. The selection of the name Altria was made not to communicate a heritage or an identity but instead to provide a blank canvas on which any identity or image could be built.

This is one reason the new global marketplace features "neutered" brands such as Accenture, Acura, Lenovo, Infiniti, Asics, and H&M, where the connection to companies and their products and services has to be learned. Some of these have a literal meaning—Asics is Latin for "Healthy spirit in a healthy body" and H&M stands for Hennes & Mauritz, two merged stores in Sweden—but what they are selling is not immediately clear. But some have been generated by computer algorithms and selected from an output list of many alternatives by managers on the basis of focus groups and internal discussion. Altria, the new name designed for Philip Morris, partly to avoid the connection to tobacco, is a name that probably only a computer could invent.

Artificial Brand Names

The advantage of an artificial name is that the brand identity and image can be created *de novo*—from scratch. The product or service offered—and the value proposition—still limits how extravagant the associations and brand promises can be, but basically the brand meaning is created by marketing communications. Over time, product experience will show customers whether the promises were kept, and the users attracted will set the style and image for the brand, but essentially the neutered brand is an empty bucket for managers to pour meaning into.

This logic might seem counter to the more common notion that brands have a personality (Apple) and are warm (Hello Kitty), exciting (Music Television, now MTV), or traditional (L.L.Bean); have strong associations with product characteristics (Volvo); make customers think of beaches (Corona), luxury (Louis Vuitton), and value (IKEA); and so on. But these are associations built up over time through brand communications, product trial, and word of mouth. Brand meaning is manufactured by what we see in the media, hear from others, and experience ourselves.

Over time, the brand name will be disassociated from its early beginning. This is why it does not matter that an Apple computer is actually named after an apple or after the Beatles' choice, which has also been suggested (Linzmayer, 2004). It does not matter that Mercedes was the name of the company chairman's young daughter. It does not matter that Nokia is the name of a town in Finland and that the company started there actually was a pulp and paper mill. Nor does it matter that according to companies' websites, Volvo came from "rolling," or that Maxim coffee is supposed to remind you of Maxwell House, or that Accenture is supposed to suggest "accent on the future." These roots will be forgotten, and the name will be invested with its own meaning, which might or might not connote the same associations as the origin.

But when choosing a new name for a brand, these connections do matter. This is where one might agree that the Ford Edsel was a bad choice because the Edsel name itself suggests old-fashioned stodginess and lack of excitement (which might of course have correlated with the upscale identity aimed for). At the beginning, it is worthwhile to try to find a name that intrinsically calls to mind the associations aimed for—thus, Accenture and Volvo as well as DKNY (Donna Karan New York), Nike (Greek goddess of victory), Lenovo ("legend renewed"), Acura ("accurate"), Lego ("LEk GOdt," Danish for "play well"), and Lexus ("luxury") (Tart, 2011). They are all strong brand names but not because of their semantic roots—because of what the brands stand for and promise now.

Global Brand Names

In today's global markets, the naming of a brand can be complicated. The name should be easy to pronounce in many languages. For example, the Swedish Electrolux company had to give up its quest for a truly global brand, realizing the difficulties in translating and pronouncing the name in China and other Asian countries. While Coca-Cola can use its name and logo (the cursive writing of its name in red-on-white or white-on-red colors) in most countries, it needed to be written in Mandarin for the Chinese market. Because the proper-sounding kanji characters called up images of tadpoles, the characters and the pronunciation was changed to "Ko-ku-ko-lee," with the meaning "delicious happiness" (Zhang & Schmitt, 2001).

The name should also be legally available in all countries. Philips, the large Dutch multinational electronics firm, was prohibited from using its brand name in the U.S. market where Philco was already registered as an electronics company. One advantage of using the computer for the new name search is that new combinations can quickly be generated and tested for legal acceptance in different countries. The problem also hits established brands. Copyright laws will usually protect an established brand in most countries, but the name has to be registered. Missing that, the company might find that the brand name has already been registered and have to buy it back. McDonald's found that in Venezuela a daring entrepreneur had already opened a McDonald's look-alike restaurant there before its entry.

Computer-generated names do not typically reflect the heritage of the brand. In some cases, this can be a drawback when the brand comes from a leading market. In fact, most strong brands do have a home country. Even though global manufacturing has made the country-of-production quite irrelevant, well-known brands are typically associated with their original home country. A Sony television made in San Diego is still a Japanese television to most people. This is not a mistaken notion since multinationals try to make sure that the manufacturing, wherever it takes place, is managed well enough to maintain high quality standards of the original country.

The development of the stylized Sony brand name is in itself an interesting story. Until 1958, the company was till Tokyo Tsushin Kogyo, when CEO Akio Morita led an effort to make the name more globally acceptable. Wanting a name that was short, easily pronounceable, and with a "ringing" sound to signify the audio products, Morita combined *sonus,* Latin for sound, with *Sonny* from English to produce Sony (Okuda, 2001).

Strong brands tend to develop a country of origin connection over time, especially among loyal customers. Uniqlo, Audi, and Natura might not directly suggest their home countries, but the satisfied user will know (Japan, Germany, and Brazil, respectively). Of course, the same is true for Ugg, Haier, and Ecco (Australia, China, and Denmark, respectively). On the other hand, there is also Hyundai, Stolichnaya, and Volkswagen—brand names that more clearly reflect their home countries.

Ugg is one brand that has adopted its Australian country of origin in the logo from the outset (see Figure 4.4).

Making the origin a part of the trademark might have been prompted by the fact that in Australia, Uggs are a generic term for sheepskin boots with fleece inside and tanned outers. The country of origin helps give the brand both an outdoor identity and authenticity.

Figure 4.4   Ugg Logo

Source: http://sheepskinshoestore.com

Despite the need to establish congruence between brand identity, image, and the name—a good fit between "what you are" and "your name"—firms sometimes opt for memorable names. In certain commodity-like categories where involvement is very low, consumers do not pay much attention to much of anything except price. Insurance tends to be a case in point. Insurance companies do a lot of advertising to place their brand names at the top of the mind among people. Still, the low involvement often defeats these efforts. One company's CEO admonished its ad agency to come up with something that would make their brand name "stick" in people's mind. The result was the notorious Aflac duck, a mascot bird whose quacking sounded just like the name of the company. The company has done very well not only at home in the United States but also elsewhere, including Japan, a success attributed to the award-winning duck commercials (Krippendorff, 2010). The odd "fit" with the insurance business has made the duck a fun surprise to consumers in a boring product category. The ads raised the brand awareness in the United States from 11 % in 2000 to 94 % today (www.aflac.com).

Basic Brand Name Rules

There are some general rules to follow and check off:

- Does the brand name fit with the value proposition and the intended positioning? A "hip" positioning might necessitate a noncorporate brand name. Even Apple launched the path-breaking "Macintosh" to separate it from the original Apple computers. Fit is partly a matter of subjective assessment, but the subjective perceptions that matter are those of the target consumers.

- Is the brand legally available in all potential market countries? Budweiser's problems with its Czech counterpart Budvar are well known, limiting the ability to use the flagship name everywhere (www.brandchannel.com).

- Can people pronounce and understand the name? Stella Artois beer might do better dropping the *Artois*, which happens anyway in social media abbreviations.

- Is the brand name easy to hear and easy to spell? Even if the online search engines attempt to correct misspellings, texting might misspell it and word of mouth on the cell phone might not be heard. "Yoox," the Italian fashion brand, is a short and clever name (www.yoox.com) but becomes an obstacle for word-of-mouth diffusion.

- The brand name should be unique and memorable. Unique comes partly from the need to be legally different, but memorable means that it should be noted and slightly surprising. On this count Yoox certainly could make some claims.

BRAND LOGO

The brand logo is an integral part of the brand and is also legally protected. In some cases, the name itself is used as the logo. Coca-Cola's cursive red lettering is one such logo. Sony is another brand where the logo is the stylized lettering of the name. Its lack of Japanese semantic roots and its early success in America meant that in the beginning some Japanese assumed it was an American brand (Fields, 1988).

Logos are meant to give a visual representation of the brand, with more subliminal "right-brained" impact than the cognitive "left-brained" representation of the name itself. In brand research, logos are typically measured in terms of "recognition" while brand names are scored according to "recall." Brand identity is cognitively tied to the brand name; brand image is often connected closer to the more visual logo.

In many low-involvement purchase situations, including most consumer packaged goods (CPG), the brand primary effect comes mainly from a logo recognized—perhaps not consciously—than from the brand name. Even when buyers pay attention, it is sometimes easy to make a mistake between logos of the same color, shape, and lettering—an opportunity exploited by counterfeits and pirated products, but also by aspiring competitors. Starbucks' success has encouraged the opening of many new coffee shops around the world and has also inspired many similar logos, including these from various countries (see Figure 4.5).

Not all such imitations can be successfully prosecuted even where the evidence is clear. When Korean automaker Hyundai created its logo, the slanted *H*, its obvious blueprint, was the already established Japanese Honda's straight *H* (see Figure 4.6). Still, according to a Honda representative, its attempt to forestall the use of the logo by Hyundai by legal means was given up after a year of fruitless negotiations and litigation.

The design of a stylized logo is usually done with the help of specialists. The Federal Express company's branding effort is a case in point (see Figure 4.6). With the help of the Landor agency, the company first shortened its name to FedEx, maintaining its essential identity but making the name more globally acceptable. A new logo was then designed, maintaining the red, white, and blue coloring but more compact and still visible at a distance (important because the trucks need to be seen by receptionists allowing access to office buildings). By the choice of the font and allowing the letters to touch, the design also created a directional arrow between the letters *E* and *x,* a subliminal symbol of express motion (Adamson, 2006, p. 189).

Figure 4.5   Coffee Shop Logos

Source: http://silencedmajority.blogs.com/silenced_majority_portal/2009/07/starbucks-testmarketing-under-fake-names.html

Figure 4.6   Four Global Logos: Hyundai, Honda, FedEx, and Orange

Sources: http://autocarsconcept.blogspot.com/2012/12/hyundai-logo.html; http://vannyorkhonda.com/WinstonSalem.aspx ;
http://www.etsu.edu/centralreceiving/shipping/manager.aspx; http://www.logostage.com/logo/orange/

Another prominent example of brand and logo creation is France Telecom's Orange, a mobile phone provider (see Figure 4.6). The Orange brand, at the time an unusual name for a telecommunications firm, was created by an internal team at U.K.-based Microtel headed by Chris Moss (marketing director), hired there from Richard Branson's Virgin Group. Rather than calling the new brand Microtel and likely becoming an also-ran follower, Moss wanted something that stood for a whole new set of values in the market. Orange was born with the Apple name as a model and with the orange seen as a strong feng shui color (Tylee, 2003). The brand consultancy firm Wolff Olins was charged with designing the logo but switched from an actual orange (to avoid being seen as a fruit) in favor of a simple square. Another advertising agency, WCRS, created the Orange slogan "The future's bright, the future's Orange," which simply plays on the color itself.

The brand name and logo together represent a brand's identity and image. When recognized and recalled they should evoke, whether consciously or subconsciously, the associations and promises that constitute the brand identity, image, and, in the end, personality.

Many companies have quite elaborate and precise instructions for how the brand name and logo should be depicted. This includes what fonts and color for the name are acceptable, the proper position in an advertisement, how to feature the logo in a commercial, and so on. These tasks fall under what is typically called "Brand Asset Management." **Brand asset management** involves not only establishing rules to ensure consistent consumer exposure of brand and logo, but also instructions for how relevant distributors, suppliers and vendors should depict the brand and logo in their communications. It also, of course, involves monitoring to make sure the guidelines are followed.

BRAND SLOGANS

As we saw in Chapter 3, slogans are the short and memorable one-liners that are meant to capture the imagination of the consumer and reflect a unique selling point of the brand. For new brands, they have to point to specific product benefits to be useful. "Good to the last drop" suggested a specific benefit for the new Maxwell House coffee in 1917; the less specific "We bring good things to life" from General Electric (GE) works only because the company is already well known.

Even more than the brand name and logo, the slogan should "fit" with the value proposition and the intended positioning of the new brand. They are, more or less, shorthand for the promise of the new brand. Sometimes presented with a cartoon character and special music (jingle), slogans become influential on brand image and personality. Jingles are useful primarily for children's brands, appealing as they are to the not yet literate. They offer the reassurance of a familiar and comfortable sound (Yalch, 1991).

Slogans are typically created by professionals—usually the advertising agencies' copywriters. They often begin as the tagline in the advertising copy. It is rare that the very first tagline becomes the long-term slogan, but once the copywriter hits on a winner, they tend to remain. "Good to the last drop," Morton's Salt's "When it rains, it pours," as well as "All the news that's fit to print" for the *New York Times* have had a long life. The ad agency creators of the best slogans are pronounced advertising "geniuses" by their peers. "Vorsprung durch Technik" from Audi was given an award in 2003 as was "Just do it" from Nike in 2000.

SPOKESPERSON

A new brand will not yet have an established brand personality, but the early decisions made by the brand manager will help create this personality.

Perhaps the most important determinant of brand personality will be the spokesperson selected. To find an appropriate spokesperson depends partly on art, imagination, and luck but also managerial judgment. There has to be a "fit" between the spokesperson and the intended brand style and personality. But it is also important that the pioneer customers, early adopters, and opinion leaders find the spokesperson more than satisfactory and are willing to help spread the word. Of course, not all brand communications employ a spokesperson. In fact, the cost of one sometimes prohibits their use. Tiger Woods was paid an estimated $100 million over 5 years in his 2001 contract with Nike. The contract was extended in 2006 and, even after his marital problems, was renewed in 2013, with terms undisclosed (http://espn.go.com/golf/story/_/id/9485529/tiger-woods-signs-new-endorsement-contract-nike-agent-confirms).

The best spokespersons fulfill four basic criteria:

1. They are attractive—at least to their target customers. The audience will like them.
2. They have focused energy. They can convince people. The message will come through, whether verbal or visual.
3. They have expertise in the product. They know what they are talking about. Preferably they use the product themselves.
4. They are somebody that the audience can identify with or aspire to.

A new brand will typically use a celebrity spokesperson to raise its credibility and validate its claims. For example, when Bell Atlantic merged with GTE to form Verizon in 2000, it used famous basso James Earl Jones as a pitchman. A legendary actor who also gained fame for the sinister voice of Darth Vader in the *Star Wars* films, Jones lent instant credibility to the new Verizon brand. When the Paul Masson wine brand from California wanted to establish a new level of premium wine image, it used famous actor Orson Welles, another basso, who promised for Masson the following: "We will sell no wine before its time." As we have seen, L'Oréal uses many different celebrities to help introduce its various cosmetic brands.

Some celebrities are better than others. Nike's use of Michael Jordan, one of the greatest basketball players of all time, allowed the company to introduce a number of models under its "Just do it" tagline. By contrast, Shaquille O'Neal was Reebok's spokesperson for some time, with less impact. Part of the reason for the differences may have been Jordan's more attractive demeanor. Another possible reason relates to the promise of great basketball shoes. Since the introduction of "air Jordan" shoes, the most common promise of high-end basketball shoes has been their lightness—a trait that allows their wearers to jump higher and farther. But Shaquille O'Neal was never know as a leaper and so the shoes he wore never reinforced this promise. Eventually, Reebok moved further into apparel and became the NBA supplier of warm-up gear and game uniforms (Morse, 2001).

Not all spokespersons have to be celebrities, of course. When the Mexican beer Dos Equis (now owned by the Heineken company) decided on a campaign to relaunch the beer anew in the United States, the ad agency decided to have someone play "The Most

Figure 4.7   The Dos Equis "Interesting" Man

Source: http://www.highstrangenessufo.com/2012/06/ufos-on-radio.html

Interesting Man in the World." Out of the hundreds of actors who auditioned in cities countrywide to make a case for why they should play the role, Jonathan Goldsmith, who was an unknown, got the role. Why? He had the requisite burrowed face and beard and looked vaguely Hispanic (see Figure 4.7). Another reason was that he left a lasting impression; he took off a shoe and sock to audition barefoot. The successful campaign has now made the actor a celebrity (Paumgarten, 2011).

There are other spokespersons who leave their mark on the brand personality but do not necessarily follow the rules for a successful spokesperson. One example is from Isuzu, the Japanese carmaker. Its new SUV was launched in the United States in the early 1990s with the help of a legendary campaign, featuring Joe Isuzu. Played by actor David Leisure, Joe Isuzu was a caricature of a car salesman. Clad in white shoes and a plaid sport coat, Joe Isuzu made the most ridiculous claims about his products, such as "It has more seats than the Astrodome!" His trademark signature phrase was "You have my word on it." The campaign was very successful. In fact, as late as 1994, Isuzu sold more SUVs than industry giant, Toyota. But the company failed to produce new competitive models and finally left the U.S. passenger car market in 2009.

A brand can appeal through a friendly and wholesome spokesperson, to project honesty and small-town feeling. Budweiser beer does this in some of its ads with the Clydesdale horses. But Budweiser also tries to appeal to the large heavy drinker mass market with its over-the-top frog commercials. This would make the brand score high on cool, spirited, and daring, making it an "exciting" personality as well—actually, giving the brand possibly a split personality.

The people in the organization behind the brand, the salespeople, and the CEO also help define the brand personality. The UPS brand has a personality that derives very much from its delivery trucks and brown uniformed personnel that can be seen in most cities every day.

One could infer that UPS "Big Brown" brand personality shows high scores on "competence" and "ruggedness." Advertising and press conferences can be used to feature the people in the organization to demonstrate the brand personality: Steve Jobs at Apple provides one striking example, with his carefully scripted introductions of new products.

CAMPAIGN PLANNING

The objectives of the introductory campaign for a new brand are typically limited to creating awareness of the brand name and hopefully also generate some interest and knowledge of one or two points of difference (POD). More ambitious campaigns will aim for attitude and preference changes and possibly even trial intentions. A useful framework is the hierarchy of effects model in Figure 4.8, which is a simplified version of the brand pyramid in Chapter 2 but adapted for a new brand.

Figure 4.8 New Brand Penetration Goals

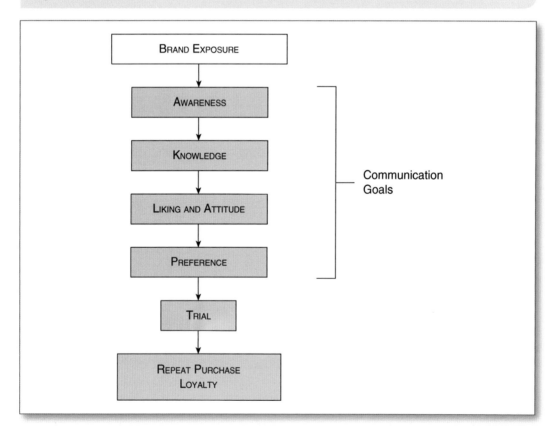

"Awareness" involves getting consumers in the target market to recall or at least recognize the new brand name and logo. "Knowledge" usually involves trying to get consumers to remember a few specific features of the new brand. In goal setting, the brand manager will usually specify a desirable level of these communication goals. The objective might be to reach a level of awareness among at least 60% of the target audience, with at least half of them also remembering some particular aspect of the brand. Setting these kinds of quantitative objectives allows the manager to also develop measures that can be used to track the gradual penetration of the new brand in the market (see the postlaunch tracking section later in the chapter).

The launch planning also involves decisions about what audiences to target and when to target them, what message to communicate, and what the appropriate timeline is.

Target Audience

In the early stages of the brand's development, the important audience members are the pioneers and early adopters. Thus, the target audience is usually the more expert and interested customers, who might be more involved in the product category and would be more receptive to the functional attributes of the new product. The expertise of the spokesperson, if any, does help here.

Message

Communications about the brand should be designed to highlight the benefits to consumers of selecting the brand and to reinforce the brand's intended positioning. These are the POD and points of parity (POP). The communications should help the target audience overcome perceived risks (functional and psychological) while highlighting how the brand can be used for self-expression purposes. In terms of brand positioning, the communications should provide a compelling value proposition for that brand that gives some reassurance that the company is a viable competitor and the product can be guaranteed to function well. Thus, it is not surprising to find the new automobiles from Korea touting their long-term warranties.

Timeline

The campaign timeline has to be carefully mapped out. What is realistically the introductory period? How long should the launch campaign be scheduled for? When should the target change? The planning horizon depends critically on the repurchase rate of the product or service. For durable products, the immediate sales effect will not be very "immediate." New buyers will come into the market, but in mature markets existing buyers might not rebuy soon. In this respect, the new Vizio brand in flat screen televisions has reached a surprisingly rapid take-off in a durable product category, starting in 2005. But the company capitalized on a couple of favorable events. For one thing, with regulatory help, the market was forced to shift from analog to digital, making high definition TV possible and opening up a new market. Also, the new flat screens were becoming affordable for the vast majority of the market; the product was in the growth phase in the U.S. market.

As production technology quickly diffused throughout Asia, Vizio could establish low-cost manufacturing in low-cost locations. First competing on price by using low-cost distributors such as Costco and mass outlets like Walmart, Vizio in 2010 turned to media advertising to establish the brand and avoid margin erosion (Strauss, 2012).

This is an exception, however. It took from 1958's Toyopet to the 1968 Corolla 10 years before Toyota was safely established in the U.S. market. Nor is success guaranteed. Peugeot, the French carmaker, also entered the U.S. market in 1958 but withdrew from the market in 1991. The low quality of the Yugo car from Yugoslavia coming on the market in the 1980s made the brand name a punch line in bad jokes (Vanderbilt, 2010).

These and many similar cases show how important the product is in creating a new brand. A consistent quality product is not enough, but without it, no brand can be sustained.

The fast-moving consumer goods categories are a different story. There are a large number of new product launches each year, not only in the United States. According to Forbes, the number of new product launches has reached a staggering 250,000 each year globally, although many are simply extensions and product modifications. Of these, observers say that about 85% to 95% will fail (Wong, 2010). Most of them will be pulled from the market within a year. Such a short decision horizon only makes sense for frequently purchased items. Ben & Jerry's quickly discontinued two new ice cream varieties, Papaya Angelou and Citron Kundera, after realizing that a lot of the young target market (younger than 35) does not read books anymore.

In general, for products with long periods before repurchasing, the timeline for a new brand has to be extended and top-line revenues and bottom-line profits can be a long time in coming. The same problem also affects many services, including financial services, insurance, and health care. By contrast, a new brand in a convenience category can be established quite quickly with the right event, sponsorship, and mass distribution.

MEDIA CHOICE

The key issue for the media decision is what media is appropriate for sending the message to the opinion leaders in the target audience.

To pioneers and opinion leaders, media advertising on television is less convincing than independent tests reported in trade magazines. New brands aiming for a teenage segment may do well with social media and less well with traditional media. It is not simply a matter of reaching the right audience but of creating the appropriate associations. Internet media will be inherently more suitable for portraying excitement, up-to-dateness, and technology and less so for communicating reliability, strength, and safety.

The launch will typically employ a number of vehicles, including television, magazine advertising, social media, and so on. Networking sites like Twitter, Facebook, YouTube, and blogs facilitate and enhance the word-of-mouth process. Individuals can retweet or repost comments made about the brand being promoted. By repeating the message, one individual can diffuse information rapidly through his or her "friends" and one posting can reach many more people. Social networking sites create word of mouth, and it is not surprising that many companies now employ social media to post informational *seeds* that grow exponentially through networking sites. Slogans can become memes—that is, getting repeated and (implicitly or explicitly) endorsed by friends, the brand image can be at least partly controlled by the firm.

For brand managers, it is important to recognize how social media has changed the traditional model of opinion leadership. While in the past, word of mouth meant the sharing of information between peers and vetted by an opinion leader, it has now come to also mean a wide diffusion of hearsay and rumors, potentially jeopardizing the intended brand position. The new model involves many more influencers (see the Word of Mouth in Social Media box).

Word of Mouth in Social Media

The traditional model of word of mouth is based on what is called the two-step flow of communications (see Figure 4.9). The model was derived from research on mass communication effects during World War II when the Nazi propaganda machine was in full gear (Katz & Lazarsfeld, 2005). What the research uncovered was that information (or propaganda) disseminated through broadcast radio did not necessarily penetrate directly to the individual person. Instead, the message and ideas were "vetted" and checked out against other people's opinions and thoughts. These people were typically those among friends and family (or peers) whom the individual thought possessed some impartiality or expertise in the issue. These key people became gatekeepers who helped validate the information received; they were the original "opinion leaders."

Figure 4.9   The Two-Step Flow of Mass Communications

Over time as television became a stronger force and the information transmitted turned from political propaganda to less threatening consumer advertising, the new opinion leaders gradually became not peers or friends but TV personalities and celebrities endorsing the brand. This is when the expert and kind doctor and attractive spokesperson became the natural presenters in advertisements and TV commercials. They substituted for the original "opinion leaders," giving the brand manager more control over the message.

With interactive and social media, the pendulum has now again swung back to consumer control over the message. In many ways, social media is the new "word of mouth." Facebook basically creates

(Continued)

(Continued)

the buzz around the brand, and the consumer decides whether or not to follow the recommendation (Sengupta, 2013). Clearly, the larger network of friends in social media makes word of mouth a bigger force than in the past. It is getting increasingly clear, however, that still only a few "close" friends carry most of the weight and that that and information and suggestions are "vetted" with those "opinion leaders" (Scott, 2010). As in the traditional consumer model, these opinion leaders become the "gatekeepers," filtering and validating the shared information. They are at the "Some friends" level in Facebook.

Social media has in fact introduced a new validating "gatekeeper" in the traditional two-step flow of communications. Marketing communications from the company—advertising, events, sponsorships, promotions—are first filtered through the consumer's network of "friends" in social media and then brought to the attention of the opinion leaders for validation. Then the information is "actionable" and the brand is included (or not) in the consumer consideration set. This three-step flow of communication can be shown as in Figure 4.10.

Figure 4.10   The Three-Step Flow of Social Media Communication

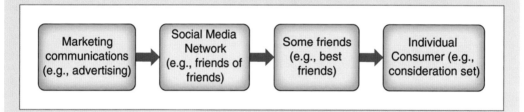

Note that this communication process shows how company communication is filtered through the social media network. Because of the speed of communication, this "filtering" does not simply validate the content but also accelerates the diffusion. Word of mouth goes through several intermediaries and recycles back but does so in real time, increasing the speed with which information spreads.

To have some control over the message, the new brand needs to become a participant in the wider network created by social media. The brand needs to provide not simply promotional messages and refutations of unwarranted rumors and also provide honest and informative material for discussion. In the social media, any misrepresentation will be quickly uncovered, compromising any new brand introduction.

Offbeat Media

Since one of the objectives of a new brand's campaign is to create awareness of its name and logo, it is important to make consumers pay attention. A number of new offbeat media vehicles have been invented by practitioners with imaginative mind-sets. A few examples include the following:

- *Brand blogging:* Creating blogs and participating in the blogosphere, in the spirit of open, transparent communications; sharing information of value that the blog community may talk about

- *Buzz marketing:* Using high-profile entertainment or odd news to get people to talk about your brand.

- *Conversation creation:* Receiving interesting or fun brand information via e-mails, catchphrases, entertainment, or promotions designed to start word-of-mouth activity

- *Product seeding:* Placing the brand into the right hands at the right time, providing information or samples to influential individuals

- *Guerilla marketing:* Appearing and promoting the brand at events sponsored by competition

- *Viral marketing:* Creating entertaining and suggestive brand messages that are designed to be passed along in an exponential fashion, often by e-mail

- *Stealth marketing:* Using nontraditional media—blogs, announcements, seeding—to hide promotional intent

These efforts usually serve as one-time stunts and are not typically meant as long-term brand building efforts. Still, they can serve their purpose, getting consumers involved and making the name memorable.

EVENT SPONSORSHIP

Although most common for established brands, event sponsorship is a popular way to create buzz and brand character for new brands. Many such events fall under the heading of "cause marketing," meaning that the brand is sponsoring a fund-raising effort for social and other charitable causes. The Japanese automaker Subaru has made its support of gay people one of its causes, using tennis star Martina Navratilova as a spokesperson. Rock bands' tours are routinely sponsored by one or more brand, and companies sponsor a wide variety of events and organizations in the entertainments and arts industries. Sports events sponsorship is common, although sometimes costly. The World Cup in Germany was sponsored by 15 companies and charged on average about €46 million (about $60 million) each for a sponsorship. The sponsors included American Budweiser for the exclusive beer commission to the dismay of German beer brewers and fans. After Anheuser-Busch was taken over by InBev, the AB InBev company has avoided antagonizing soccer fans by emphasizing local beer favorites in addition to Budweiser. So, for example, Brazilian fans will see Brahma advertised, and for Germany's matches, Hasseröder, a provincial beer from former East Germany will be promoted (see Figure 4.11)

Figure 4.11   The German World Cup Beer

Source: Anheuser-Busch. http://thegravityflux.com/hasseroder-in-wernigerode/

These global events are rare enough and reach such a vast number of people that competitive rivalry can be severe. Visa outmuscled previous MasterCard for the sponsorship at the 2010 World Cup in South Africa. Its contract includes the World Cup 2014 as well, for a total price of about $170 million (Reuters, 2007).

The sponsorship effort is sometimes connected to frequent user benefits. American Express sponsors the Radio City Music Hall events and offers preferred seating to customers paying with American Express cards. On special events such as late stage World Cup matches, the lottery used to distribute tickets is reputedly (although not officially verified) tilted in favor of customers paying by the sponsoring credit card.

PRODUCT PLACEMENT

Getting the brand featured with a famous movie star or television personality can go a long way to generate the kind of "buzz" that helps define an image and help introduce the brand. Product placement is a form of advertising where branded goods or services are placed in a context usually devoid of ads, such as movies, music videos, the story line of television shows, or news programs. The most prominent example of a successful placement is still probably E.T. tasting Reese's Pieces in the 1982 Spielberg film. Sales shot up 65% afterward. Mars, the maker of M&M's, had passed on the opportunity (www.businessweek.com/archives).

There are several reasons for brands to use product placement:

1. Fewer commercials are being watched. This is partly because of the lower "eye share" for network television in favor of cable TV. It is also because DVR/TiVo and On Demand have empowered the audience to avoid commercials.

2. There is the ability to build a stronger or emotional connection with the consumer because the product is used by a favorite character.

3. The consumer can discover, learn about, and build an affinity for a brand without the doubts that a commercial might evoke.

There are also reasons why a film studio would use product placement:

1. The brand used can "shed light" on characters; look for brands that best relate character lifestyle (e.g., Apple products are "young and cool").

2. It helps defray the costs of producing a movie.

There are risks for both parties. The film might be compromised if the product placement becomes obvious. For the same reason, consumers might turn against the brand. Also, the brand might not be used in a very complimentary way; a smashed up Mercedes-Benz might not be a very positive image for viewers to see.

Among brands that often use product placement tactics, Apple tops the chart with its products appearing in 30% of the number one films at the U.S. box office in 2010 (Burrows & Fixmer, 2012). Nike is tied for second, with Chevrolet and Ford. By contrast, Mercedes-Benz has been reluctant to have its cars used (and abused) in movies; it famously rejected an offer for product placement in *Slumdog Millionaire,* an award-winning movie set in India (Brodesser-akner, 2008).

There are usually two options to pay for such placement. One is to pay directly. Alternatively, the client provides the products in exchange for the placement (also known as a barter arrangement). Despite its top position, Apple allegedly never pays for a product placement. Its easily recognized logo has become a useful prop to characterize a creative and offbeat individual. Other brands are not so fortunate.

According to estimates, companies spent around $7.4 billion for product placement in TV, movies, Internet, video games, and other media in 2011 (http://www.pqmedia.com/about-press-201212.html). For example, the now legendary 1995 launch of the new BMW's Z3 roadster as James Bond's preferred vehicle in the movie *GoldenEye* cost the company $75 million in joint promotions (Dolan & Fournier, 2002). To secure the placement rights in the film, BMW also had to sign a three-movie deal with the production studio. The company used the films to promote its BMW 750iL, the R1200C motorcycle, and the Z8 (http://www.carenthusiast.com/news0910/bond_2.htm).

But product placement also occurs without any direct involvement from brand management. After all, even in the old days, movie actors needed to use brands whether driving a car, smoking a cigarette, or just having a drink. A classic early case is Humphrey Bogart's preference for Gordon's gin in the 1951 movie *The African Queen* (see Figure 4.12). As so often, not all the exposure is positive. In the movie, his costar Katharine Hepburn is seen throwing a bottle into the river.

There is no specific legal prohibition against such use of brands. But it means the brand owner has limited control over the exposure. For example, in the 2012 movie *Flight,* an alcoholic pilot (played by Denzel Washington) opens and drinks a can of Budweiser beer while at the control of the airplane, which soon runs into trouble. To avoid a negative fall-out, the maker of Budweiser, Anheuser-Busch, has asked the film distributor Paramount Pictures that the brand logo be hidden or obliterated (www.guardian.co.uk/media/filmblog/2012/nov/06).

As regular advertising media suffers, product placement has become increasingly attractive to build brand image and personality. But it is not always very clear whether the

Figure 4.12 "I'll Have Another One," Humphrey Bogart in *The African Queen*

Source: http://www.creammagazine.com/2012/03/online-agency-pushes-for-more-product-placement-in-movies-and-television/

positive impact is as big as hoped for after the Reese's Pieces' success or whether poor placement is as negative as feared.

TRACKING RESULTS

The gradual penetration of the new brand into the marketplace needs to be tracked carefully. In the typical case, the introductory campaign will lay out some checkpoints along the path from initial awareness to increased familiarity and liking and preference. The introductory campaign cannot really aim at the higher commitment levels of loyalty and bonding directly. But tracking measures should involve trial and initial satisfaction. Then, over time, it is very important to track repeat purchases or, for less frequently purchased products, positive word of mouth and recommendations to others.

It is important to track the speed and depth of penetration. Where store data and scanner data are available, actual sales data can be obtained and tracked almost daily. The trend in the sales data can usually be projected out using extrapolation of the standard product life cycle pattern (see Figure 4.13).

But sales data do not capture the whole picture of the brand building process. More important for branding purposes is the tracking of how consumers move through the brand equity pyramid from awareness and up (see Chapter 2). To get that information, it is necessary to do periodical surveys of actual and potential customers. Mapping out the findings in a bar diagram and drawing on the hierarchy of effects model used to set objectives can give a much better sense of how the brand acceptance and allegiance is progressing. The following figure is representative of such diagnostic tracking of both reach and depth (see Figure 4.14).

The vertical axis shows the percentage of target consumers who have been reached by the brand message at a particular point in time. The percentage of target customers "aware" shows how well the campaign has managed to penetrate consumer consciousness. The percentage "familiar" are those consumers who do feel familiar with the brand, a deeper sentiment. The next step involves what perceptions the consumers have of the brand. "Features" represent the percentage of consumers who know some of the functional features of the brand—for example, its two main differential advantages. Similarly, "imagery" might involve the percentage of consumers who recollect the two primary

Figure 4.13 Tracking the Speed and Depth of Brand Penetration

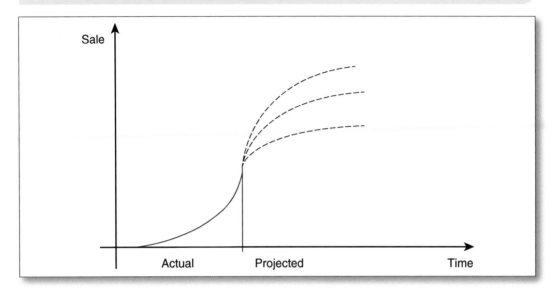

Figure 4.14 Tracking the Penetration Process of a New Brand

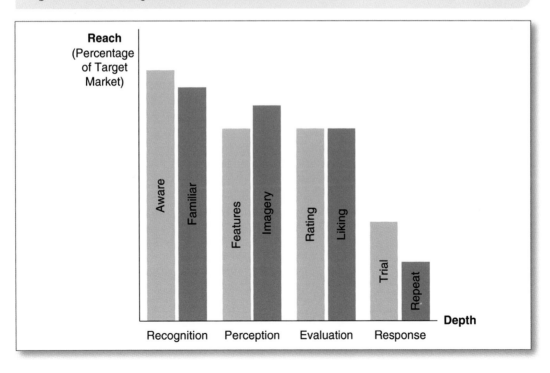

design features of the product or the logo. The "rating" and the "liking" scores represent the consumers who rate the brand highly and those who like the brand.

In the brand building process, it is usually premature to try to get deeper into any bonding or loyalty sentiments. Questions can at least tap into the likelihood of inquiries about wanting to try the brand. The conversion rates between the successive stages are important. For example, it is useful to try to develop a sense of the likelihood of a conversion from favorable perceptions to liking and trial. Past brand introductions can help give a sense of the percentage of consumers with favorable "liking" scores will usually be converted to "trial."

Using this kind of tracking tool and repeating the measurement over time, the firm should be able to identify the extent to which goals of awareness and familiarity have been met, at what level in the brand equity pyramid the drop-off is most severe, and what adjustments to the campaign might be called for. For example, if the drop-off from familiarity to features and imagery is great, the campaign has not managed to convert basic recognition into deeper perceptions and knowledge about the brand. Thus a level of 80 % familiarity, which is quite close to saturation, should not be followed by very little (say, 30 %) knowledge of specific features. This suggests a modified campaign with a stress on the unique selling propositions. Similarly, if rating and liking is high, but trial is low, the campaign might have to shift from communications to in-store promotions. It usually means that consumers like the brand but cannot find it in the store.

SUMMARY

Creating a new brand offers a serious challenge to a brand manager. A new name, new logo, and new slogan will need to be invented. All three should reflect the product's value proposition and target positioning. The new brand identity should reflect company values in some form, and the intended new brand image and personality will suggest but also constrain the selection of appeals and spokesperson.

With so many loose parts to the puzzle, the brand manager needs to be very systematic but also imaginative. Usually the name and logo will be decided first, focusing on finding a suitable and available brand name, and then a logo that relates to the brand identity. The slogan typically comes next, from the advertising agency's copywriter, and should express the value proposition in a shorthand "unique selling proposition" manner.

The appropriate brand image and brand personality require particular attention to media choice, message, and spokesperson. Event sponsorship and product placement will factor in as well. Brand image will be based not simply on functional characteristics but also on media choices and word of mouth from early adopters and opinion leaders, filtered through both social media "friends" and the social network at large. Although the brand personality will only emerge in time, it will be influenced by the spokesperson, product placement, and the traits of the typical user.

A brand can be said to be *established* when it has a clear identity, image, and personality. How *strong* it is depends on its depth of affinity (level of loyalty) and its reach across markets. Getting there will take time, effort, and strategic flexibility. The necessary adjustment will depend on what brand tracking reveals about the acceptance and growth of brand penetration. Consumer survey or panel measures of the percentage aware of the brand name and percentage knowledgeable about at least some brand features serve to track the success of the launch. Tracking penetration should begin at the inception of the brand and continue until the brand is divested or harvested. An effective tracking instrument would provide feedback on consumer perceptions that relate to tactical decisions, including questions about image (trustworthiness, good value, dynamic, etc.), personality (honest, rugged, etc.), and position relative to the competition (POP, points of superiority).

KEY TERMS

Brand name, Brand logo, Brand penetration, Brand slogans, Brand asset management, Event sponsorship, Offbeat media, Product placement, Spokesperson, Tracking penetration

DISCUSSION QUESTIONS

1. Starbucks is a relatively new brand, allegedly created without any advertising. Do some research (on Google, for example) to try to find out how the brand was built. What are the lessons for other new brands?

2. Pick a strong brand with a prominent spokesperson (an example would be Dennis Haysbert at Allstate Insurance). Discuss how the brand positioning and the spokesperson fit together. Do competitors also have strong spokespersons? Can you explain why or why not?

3. The three-step flow of communication model suggests that "friends" in the social network can serve as opinion leaders. Can you think of examples of products where this is likely to be the case? How could you use buzzmetric data (see Chapter 3) to identify who might be an opinion leader in a social network?

4. Use the diagram in Figure 4.14 to discuss how a drop in the new brand penetration process at different stages (from awareness to repeat) can be remedied.

MINICASE: SHARAPOVA BUILDS A BRAND

Most of us are probably tired of reading about the riches of tennis champions. Roger Federer, until recently the number one men's player, is said to be worth $180 million net. He made a reported $71.5 million in 2013, of which $65 million came from endorsements. Maria Sharapova, a leading

(Continued)

(Continued)

woman tennis player, is said to be worth about $90 million (figures from the CelebrityNetWorth.com web-site).

Tennis champions are of course not new. There have been a number of outstanding champions over the years, and experts still argue about whether the present crop is that much better than past years. What has changed is the money collected by the stars. Tennis champions are now "brands," and these brands are being monetized. The brand-building process follows some pretty straightforward but strict and often unforgiving guidelines.

The first requirement is outstanding performance in competition and especially the main Grand Slam events. The four slams are the Australian, French and U.S. Open plus Wimbledon. These four are globally televised events, and it is primarily because of the TV rights that the available money to dole out has increased significantly. Global television has increased the audience exponentially, leading to increased advertising spending, which, in turn, has made the tournaments' coffers richer and the prize money higher. Furthermore, for the individual athlete, a strong performance will not only mean money, but will also make his or her face (and the body) exposed around the world. The higher recognition level translates into potentially more earnings through endorsements. Sharapova, with three grand slam titles, has several endorsements, including an 8-year deal with Nike for $70 million.

All this does not really need more from the athlete than a strong performance on the court. Recently, however, some athletes have gone further and attempted to create their own brands. Given what we know about branding, this is a quite natural step. The personal brand identity is already well established—the player is well recognized for his or her achievements. The image is well honed through television interviews and attitude on the court, as is the personality. What remains is to leverage this brand equity through products which naturally fit with the brand—not just via endorsements, but via direct ownership and licensing of the brand name. Not all athletes are willing to take this step, in fact most are content staying simply as spokespersons for others' products.

Sharapova is one athlete that has embraced the new brand ownership role. In addition to her prize money and endorsements, she collects revenues from more daring enterprises. The first step has involved creating collections for the brands she already endorses. Thus, she has her own designer clothes collection (which she wears in play) sold by Nike, She created a line of shoes for Cole Haan and her "ballerina flat" was one of the top-selling shoes for the company. For TAG Heuer she has designed a line of sunglasses, and she might design jewelry for Tiffany.

The next step is naturally to develop completely new products independently. Her first effort, however, seems somewhat curious. In 2013 she launched her own line of candy, "Sugarpova," a product that she has painstakingly developed over more than a year. The jury is still out on its success. One promotional effort that backfired was an appeal to the U.S. Open officials to allow her name to be listed as "Sugarpova," a request that was later withdrawn.

Sharapova's efforts have not gone unnoticed. A Harvard Business School Case has been developed covering her brand. Her competitors, notably Serena Williams and Li Na (the leading Chinese woman player) seem to be following in her footsteps (with Li Na in fact managed by Sharapova's agent). Serena Williams' own 2005 line of clothing, named Aneres (Serena spelled backward), was later dropped but is reportedly being re-introduced. Li Na is focused still on endorsements, particularly targeting the China market.

The players are competitors on and off the court. An exchange of incendiary comments between Sharapova and Williams at the 2013 Wimbledon brought on a slight media frenzy, with reports that the Sharapova "brand" had been damaged. Passions can easily rise with competitive pressure, especially when the stakes are so high.

Discussion Questions

1. How important is performance on the court to the champion's brand equity?

2. In what ways might the endorsements and the brand building interfere with the on-court performance?

3. How important is the off-the-court behavior of the athletes?

4. How likely is it that the brand will continue after the athlete retires? How can brand building help?

Sources

Hyde, M. (2013, August 21). Maria Sharapova's brand strategy is shameless but at least it's honest. *The Guardian.*
Kelner, M. (2013, June 22). This time it's personal as SW19 stars Sharapova and Williams go to war. *Daily Mail.*
Lattman, P. (2012, August 26). Dealmaker for the Shotmakers. *The New York Times,* p. F4.

SUGGESTED PROJECT

Image and Personality Exercise: For two brands in a category of interest (say Brand X and Y), have 20 people answer the following question: What three words come to mind when you think about Brand X? Brand Y? Organize the 60 words about each brand into nonpersonality traits (e.g., powerful, quality, inexpensive) and personality traits (e.g., smart, kind, hopeful). Note: You will likely need to combine words that are synonyms. Within each category, compute the frequency of each word and its proportion of all the words in the category. Order these percentages from most to least for the image and the personality groups separately. Compare and contrast the images and personalities of the two brands.

PART II

Branding Strategies

107

CHAPTER 5

Managing an Established Brand

For a brand to sustain consumer interest, it can't just be different; it has to keep being different.

—John Gerzema and Ed Lebar[1]

LEARNING OBJECTIVES

In this chapter, you will learn the following:

- About the main growth strategies of established brands
- How **loyalty programs** help and maintain and grow brand allegiance
- The important branding role of corporate social responsibility
- How competitive position influences the choice of strategy
- When a brand should respond to a low-price private brand attack
- How to fit the media mix to the brand personality

Once brand awareness and product knowledge have reached saturation and the brand positioning, the brand identity, and image are firmed up, the brand management task changes. The brand has now established its position; it has a definite brand identity and a

---

[1]John Gerzema is chief insights officer and Ed Lebar is CEO of BrandAsset Consulting, both at Young & Rubicam. The quote is from Gerzema and Lebar (2008, p. 41).

unique brand image. It is a player in its market. This increases the options available to the brand manager but also the challenges.

The first option is whether to grown the brand and if so how. The second is how to prepare for and respond to competitive threats. And the third is how to manage the communications mix to support the brand in maturity. This chapter addresses each of these in turn, beginning with market penetration as the basic growth strategy for existing brands.

MANAGING MARKET PENETRATION

The Ansoff Matrix

Before getting too far into the management of an established brand, it will be useful to spell out more precisely what the basic strategic alternatives are. To do this, we can use the classic Ansoff growth matrix (see Figure 5.1).

The matrix identifies four alternative growth strategies for a company's product. An existing product can penetrate further into the existing market—the *market penetration*

Figure 5.1   Four Alternative Growth Strategies

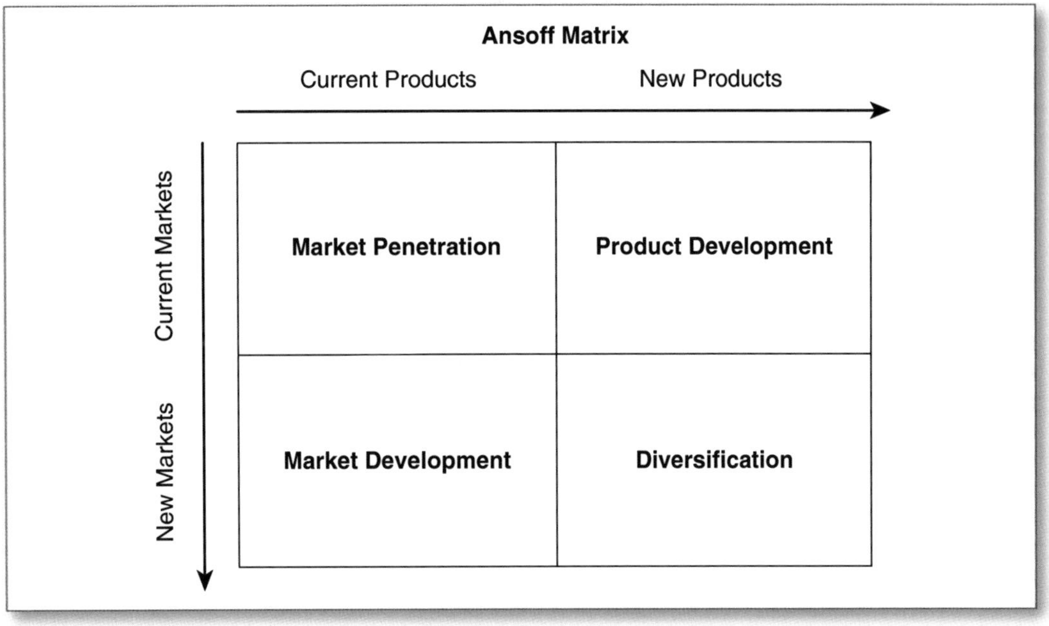

Source: Ansoff (1965).

alternative in the upper left-hand corner of the matrix. Alternatively, new products can be developed (*product development*) or new markets can be entered (*market development*). Finally, the company can grow by getting into new products and new markets completely, a *diversification* strategy.

We can apply this framework to a company's established brand to show the different strategic options. In the first four chapters of this book, we essentially developed and built the brand that the company now possesses. In this chapter, where we discuss the management of an established brand, we are dealing with what Ansoff called "market penetration." The tasks include growing loyalty levels among existing customers, upgrading and extending the product line, and taking other actions to essentially penetrate the market further. In Chapter 6, we discuss the strategy of using the existing brand to endorse new products, similar to the product development quadrant of Ansoff's matrix. Then in Chapter 7, we leverage the brand by going into new markets, moving into the market development corner of the matrix. Finally, what Ansoff called "diversification" corresponds to what we discuss in Chapter 8, where we extend brand management to several brands, not just one.

Penetration and Brand Allegiance

Market penetration with an established brand means in part simply doing what has already put the brand into its desired position. The advertising and promotional strategies used to create the now-established brand identity and image need to be continued—although not necessarily at the level used in the introductory campaign. A strong brand needs continuity and consistency, keeping the trust of its initial customers. It needs also build deeper relationships with its current customers through customer engagement and customer relationship management (CRM). It can also build an image of caring by through corporate social responsibility (CSR) programs.

In some ways, sustaining and deepening the allegiance of an established brand can be the most challenging brand management task. It means maintaining the initial brand excitement in the company, keeping the brand relevant and in the minds of consumers, and fending off intruding brands from competitors and private labels. The task is complicated because it involves a basic conflict between keeping the current customers happy and excited but also keeping them away from exploring other brands. It's akin to sustaining the joy in a marriage. It involves a call to action and inaction.

There are three basic and complementary strategies to increasing brand allegiance (see Figure 5.2).

The first strategy is to raise brand loyalty directly among existing customers by establishing loyalty programs, such as frequent-flier awards, membership discounts, and so on. CRM is a cornerstone of a loyalty strategy.

A second allegiance strategy is to maintain engagement with one's customers by frequently refreshing the product line. Upgrading the line with new and modified products will keep the brand dynamic, exciting, and relevant to maximize customer engagement. Extending the product line by adding new models, package sizes, and accessories will

Figure 5.2   Increasing Brand Allegiance

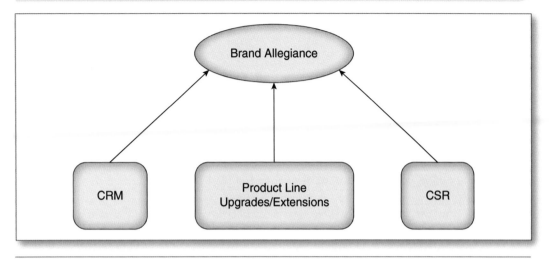

Note: CRM = customer relationship management; CSR = corporate social responsibility.

increase penetration and offer more variety to customers. The loyalty programs and product line strategies are complementary; loyalty is easier to kindle when the customer can rely on up-to-date products and models.

But brand loyalty does not simply mean repeat purchases and CRM. It is important to recognize that any allegiance implies a broader mutual commitment between the brand and its customers. Today, that allegiance transcends products and services. The brand has to grow with the consumer, to anticipate and help lead the consumer to where the market—and society—is going. This means that the brand has to engage with the consumer over and above purely functional and emotional needs. The brand has to reflect and speak to more general consumer concerns. This third "penetration" strategy involves ethical conduct, "green" products, support of environmental efforts, CSR, fair trade, and cause marketing. The brand should reflect concerns over and above the immediate profit-and-loss bottom line. The larger concern of the company will yield affection and allegiance for the brand over a longer run than just the next product cycle.

Customer Relationship Management

CRM is the main way of maintaining and increasing loyalty. CRM involves the creation of special benefits for preferred customers (Boulding, Staelin, Ehret, & Johnston, 2005). Examples include frequent-flier programs, store membership cards, dedicated service personnel, and similar efforts that favor preferred customers. The aim of CRM programs is to make the loyalty "stickier," meaning that the customer will engage in some effort to patronize the brand. We all know somebody who is willing to skip a nonstop flight in order to travel across three stops with another airline where he or she needs just a few more miles to qualify for a free trip. Apple's refusal to use shared software is partly an effort to make the customer more dependent on Apple—aka "loyal fans" of Apple.

In the CRM effort, brand communities and customer clubs can be very helpful. Connecting people who are linked by a common brand has become prevalent in the automobile and motorcycle industries. General Motors' (GMs)' Saturn Forum and Harley-Davidson's bikers groups are well known. Other companies have also formed user communities. Pampers Village is an online community with a newsletter, small gifts, and a support group of mothers with newborn and small babies (www.pampers.com). Weight Watchers offers a customized online weight loss plan that offers advice on recipes and products (www.weightwatchers.com). A Hello Kitty fan club (www.hellokittyfansunits.webs.com) offers members pictures and videos of Hello Kitty, access to special content and new products, and connections to other fans. Companies play a role in these communities, but their presence has to be carefully calibrated. Groups such as Pabst Blue Ribbon drinkers do not want the stigma of corporate involvement (Kowitt, 2009).

Loyalty programs have been particularly active in mobile marketing. One mobile app serves to connect all the loyalty programs a consumer is signed up for and also enables the consumer to add more loyalty memberships (www.keyringapp.com). Other apps are designed specifically for a particular company and add value for the loyal customer by offering specials and deals tailored to the individual consumer. For example, many retailers and chain restaurants let shoppers get points and loyalty benefits using branded smartphone apps, including indie bookstores, coffee shops, and local restaurants.

There are also so-called third-party app makers who help companies create the mobile loyalty programs for clients. Shopkick is one such example (www.shopkick.com). Its app for the iPhone leverages the popularity of "checking in" at various retail locations to earn points and other rewards by entering or exploring specific areas of the store. The Target chain is an early client. Target customers can download the free shopkick mobile app from the iTunes App Store to their iPhone (see Figure 5.3).

Target makes offers via shopkick on a wide range of everyday items like food and cleaning supplies, to specialty products like electronics and toys. When customers enter a participating Target store, they instantly receive points, called "kicks." Consumers also can scan select product bar codes in-store to earn additional kicks. Target is also able to deliver scannable mobile coupons to guests for redemption at checkout (www.screen mediadaily.com).

Brand loyalty programs aim to retain current customers to the extent possible. A well-known maxim is that it costs five times as much to acquire a new customer as it does retaining an existing customer. The sentiment is expressed in an article in the *Harvard Business Review* that argues that customer retention strategies should aim at

Figure 5.3   Target's Shopkick Consumer Mobile App

Source: http://www.mobilecommercedaily.com/wet-seal-target-ramp-up-mobile-lbs-to-drive-customer-acquisition-loyalty

"zero defections" (Reichheld & Sasser, 1990). However, as we saw in Chapter 2, such a strategy is often too optimistic. As the empirical evidence shows, many brands exhibit rates of defection around 50%, meaning that about half of the current customers will next time buy a competing brand (Sharp, 2010, pp. 32–33). This happens even when a brand does have a loyal following. The reasons are several. It may be that the customer wants variety, or that the brand happens not to be available at the point of purchase, or that the purchase is for a special occasion, and so on. Thus, even though brand loyalty is the aim of a CRM strategy, it does not necessarily lead to a 100% share of the customer spending.

PRODUCT STRATEGIES

A second major strategy to raise brand allegiance is to upgrade the products and extend the product line. This allows the brand to keep the brand relevant among current customers and also to attract new customers from competition. We will distinguish between two main strategies: (1) upgraded products and (2) line extension.

Upgraded Products

The most common way of maintaining the initial "buzz" used to establish the brand is to introduce innovative product modifications, new versions, improvements, and new models. For many brands, this is the major means by which brand excitement and relevance is maintained. For many years in the past, product introductions were relatively rare and routinely planned. New automobile models would be introduced in the fall each year, new fashion would be timed to the seasons, and television series would start and close at pre-determined times. Nowadays, these cutoff dates are extended or completely ignored, and new product versions are likely to happen any time.

In addition, new and modified versions have to be pre-announced and release dates set, occasioning additional publicity and excitement before and after the actual introductions. The rampant rise of me-too products and imitative features also means that product innovations do not simply come from the brand owner but are the result of competitive successes.

When Japanese electronics maker Sharp put a camera on a cell phone in 1997, other cell phone producers soon followed. Virtually all phones need a camera now. Motorola's and Samsung's success in the late 1990s with the clamshell cell phone was soon copied by other manufacturers. The exception was the leader Nokia, who did not offer a clamshell model until 2004. Nokia lost a significant piece of market share in that period, going down from 37% to 30% worldwide (Cheng, 2012).

The brand excitement aroused by product innovation at this level can be further heightened by tactical moves. One way is to make some of the new options available only in limited quantities. This is a standard tactic of Swiss watchmaker Swatch. The special designer models procured by Swatch for its fashion watches are produced in limited quantities and are available for a short time only. Some beer brands also use this tactic—spring beer, or Christmas ale, for example—as do winemakers introducing the new Beaujolais every year with a slogan "The New Beaujolais has arrived." Zara, the Spanish fast retail apparel maker, has become famous for limited series, enhancing the uniqueness of the designs (Hansen, 2012).

Product innovation with the help of customers and product users is another way to create involvement and affinity with the brand. The rise of the Internet allows the use of interactive websites where users can suggest product modifications and improvements and even design their own versions of the product. Automobile and other durable goods manufacturers find this particularly useful. It is, of course, important that suggestions be acknowledged in some form, and even though the setup of an interactive website can be done with relative ease, the maintenance and updating of the site require dedicated personnel. Weak feedback, outdated websites, and bad customer relations are negative news that can reverberate quickly on the net.

Line Extension

Product **line extension** means the firm will develop and introduce new models and products that serve to fill out and expand the product line offering to existing and new customers. It is exciting and satisfying for current customers to see the brand attracting new customers from competition. It means the brand loyalty is not misplaced. When you choose an Android smartphone and see others with the similar phone, the cognitive dissonance and doubts that all of us consumers feel are assuaged. This so-called demonstration effect is important for brand loyalty. "We made the right choice," and we are happy to tell others about it.

The basic attraction of product line extension is that the brand becomes relevant for a larger market. The famous slogan "A car for every purse and purpose," minted by Alfred P. Sloan in the 1920s, was used to explain the branding strategy of GM in opposition to Ford's idea that the customer can have "any color he wants as long as it is black." GM's approach with five main brands (Cadillac, Oldsmobile, Buick, Pontiac, Chevrolet), each managed as a separate division with its own model lineup, set the standard for product line branding for years to come (see Figure 5.4). It is fair to say Alfred P. Sloan's "ladder of success" with an entry-level buyer starting out with a "basic transportation" Chevrolet, rising through Pontiac, Oldsmobile, Buick, and ultimately to Cadillac represented one of the earliest efforts to differentiate a product through branding (Sloan, 1965, pp. 62–69).

Line extension leads to closer adaptation to different user requirements. "Versioning" is a popular term for the proliferation of the same branded product for a variety of uses and

Figure 5.4   Five General Motors Brand Logos

Source: General Motors. www.gm.com

users (see, e.g., Mohammed, n.d.). So, for example, Bayer's successful One A Day vitamins have grown from simple multivitamins to versions for males and females, to versions for women's prenatal, women's skin support, women's petites (smaller tablets), and so on. The same pattern can be observed in many product categories—shampoos, breakfast cereal, teas, and so on. The brand is "revitalized" by a seemingly continuous stream of new product options.

Product line extensions allow for the fact that current customers are not necessarily staying put in their needs, desires, and preferences. Existing customers grow older, unavoidably, life cycle shifts as singles marry, have children, who then leave home (or not). These changes will also change the market. The segments move. To follow the loyal customer, firms have to introduce new and adapted products with different features and new functions to keep the brand relevant. Watches will have larger faces, soft drinks will have less sugar (or more), new designs will feature easy opening or childproof caps, and cute cell phones for teenage girls will grow into more rugged designs in order to follow their customers.

However, it is not always clear that brand managers should follow their customers into new segments. The threat to the brand name may simply be too great. The ladder of success branding policy of GM reflects the notion that one single brand should not be stretched too far.

A small niche market may be attractive from a brand loyalty standpoint because it becomes possible to customize designs and features for a select few. This raises allegiance and brand loyalty, but as a business strategy it is risky. Automobiles provide some examples of this. A brand such as Saab 900 was long a front-wheel drive pioneer with a unique aerodynamic styling reflecting its airplane heritage. It had a very devoted following in several markets around the world, with customers who claimed to greet each other as they met on the highway and a dedicated website: www.saabsunited.com. As a brand, it was strong in terms of allegiance, but the car was simply too dependent on a small set of existing customers. When the brand executed a product line extension with a larger, more luxurious model, Saab 9000, product deficiencies prevented it from breaking into the new segment and the larger model was discontinued. Although an independent company agreed to buy the Saab marquee in 2010, the car's future has been uncertain since 2008, when GM, its then owner, decided to put it up for sale. In May 2012, it was acquired by a Hong Kong-based consortium with plans to launch an electric car on the same platform (http://www.saabsunited.com/category/news).

CORPORATE SOCIAL RESPONSIBILITY

CSR is the notion of achieving company success through supporting community efforts. It is "doing well by doing good." CSR has become increasingly important in sustaining and deepening the allegiance to brands (see, e.g., Klein & Dawar, 2004; Sen & Bhattacharya, 2001). For example, event sponsorships for good causes are common. Thus, Avon sponsors a walk for breast cancer, *Sports Illustrated* sponsors "National Breast Cancer Awareness Month," Continental Airlines sponsors a "Multiple Sclerosis Walk." Cause-related marketing can be a very effective strategy to help cement a brands reputation. The lack of an obvious profit-oriented motivation and the added publicity can be very useful to further enhance the "mind share" for an existing brand. This can also help soften the image of a big brand that might otherwise seem distant and arrogant. For example, IBM and The Nature Conservancy have launched a website called "Rivers for Tomorrow" where watershed managers can map, analyze, and share detailed information about the health of local freshwater river basins to inform cleanup programs (http://www.ibm.com/smarterplanet/us/en/water_management/ideas/).

Some companies go beyond cause marketing and use social media and interactive marketing to open new relationships between brands and consumers. The Pepsi Refresh Project exemplifies this trend. The project was designed to give away more than $20 million in the United States to fund good ideas—big and small—that move communities forward. People can register and submit their ideas and vote to promote ideas that they care about. For PepsiCo, this will generate a steady stream of national, local and online media buzz, keeping the brand relevant and vibrant (Zmuda, 2010).

In order to reap the benefits from these social and cultural sponsorships, it is important that the rest of the communication mix integrates these events with the other media components—advertising, promotions, PR, and the Internet. The sponsorship effort is sometimes connected to frequent user benefits. American Express sponsors Radio City Music Hall events in New York City and offers preferred seating to customers paying by American Express cards.

It is important to establish a direct link online between the event itself and the brand's website. In some cases, the event website may be reluctant to do this, for instance in an artistic context where it might desirable to avoid the association with crass commercialism. The Berlin Philharmonic's website (www.berlin-philharmoniker.de/en) posts its sponsor's name (Deutsche Bank) in a corner with a very small font; however, the New York Philharmonic displays its sponsor (Credit Suisse) in a similar place but with slightly larger font (www.nyphil.org). By contrast, the sponsorships should be posted prominently on the brand's website and links to the events created. Deutsche Bank provides a web gallery of its many "doing good" efforts—not only the Berlin Philharmonic but a golf tournament (in Dubai) and other CSR-oriented efforts (www.db.com/csr/en/art_and_music).

The impact of CSR efforts is generally positive and consumers tend to ascribe a caring attitude to the company and its brands (e.g., Klein & Dawar, 2004). However, the effect is limited by the extent to which the issues supported are congruent with consumers' attitude. Where there is discrepancy between the cause supported and consumer sentiment, the effect is minimal and can even be reversed. For example, a company portraying itself as a supporter of a fair workplace among its overseas suppliers need to back up its claim with supportive efforts also at home for women and minorities (e.g., Sen & Bhattacharya, 2001). To be successful, CSR efforts should be a manifestation of a serious and authentic commitment (see the Conscious Capitalism box).

Conscious Capitalism

Some companies go further beyond simply sponsoring worthwhile causes and events. They try to infuse their entire mode of operation with an ethical component that then spills over into their brand. **Conscious Capitalism** stands for this idea. For example, employees are told that they are doing inherently good work and that by doing good work the business will also do well financially. The basic credo of the movement involves four tenets:

1. Business is inherently good because it creates value.
2. It is ethical because it is based on voluntary exchange.
3. It is noble because it can elevate our existence.
4. It is heroic because it lifts people out of poverty and creates prosperity.

One leader in this movement is the co-CEO of Whole Foods Market, John Mackey, who has also written extensively about the movement (Mackey & Sisodia, 2013).

Figure 5.5   The Whole Foods Market Logo

Source: Whole Foods Market.

As always, once such lofty goals are announced, the brand and the company will attract more than usual scrutiny, making it extra important that the management delivers on the promises. So far, Whole Foods Market has done quite well.

Green Products

Extending the product line into so-called green products and services has also become a popular way for brands to achieve a more "caring and responsible" image and personality.

Many green and organic products and product lines have now been developed by several manufacturers. In 2009, the number of green product on retail shelves in the United States grew by 72 % according to the environmental marketing firm TerraChoice. "Going green" with existing product lines also helps the bottom line as consumers increasingly pay attention to environmental impact of their choices.

Examples of such line extensions abound. Unilever reignited its Surf detergent brand by Surf Excel Quick Wash, cutting water consumption in half. Procter & Gamble (P&G) similarly cut water consumption by raising the power of its liquid detergent and reducing package sizes. It has also shifted to biodegradable plastics in some of its packaging, including Pantene shampoo.

The efforts by major automobile companies to develop hybrid and electric cars also help to change brand image. Offering lower calorie meals has helped McDonald's image, although competitors such as Subway have still higher ratings on "greenness."

The green product line extensions are not always quite what they seem. For example, *Huggies'* new Pure & Natural disposable diapers come in green-colored boxes. Disposable diapers add tons of waste to America's landfills every year. They also contain chemicals, including carcinogens like dioxin. But the only difference with regular Huggies is a small piece of organic cotton on the outside of the diaper (TerraChoice, 2007). This is not very "green."

Fair Trade

A Fair Trade brand such as Starbucks or Honest Tea means that the brand tries to make sure the original growers (of coffee and tea, respectively) in the developing world capture more of the total price than before. The movement has been largely successful and has made a difference for consumers. For example, according to some research, consumers are willing to pay 10 % more for a fair trade product such as coffee (De Pelsmacker, Driesen, & Rayp, 2006). However, there have been suggestions that the middlemen, including the companies, are not always passing through the money (Hamel, 2006).

In general, the green and fair trade efforts have apositive and enduring effect on brand equity (e.g., Castaldo, Perrini, Misani, & Tencati, 2008). However, if abuse or inconsistent practices are uncovered, the potential negative spillover effects need to be considered. In fact, *greenwashing* has become a new pejorative term to describe company efforts to capitalize on the desire for consumers to choose environmentally friendly and organic products (TerraChoice, 2007). Watchdogs such as TerraChoice are trying to police the most egregious breaches of the public trust. From a branding perspective, being accused of greenwashing would be very detrimental to the firm, easily leading to a dilution of brand equity. As always, ethical conduct and honest dealings are the best antidote.

MANAGING COMPETITIVE RESPONSE

So far we have said very little about competition. It is useful to keep in mind that with a penetration strategy, the brand is basically involved in what Porter (1980) called competitive "rivalry." Increased penetration is basically a "red ocean" strategy as Kim and Mauborgne (2005) described the intense jockeying for market share. While CRM and CSR strategies can be usefully applied for an established brand in any type of competitive position, the product strategies (product upgrades and line extensions) have different effects depending on the competitive power and position of the brand.

The Role of Market Position

To see how competitive power matters, it is useful to distinguish between three types of market positions: (1) a category leader, (2) a major "runner-up," and (3) a midlevel niche brand. The competitive power runs basically from the market leader to the runner-up brands and then to the midlevel niche brands. The competitive reactions differ for each of the three brand categories.

The basic strategic choices and how they relate to the competitive reactions are indicated in Figure 5.6. In what follows, each position is discussed in more depth. Later in the chapter, we will also discuss the competitive threat from private labels and store brands.

Category Leader

The overriding concern for an unquestionably leading brand in a category—say, Coca-Cola in soft drinks, Heinz in ketchup, Starbucks in coffee, and McDonald's in fast food—is not to

Figure 5.6   Competitive Strategy Depends on Market Position

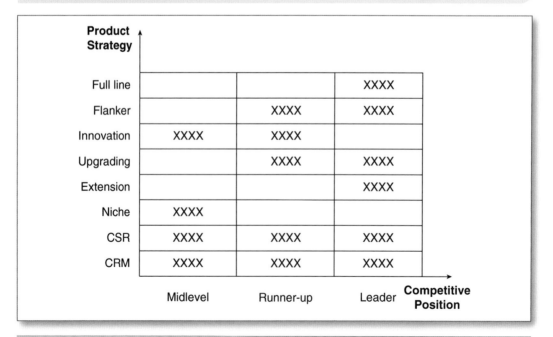

Product Strategy	Midlevel	Runner-up	Leader
Full line			XXXX
Flanker		XXXX	XXXX
Innovation	XXXX	XXXX	
Upgrading		XXXX	XXXX
Extension			XXXX
Niche	XXXX		
CSR	XXXX	XXXX	XXXX
CRM	XXXX	XXXX	XXXX

Note: xxxx indicates an appropriate strategy; CRM = customer relationship management; CSR = corporate social responsibility.

call attention to other brands in its promotions. Reinforcing the image of superiority is best done by standing "head and shoulders" above the fray of competition. Marketing communications need to focus forward and upward as the leadership position mandates. The upshot is that product upgrading and line extensions become natural strategies, the brand becomes a spokesperson for the category, and it should champion the generic growth of the category.

These are tall tasks. Once a brand reaches the top, most roads go downhill. Most competitors will tend to benchmark the leading brand, defining their strategies in some relationship to the largest shareholder. For example, major competitors go head-to-head against the leader with comparative advertising, a quite successful strategy that should not be used by the leading brand (e.g., Pechmann & Stewart, 1990). There are advantages to being the leader, however. Marketing communications that increase the generic market will naturally fall mostly to the lead brand. One reason is that a leading brand will typically be more easily available in distribution channels than other brands (Sharp, 2010). Also, the leading brand does not necessarily have to be in the forefront of creating new products or upgrading features, but the brand has to introduce new successful features quickly to maintain brand allegiance. In order to sustain the leadership position, companies like McDonald's have to be green and healthy too when Subway challenges, and Starbucks has to improve its quality when higher quality coffee chains such as Illy coffee appear. The Nokia debacle with the clamshell phone shows what can happen if the leader does not respond.

At the same time, the leader has to be selective when adopting new features from competitors since their adoption means that the new features are *endorsed* by the leader. When Toyota produces front-wheel drive cars to match Honda, front-wheel drive cars become the de facto standard for intermediate sedans. In this way, leaders tend to be the standard-setters even if they are not the most innovative. It is important that the leader recognizes its own resource limitations when setting these new standards. If they cannot deliver to the new standards, the leaders have to try to stop them. For example, when digital watches emerged from the United States and Japan in the 1970s, they disrupted the leading Swiss watch industry. Since the Swiss had no capability in electronics, they mounted a massive countercampaign to (successfully) convince consumers about the aesthetic superiority of the round clock face over the more precise but mundane digital watch. Similarly, Gillette has (also successfully) spent millions of promotional moneys to convince consumers that an electric razor does not give the same smooth shave as a wet shave with a blade. Just to hedge its bet, however, Gillette also has acquired German Braun, a leading electric razor manufacturer.

The upgrading and line extensions by the leading brand essentially will be a combined growth and defense strategy. Versioning and full-line strategies, with so-called flanking brands to protect the main cash cow will be the main components. Versioning was discussed previously with Bayer's One A Day vitamins. Bayer is the leading vitamin brand in Europe and the United States. Other examples include the many versions of Head & Shoulders shampoo from P&G, a global leader in the "scalp health" hair care category. In full-line policies, these extensions fill the "gaps" with fine-tuned features for discerning and segmented customers, the way close shades of red color can be found for most lipstick brands.

Flanker brands are added sub-brands that serve to essentially close off the extreme positions of the main brand itself. For example, when Starbucks adds hot chocolate and tea brands (Tazo) to its product line it follows a flanker strategy. In versioning, the brand name tends to remain the same while flanker brands tend to have other names (although the chocolate at Starbucks is its own). In the next chapter, we discuss brand extensions, which is the use of the same brand name in a new product category. The Starbucks hot chocolate could be seen as a brand extension but is not really advertised separately and serves more as a flanker brand because of the similarity between coffee and hot chocolate. Some experts would also consider Gillette's acquisition of Braun as a flanker brand strategy.

Full-line product policies become a natural strategy for a leading brand. It helps leverage an already strong brand among existing and new customers, it prevents competitors from attacking in a weak spot, and it helps grow the generic market. It is a strategy designed to dominate a particular product category, and ensure monopoly pricing power. For economists, these kinds of leading brands (such as Kodak in film at one time, Nike in athletic shoes, Intel in microprocessors, etc.) are easily attacked as global imperialists. But for the corporation, the threat from competitors is usually enough of a challenge to prevent any sense of imperial power. It is competition that keeps check on the would-be monopolies in free markets.

Runner-Up Competitor(s)

In many product categories, there is one or maybe two runners-up, second-place competitors who are "pretenders" to the leadership. Coca-Cola is followed by Pepsi-Cola, McDonald's by Burger King and Wendy's, iPhone by Samsung, BMW by Audi, and so on. The order is not always clear, and over time the names change. For example, while in the 2006 rankings, Dell was leading Hewlett-Packard (HP) in personal computers; in 2012, it was HP over Lenovo with Dell far behind (http://www.icharts.net/chartchannel/top-5-worldwide-pc-vendors-market-share-4q12-unit-shipment_m37bzspdc/). Nevertheless, being the runner-up impacts what the brand can and should do.

The natural instinct to claim "we are as good as the leader" is usually not a very good strategy for the runner-up. First of all, it is obviously self-serving so lacks credibility and persuasive power. Even if the second-placed brand's quality and features match up quite closely with the leader, such functional parity could mean that the advantage of the leader is in better distribution coverage or better supply chain. If so, the second-place brand's strategy is probably best focused on first eliminating such deficiencies. In the more typical case, however, the difference between leaders and followers lies in the brand, its identity, image, and personality. The leading brand might be more attractive, more in tune with the audience, more prestigious, perceived as cooler, the *in* thing and so on.

This suggests an alternative strategy for runners-up: Make your brand as attractive as the leader's. There are several recent examples of this strategy. They include Samsung's recent efforts to directly attack the iPhone aura in the advertising. One typical commercial demonstrates the fun and superiority of the new Galaxy phones to a tired line of consumers waiting for the next iPhone model. "The new cool is already here" is a tagline that takes direct aim at the iPhone leader. In a similar kind of effort, Burger King tried to raise its image among "real men" by offering more beef in its Whopper than McDonald's Big Mac but failed—and now has resorted to copying the McDonald's menu (Brush, 2012). BMW has tried—also unsuccessfully—for years to rise up to the Mercedes-Benz image of a luxury car and has in the meantime been attacked from below by Audi. Audi has parlayed its Quattro four-wheel drive into a technical advantage over BMW and is underway with a campaign to become a new icon for the young urban professionals (yuppies, for short) that constitute the core of BMW's traditional base.

Midlevel Brand

Most "average" brands have to rely on one of two alternative strategies: (1) lower price or (2) special features. Special features usually means that the brand will appeal to only a subset of the market, and thus, it becomes a niche brand. There are some specific characteristics or benefits that stand out and that might appeal only to a segment such as heavy users. An example would be a car battery with very high durability, a very thin and light cell phone, or a backpack that can double as a baby carrier. The special feature might initially be attractive to only a subset of the market, but in some cases it becomes the new standard, and even the leading brand will have to offer a version. Something like this happened with smartphones (where leading BlackBerry was very slow in adapting) but also with simpler products such as baby diapers (where leading Pampers first shifted to thinner diapers to follow Japanese competitors Unicharm and Kao).

For these brands, the promotional effort naturally involves comparative advertising. For the consumers to recognize the special feature(s), comparisons against leading brands is a logical communication mode. When Sears first launched its DieHard car batteries in 1967 it used comparative TV advertising to demonstrate the long-lasting batteries against existing brands, with memorable images of cars stranded in the snow.

Comparative ads can also be used to leverage brand that is built on low price. Vizio, the new television maker, uses comparative ads to demonstrate its picture parity with more established brands, showcasing its much lower price. As sales have risen, Vizio has smartly endeavored to upgrade its low price image by sponsoring high profile events, including the 2008 Olympics and the annual Rose Bowl game in Pasadena.

The midlevel "also-ran" brands often face a vicarious existence. There is compelling evidence across a large number of product categories that over time only three main brands can survive and make a profit. Some authors point to the regularities in a number of categories: United Air, Delta, and Southwest in airlines; McDonald's, Burger King, and Wendy's in fast food; GM, Ford, and Chrysler in automobiles; P&G, Unilever, and L'Oréal in personal care products, and so on (Sheth & Sisodia, 2002). While the top three names may change over time, it is argued that there will still only be a threesome that will be profitable as mainstream brands, with some niche brands on the margin. For our purposes here, the implication is that most midlevel brands need to either develop a stronger brand (as Vizio seems intent on doing) or focus on developing a particular niche in the market by offering special features. This will allow raising prices and higher margins. The low-price position is just very difficult to sustain over time in a market with international competition (Porter, 1996).

The competitive pull of the various strategies can be depicted with reference to the kind of brand positioning maps we covered in Chapter 3 (see Figure 5.7).

Figure 5.7   The Competitive Pull Between Leader, Runner-Up, and Niche Brands

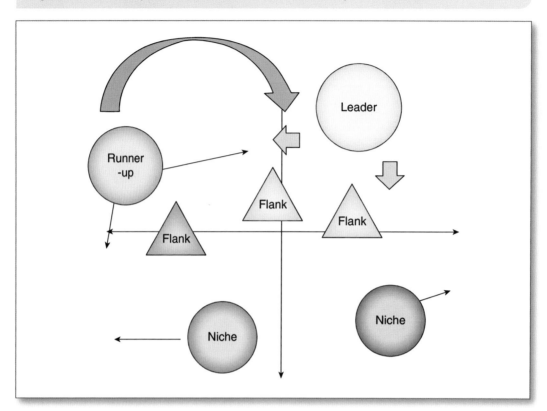

In the figure, the leading brand is firmly positioned in the upper right-hand corner of the market, protected by two flanker brands. The runner-up brand is positioned on the left-hand side, but the typical competitive pull is for the firm to challenge the leading brand because that is where the main market is. The leading brand will defend itself against the runner-up, who will try to disrupt the market with an innovation, while also attacking the leader where the defense is weaker. The midlevel niche brands tend to avoid direct confrontation.

DEFENDING THE BRAND

There are usually a number of competitive threats to an established brand. Good loyalty programs and upgraded products are the first line of defense. A caring and responsible brand personality is a secondary line of defense. But competition can be fierce, and the consumer loyalty is often severely tested by tempting offers in ads and in the store. Here we focus on two major threats: (1) price discounts and (2) private labels.

Price Discounts

Strong brands usually avoid price competition. As we know, the strength of a brand usually translates into a price premium for the brand. Lowering price can easily lead to a *dilution* of brand equity, meaning that consumers will perceive the brand of lesser value. Reducing price is often interpreted as a signal that the brand is no longer delivering credibly on its promises. However, competitors often attack a strong brand through a price discount on products targeting the same segment. Should the brand match such a discounted price? The answer is usually no—or at least not automatically.

First of all, it is important to price out the various benefits (points of parity [POP] and points of difference [POD]) that our product offers relative to the discounted competing brand. This should be done first without considering the brand itself. In marketing, this is usually done as a form of "value-based pricing" (Kotler & Keller, 2012, p. 400). The comparison should be done so as to show our competitive advantages—or disadvantages—on various product attributes. Percentage weights should be assigned to these attributes according to their importance for our customers. Weighing together the deviations from the competitor's attributes, we can identify the justifiable price premium for our brand—not counting the brand.

If the sum of the weighted deviations is positive for our product, it means our product delivers more benefits than competition. This will often be the case, since the discounting competitor may well have an inferior product (which is why there is a discount). Now compare our price to the competitor's discounted price. If the percentage price difference is greater than the percentage product superiority, we are in fact asking our customers to prefer our product on the basis of the brand alone. This is a risky situation, and then a matching discount for our product should be considered. On the other hand, if the percentage discount is smaller than our competitive advantage, it is likely that our product superiority makes a price cut unnecessary.

An example of the necessary calculations is given in Figure 5.8. In the example, the price premium over the competitor is justified by product superiority up to $12.68. The actual price of $14.00 means that the brand advantage is valued at $1.32. If the competitor reduces price more than that, we should definitely consider a price countermove.

This analysis is not the final word, of course. In-store factors and other situational differences need to be considered (see, for example, Rao, Bergen, & Davis, 2000). But it provides a good starting point from which to exercise managerial judgment.

Private Labels

Private labels (also known as store brands) are brands sold by supermarkets and other retail chains as their "own" brands. They have long been ubiquitous in Europe, where strong distribution chains have power over national brand manufacturers but have risen everywhere in recent years. According to data, in Germany the share of sales gong to private labels has risen from 12% to 32% in the past three decades, and in the United States, the share of sales going to private labels is now at 20% for supermarkets and mass merchandisers (Kumar & Steenkamp, 2007, p. 4). As economic uncertainties propel consumers to pay closer attention to spending, these numbers keep rising further not only for grocery store items but for consumer packaged goods (CPG) in general (see Figure 5.9).

Figure 5.8   Responding to a Price Reduction

Competitor product	Our product
Regular Price: $9	Regular Price: $14 Product superiority: (3.8-2.8)/3.8=26.3%
Ease of Use: 3 Importance: .4	Ease of use: 4 Importance: .4
Battery life score: 2 Importance: .4	Battery life score:4 Importance: .4
Weight score: 4 Importance: .2	Weight score: 3 Importance: .2
Weighted product value: 2.8	Weighted product value: 3.8
Price cut: X	Imputed brand value: 35.7% - 26.3%=9.4% Brand value: 14 × 9.4% = $1.32

Source: Ryans (2009).

Store brands are typically not backed by promotional advertising. Although there are varieties of store brands, even premium store brands at the upper end of the price scale (Safeway stores have introduced a Safeway Select line, for example) the attraction of private labels to consumers is lower price. The consumer savings can be considerable. A study by the market researcher SymphonyIRI found savings of 64% in personal care categories; food products—fresh and perishable items—were 36% cheaper; frozen items were 32% cheaper; and general merchandise like cleaning products were 22% cheaper (Choi, 2012). Store brands such as Trader Joe's cater to a price sensitive part of the market which, according to research and observers, tends to be impervious to brand loyalty, buying basically on price (Batra & Sinha, 2000; Hoch, 1996).

The basic problem this development poses for the kind of national brands discussed here is not simply that there is now increased price competition. The basic concept underlying brand equity is that the consumer can develop a loyalty and affinity to a particular brand that carries over between store visits. These brands can typically be found in many different distribution outlets and locations. By contrast, store brands are by definition not promoted independently of the store or its chain. While branding assumes that the consumer is presold on the brand (a so-called "pull" strategy), store brands intercept the consumer in the store (a "push" strategy). Of course, over time consumers can also develop a loyalty to the store brands, which is apparently exactly what is threatening to happen once quality is high (Choi, 2012).

To counter this new competition, manufacturers' brands naturally turn to price competition, with in-store point-of-purchase promotions, discounts, and rebates. But so as not to affect brand positioning significantly, such measures have to be temporary and thus are

Figure 5.9   Store Brands as a Percentage of Consumer Packaged Goods Sales

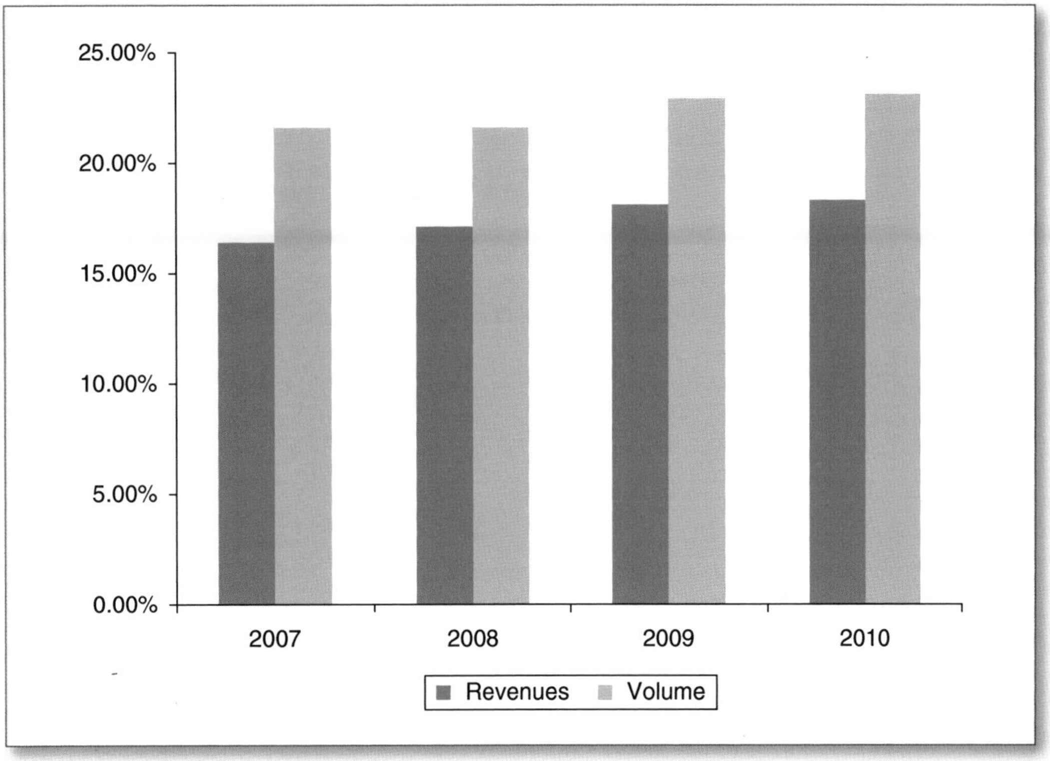

Source: http://www.storebrandsdecisions.com/news/2010/10/26/dearth-of-cpg-innovation-helps-fuel-private-label-growth

not very effective against "always low price" store brands. Longer-term price reductions and accompanying reductions in promotion tend to dilute the brand precariously. Marlboro's notorious Black Friday experiment in 1993 shows both the folly of meeting price cuts and the rejuvenation of more positive brand reinforcement. To combat the discounted price of generic cigarettes, Marlboro's price was cut by 20% and its advertising curtailed (Lubin, 2011). Even before consumers could react, stock prices for Philip Morris and other consumer goods manufacturers dropped dramatically. Investors had quickly concluded that the new "value-oriented" consumers would no longer pay extra for strong brands. Within a year, however, as Marlboro and other consumer product companies restored price cuts and increased their marketing efforts, brand importance rose even higher than before as globalization opened up new emerging markets (Lubin, 2011; http://www.businessweek.com/stories/1994-01-30/the-smoke-clears-at-marlboro).

The lesson of the Marlboro Friday incident has been that price discounts are not the way for national brands to meet the challenge of private labels. Of course, since 1993 some things have changed. Store brands are no longer simply generic brands with no discernible quality or packaging features. It's quite the contrary. Today's store brands have higher quality—some of them produced by the same manufacturers as produce the national brands. There are also special manufacturers that focus entirely on manufacturing high quality me-too generics based on the best national brands and then supplied to various chains. In addition, some companies make products based specifically on product specifications from the retail client, which can be quite demanding. For example, Ralcorp Holdings, a prominent North American manufacturer of store brands (now owned by ConAgra), has plants in Italy to produce premium pasta products.

The upshot is that the national brands mostly discussed in this text really need to go beyond lowering prices or increasing promotional spending. They need to engage the different retail chains—including, where relevant, giant Walmart—and develop some kind of symbiotic strategy. The trump card they have is the fact that many of the retailers do see a need to feature also the national brands in order to attract mainstream customers. "Value-oriented" customers might still patronize stores without well-known national brands, but for most consumers, store brands alone will not be sufficiently attractive to warrant a trip to the store.

The strategy that most experts warn against is for the national manufacturers to join up and become private label suppliers as well. There is always temptation to do this because the economics often seem very attractive. If some excess capacity is available, why should not some Heinz factory produce some extra ketchup that can be bottled by Whole Foods under its 365 store label? The answer is that the customers will soon learn that there is no reason for consumers to consider Heinz own more expensive national brand any longer. This means that once the lost opportunity costs are correctly included in the calculations, the economic advantages of supplying the extra ketchup no longer look very attractive.

MANAGING THE COMMUNICATION MIX

Letting the customers know that products have improved, new features have been added, and upgrades are available is important. It is also important to make sure that any "doing good" efforts be noted in the media. The media used can vary—from advertising in mass media to one-to-one e-mails, from sponsorship of major sport events to direct mail invitations to special parties.

The choice of particular media and media vehicles should, as always, be based on their fit with brand identity, image, and personality. Nike sponsors sports events because it is "a sports company." Events such as breast cancer walks are sponsored by companies selling products bought primarily by women. Coca-Cola and Pepsi-Cola organizes or sponsors events in the inner cities of the United States, creating goodwill among some of its major consumers. Disney organizes its own events aimed at "children of all ages" to promote its theme parks, movies, and merchandise. Its movies and television program are also designed around the brand theme. When Euro Disney faltered after its opening in 1991, one of the company's countermoves was to make an animated movie with a French theme. Disney's *The Hunchback of Notre Dame* premiered in 1996 and helped the park regain some of its glory (Redding, 2012). The strategy involved repositioning and renaming Euro Disney to the more French-centric "Disneyland Paris." The brand, in some ways, changed identity in Europe.

Advertising media choices involve allocations between television, print, Internet, and other media in a first step and selections of specific vehicles (Which programs? Which magazines? Which websites? What type of events?) in the second step. The first choice depends partly on the amount of expenditures available. For example, television ads require typically much more funding than the Internet, but the targeting on the Internet can be more precise, resulting in better response on brand recall and engagement (Morgan, 2010). The second step, vehicle choice, requires in-depth but standard analysis of the vehicle audience, effectiveness assessment, and cost. Based on audience data, does the vehicle reach the target market? Does exposure to the message register with the individual? Is the cost-per-exposure lower than other alternative media vehicles?

For brand management, there are a couple of key issues here. They involve the fit with the brand (see Figure 5.10).

Mass Versus One-to-One Media

One decision concerns whether to use mass media such as television and print media or whether one-to-one media should be employed. It is not necessarily an either-or proposition but a matter of balance. Traditional media tends to color the brands with

Figure 5.10   Communication Choice

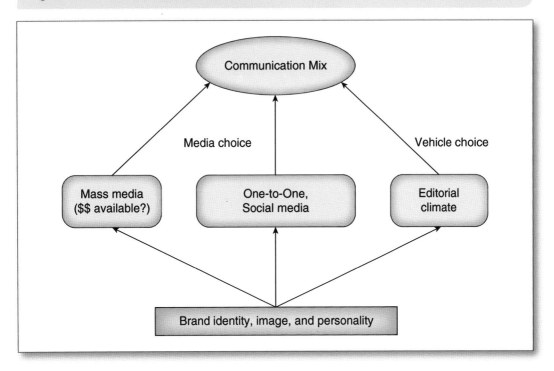

mainstream characteristics. For many utilitarian household products, this is how the brands are sustained. Frequent exposures keep the brand at the top of the mind. But such media makes it difficult to create the excitement and freshness that many hedonic and symbolic brands need. For such product categories, the emphasis should be on one-to-one type media, the Internet, events, and Facebook.

A good example is the revitalization of Old Spice. The brand's "The Man Your Man Could Smell Like" campaign kicked off with an attention-grabbing television commercial just before the 2010 Super Bowl. The commercial spread quickly through word of mouth and went viral with 7 million online views in the first week. Old Spice took advantage of the attention and continued the momentum with a variety of online and in-store promotions. There were Twitter conversations with the commercial's star, real-time video vignettes posted on YouTube, and coupons distributions through Facebook and the company's website. Old Spice gained 630,000 Facebook fans, 80,000 Twitter followers, increased traffic on OldSpice.com by 300%, and increased sales by 106% compared to the previous year (Reiss, 2010).

The campaign's success is attributable to the messaging strategy. Old Spice chose a variety of communication channels that would capture its target market of males between the ages of 12 and 34 and then maintained consistent messaging throughout the marketing mix. As an established brand, Old Spice succeeded in igniting brand excitement, reminding consumers of its relevance, and increasing consumer touch points (Bruno, 2010). The connections made through Twitter and Facebook allow the brand to maintain customer relationships and communicate brand information into the future.

Editorial Climate

Another issue of fit concerns the editorial climate of the alternative vehicles. The *editorial climate* is a term describing the general style and content of the vehicle. For brand image and brand personality, editorial climate is important because the brand and the vehicle become automatically associated. Advertisers pulling back from Fox News—as LexisNexis, P&G, and Progressive Insurance did in 2009 after Glenn Beck called President Obama a racist—provides an extreme example of the importance of editorial climate (Drivas, 2011). If a brand wants to be perceived as sincere, *Time* magazine might be a better choice than *People* magazine, even though their audiences overlap. The iPad advertises in the *New Yorker*—presumably to raise its intellectual image.

SUMMARY

Managing an established brand involves market penetration, maintaining, defending, and raising the brand allegiance and equity. This means first of all maintaining loyalty among current customers, keeping the brand vital and relevant to them. This can usually be accomplished through customer relationship programs but also needs the support from up-to-date and customized products. This means that product upgrading and line extensions become necessary. Offering an extended product line with state-of-the-art products also serves to attract new customers, helping to raise brand equity further.

But loyalty can only be sustained if the brand also offers highly visible marketing efforts such as event sponsorships and product placement. Today these efforts also need to be supported by clear and unambiguous efforts to make the brand a player on greater social causes, including environmental concerns, green products, and humanitarian issues such as fair trade. It is important in these cases that the effort is sincere and genuine. The negative spillover that may happen when the advertised effort lacks implementation can severely dilute the brand.

The product strategies to follow for the brand depends intimately on its competitive position. For example, a market-leading brand should avoid comparisons with competitors; lesser brands may well play off their differences with the leader through promotions such as comparative advertising. Leading brands need to be very active in filling out their product lines and also establishing flanking brands, which can protect their main market position. Runner-up brands, by contrast, should be more innovative and focused, looking for weaknesses in the leading brands lines and creating new options in the marketplace. For midlevel brands, the most obvious strategy is to opt for some niche in the marketplace where its profit margins can be protected against lower prices.

The established brand often faces attacks from low-price entrants and private labels that have to be factored in the equation. Here the degree of price deviation usually determines whether a response is necessary. A big threat is often private labels. Store brands are taking a significant share of many markets, and their low prices are difficult for national brands to counter. The national brands need to develop some symbiotic relationships with the private label outlets, and their best option tends to be the offering of outstanding value and ethical conduct. Although some large brands do supply similar products to private labels as well, the necessary secrecy around such arrangements make them difficult to manage, and most strong brand owners are best advised not to participate in such deals.

As always, the overall marketing effort involves a significant amount of advertising and other media promotions. The target segment and the product category determine whether mass media or social media should be used, and it is important to align the media choice with the brand character (brand identity, image, and personality).

KEY TERMS

Brand dilution, Category leader, Conscious capitalism, Corporate social responsibility (CSR), Customer relationship management (CRM), Fair trade, Flanker brands, Green products, Line extension, Loyalty programs, Market penetration, Niche brand, Private labels, Runner-up brands, Store brands, Third-party app makers, Upgraded products

DISCUSSION QUESTIONS

1. For a specific product category of your own choice (such as soft drinks, say, or automobiles), discuss the different strategies for the respective competitors. Can you find examples of flanker brands?

2. From your own experience with loyalty programs (such as frequent-flier miles, for example), what would you say are the strong and weak points from a consumer viewpoint? How important have these programs been to you?

3. Identify a company that has emphasized CSR as a way to build loyalty. Do you think the CSR program has worked? Why or why not?

4. For what products would you say store brands have been most successful for you as a consumer? Are there categories where you would never purchase a store brand?

5. Why is a price discount so dangerous for an established brand? Even premium brand companies (such as Mercedes-Benz) have at times engaged in price competition (e.g., rebates). How have they avoided brand dilution (or have they)?

MINICASE: TIM COOK DISAPPOINTS WITH IPHONE 5S AND 5C

Steve Jobs, the CEO of Apple, was legendary for his masterful performances when introducing Apple's new products—the iPod, the iMac, the iPhone and iPad. After he passed away in 2011, the man to succeed him was Tim Cook, who had served as COO with Jobs. As most everyone predicted, following the Steve Jobs act would be an almost impossible task. Judging from the reaction of news media to Tim Cook's 2013 public updating of iPhone 5, the predictions have been borne out.

The iPhone 5 release in 2012 did meet with some of the same negatives. Where Steve Jobs seemed the natural salesperson with an infectious and focused energy, Tim Cook was a more laid back and quiet individual than was Steve Jobs. Trying to perpetuate the stylized mode of presentation pioneered by Steve Jobs might not have been the best use of Mr. Cook's talents, but he seemed reasonably comfortable introducing the iPhone 5 model. Its new elongated shape and screen size offered something quite novel in a crowded market.

But for the September 2013 occasion, Apple's traditional innovative flair had turned from technology to packaging and marketing. Without offering much in terms of new features but mainly cosmetic "improvements," the biggest "new" was the introduction of a lower priced version 5c in tandem with the upscale 5s. The 5s can now be had in gold, and the lower priced 5c comes in five different colors and has a plastic case.

The marketing rationale behind the launch of the 5c is clear. The iPhone is generally positioned as an upscale high-priced phone on the market, leaving a big chunk of the world market open to lower priced competitors, as well as full-line competitors such as Samsung, the world's leading cell phone maker. Apple clearly is trying to become an important player also at lower price points, important in the large emerging markets such as China and India.

Nevertheless, the shift was met with considerable disappointment and skepticism. One concern related directly to the sense that the brand had been compromised. A comment on CNN by Ronnie Goodstein, a marketing professor at Georgetown University, was representative of that sentiment: "Apple has consistently bet the house on innovation, and has a great winning record in the past 15 years. For them to introduce a 'me too' product is against what they stand for" (http://www.cnn.com/2013/09/11/tech/innovation/apple-iphone-innovation-debate/).

Others were actually concerned that the strategy would not work. In particular, some argued that the low price was not low enough for emerging markets. Globally, in 2012 smartphone sales were still increasing and comprised about 40% of all phone sales (Pressman, 2013). But in emerging markets the bestselling phones typically cost $300 or less and run Google's Android operating system. At a $549 price without a contract, the standard in emerging countries, the 5c might not do very well.

Still others fretted about Tim Cook's lack of daring. One commentator coined him "Timid Tim" and continued: "The company that reeled off one breakthrough after another under the late Steve Jobs and wasn't afraid to kill off its own successful products to make room for new ones now seems content to just stay the course" (Wolverton, 2013). Another blogger commented that the slogan used at the launch of iPhone 4 ("This changes everything. Again!") now could be written "This changes nothing. Again." (Rai, 2013).

Discussion Questions

1. To what extent are the Apple brand identity, image and personality still tied up with Steve Jobs?

2. How do you think Steve Jobs would have introduced the new phones?

3. To what extent do you think the commentators' reaction is to Tim Cook rather than the new phones?

4. What do you recommend for Tim Cook to do? Should Apple get another spokesperson?

Sources

Pressman, A. (2013, September 10). Apple's iPhone 5C price disappoints investors hoping for something lower. *The Exchange*. Retrieved from http://finance.yahoo.com/blogs/the-exchange/apple-iphone-5c-price-disappoints-investors-hoping-something-210342168.html

Rai, A. (2013, September 11). Apple disappoints with iPhone 5s & 5c; takes the battle to Google & loses! Retrieved from http://techcircle.vccircle.com/2013/09/11/apple-disappoints-with-iphone-5s-takes-the-battle-to-google-loses/

Wolverton, T. (2013, September 10). Apple's Timid Tim once again disappoints. *Mercury News Columnist*. Retrieved from http://www.trentonian.com/opinion/20130911/apples-timid-tim-once-again-disappoints.

SUGGESTED PROJECT

Competition Exercise: Samsung sells more cell phones than anyone else in the world. Still, the leading cell phone in terms of technology and design is considered to be the iPhone, which retails at a higher price. Both the Samsung Galaxy and iPhone 5 can be considered well-established brands.

The branding strategies followed differ significantly between the two brands. While the iPhone stays with one or two models, Samsung offers a range of models at different price points. Do some research on the web and pinpoint in detail some of the differences between these two brands. Try to build a positioning map for these two brands—and other brands as you see fit (LG, Nokia, etc.). Look for what dimensions matter for consumers and where the brands differ significantly—ease of use, features, etc. (Recall the Steve Jobs initial positioning of the iPhone in Chapter 3). Use a poster board to show the map more graphically.

Then analyze the branding strategies of the two competitors in more depth. Does Samsung attack iPhone head-on? How? Does Samsung use flanker brands? To what extent do the Samsung brands cannibalize each other, or are they targeting different segments? Do consumers get confused about the choices?

Why do you think the iPhone offers so few models—surely business users require different features and designs than regular consumers, not just an option for more internal storage (16GB, 32GB, or 64GB)? Shouldn't the iPhone be more finely targeted to, say, women? The color choice is white or black—very limited, no? And why do they keep the iPhone 4 and 4S in the product lineup—defense against Samsung? Try to explain what Apple's thinking might be—and predict what will happen in the future.

PART II

Branding Strategies

Brand Extension

Brand extension is not new: it is the core of the business model of luxury brands.

—Jean-Noel Kapferer[1]

LEARNING OBJECTIVES

In this chapter, you will learn the following:

- How a strong brand supports the acceptance of a new product
- How to assess the degree to which a brand can be extended
- How **umbrella brands** work
- What to look for when researching potential extensions
- How a **brand extension** can help increase **parent brand equity**
- How **co-branding** works
- When to shift to a new brand

Brand extension describes the case where an established brand is used to introduce a new product in a different product category. This is supposed to accomplish two things. It helps the new product's market acceptance. It also helps grow the value of the extended parent brand.

Brand extension is basically a corporate growth strategy (product development in Ansoff's matrix). A well-established brand will induce corporate management to look for

---

[1]Jean-Noel Kapferer is professor of marketing strategy at HEC School of Management in Paris, France. The quote is from Kapferer (2004, p. 240).

growth opportunities by extending the brand. Although luxury brands provide the most obvious examples, many other strong brands are leveraged through extensions. Thus, Sony management is looking for ways to further exploit the equity in the brand by extending into films and computers. Panasonic, Sony's longtime competitor in electronics, is also looking to extend its brand, only in a different direction entirely, into solutions that help people live a sustainable lifestyle (http://panasonic.net/es/fujisawasst/).

Growing by brand extension is a strategy most major brands have considered. And in some cases the idea of an extension comes first and the new product later. At present, Bic, the French pen maker, is looking for ways to leverage its brand in new products. Its Bic lighters are ubiquitous, and it has already succeeded at extending its brand into shavers (http://www.bicworld.com/en/homepage/homepage/#).

WHY BRAND EXTENSIONS ARE COMMON

The most obvious reason for a brand extension—beyond growing the value of a well-known brand—is the speedy acceptance of a new product. The established brand confers immediate credibility and legitimacy on the new product. This helps explain why brand extensions are very common, especially among luxury brands. For example, the Ferragamo brand has been extended from women's shoes to men's shoes and to belts, wallets, bags, and even further to ties, eyewear, and fragrances (see http://www.ferragamo.com/webapp/wcs/stores/servlet/TopCategories_31150_35551). More utilitarian brands have followed suit. A prominent example is the Virgin brand, first established in 1972 as Virgin Records by Richard Branson, the British entrepreneur. Choosing the name "Virgin" to allude to his inexperience in business, Branson developed a cursive lettering and a white-and-red logo, which fit well with the young target segment for the record store, and then extended it with **sub-brands** (see Figure 6.1). Improbably, with great entrepreneurial flair, Branson has introduced

Figure 6.1   The Virgin Mobile Logo

Source: virgin.com.

the same name successfully to more than 50 businesses, as different as airlines (Virgin Atlantic), telecom (Virgin Mobile), and Virgin Wines (www.virgin.com).

American company Arm & Hammer baking soda's red-and-white logo can now be found on toothpaste, detergent, and pet food. Japanese Yamaha uses the same name for motorcycles and music instruments. The established brand serves to endorse the new product in the market. The strategy is particularly attractive when the original brand is strong and well known even outside its target segment and where the brand character (identity, brand image, and personality) fits well with the new product.

Once brands are recognized as major assets of firms, brand extensions become a more central business issue. Leveraging a company's main brands become senior management concerns. According to Keller (2013, p. 405), in 2009 some 93% of all new food and beverage products with first-year sales exceeding $7.5 million were brand extensions. The figure is probably inflated by a large number being simple product line extensions. Nevertheless, the fact is that building a new brand is expensive and time-consuming. Brand extensions do not always succeed, but they may lower the cost of failure by avoiding the high start-up costs of a new brand.

Successful brand extensions clearly can add to parent brand value. The brand reaches more customers in new product categories, and current customers can find the brand in new places. Greater availability and exposure of the brand will undoubtedly increase familiarity and knowledge among consumers. But whether higher order commitments are affected is not so obvious. Do Mercedes-Benz customers become more loyal because Mercedes-Benz also produces trucks and buses? Probably not. Do Apple loyals with iMacs become more loyal to Apple because of the iPod and iPhone? Probably yes—Steve Jobs' image still colors all three. Are Yamaha's customers in electronic music more loyal because the company also manufactures motorcycles? Hard to believe. Do Virgin Atlantic customers become more loyal when Virgin enters the mobile phone business? Possibly—with Richard Branson being another charismatic leader. Most research suggests that the effect is positive when the extension category fits with the existing product and the extension is successful (e.g., Broniarczyk & Alba, 1994; Völckner & Sattler, 2006). But anecdotal evidence would suggest that results vary by product category, and that brand personality matters a lot.

Similarly, the research on negative feedback from a failed extension suggests that the negative effect on parent equity is greater the closer the fit is (Tabuchi, 2012), that a failure might then negatively affect beliefs and feelings about the parent brand (Milberg, Park, & McCarthy, 1994), and that a failure can affect the corporate brand negatively (Roedder-John, Loken, & Joiner, 1998). Where the extension varies greatly from the original product category, however, the negative effect is minimal. Will Heinz's failure in Heinz Cleaning Vinegar lower the equity for Heinz Ketchup? Probably not; Heinz is not known for cleaning products.

The upshot is that for the parent brand, a brand extension is risky. Its brand value might increase as it grows bigger, but the level of allegiance among current customers might not change much, and a failure might in fact have a negative spillover. To add to the problem, current customers may get less attention and feel neglected. Thus, brand extensions are best seen as a strategy to increase brand value rather than brand equity as such. The dollar value of the brand might grow while putting brand equity among current customers at risk.

The chapter first shows graphically how brands and products are related and how the extension decision turns on the implications it has for what brands do for consumers. We then discuss the pros and cons of brand extensions and then give special attention to the two main pros, raising **new product acceptance** and increasing parent brand value. Then some actual successes and failures of brand extensions are discussed. The chapter then shows how to analyze the extendability of a parent brand and the way to handle the assessment of fit between parent brand and the new product. This is followed by a discussion of the corporate umbrella brand choice, common in brand extensions and the case of sub-brands. The final section discusses the prior research necessary to identify whether an intended brand extension is likely to succeed or not.

THE BRAND AND ITS PRODUCTS

Thus far, we have not directly addressed the issue of brand versus product. To understand when and where brand extensions are likely to succeed, it is important to understand the relationship between a brand and its products. In Chapter 1, we defined a brand as a name that is attached to one or more products or services. The name, together with its logo are registered and legally protected as trademarks. A product or service is something that the consumer buys to satisfy a need.

The more effectively a product or service satisfies the need it was bought to address, the greater its functional ability. This means that the products attached to a brand are central to the brand's ability to reduce functional risk. This relationship is depicted in Figure 6.2, which shows how attachment of a brand to its original product creates the brand's ability to reduce functional risk.

Figure 6.2   How the Brand Reduces Original Risk

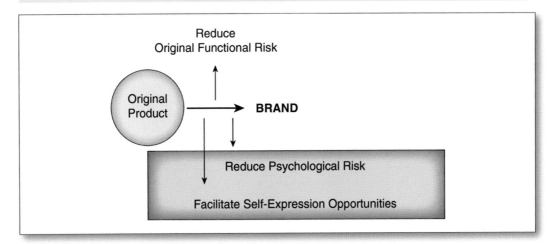

As we know, the value of a brand to a consumer depends not only on its ability to limit functional risk but also its ability to reduce psychological risk and to facilitate self-expression. This is more a matter of the brand character than of the product itself. For self-expression, a person hoping to signal affluence carries a Coach purse or drives a Lexus sedan. To reduce psychological risk, the person hoping to quell concerns about having made the "right" choice can select IBM, because, as the saying goes, "nobody ever got fired for buying IBM."

When the brand is attached to a new product designed to fulfill a functional need different from the original product, the new attachment is an extension. The first fit question then is whether the brand can be stretched and credibly be used to reduce the new and different functional risk. Where the original and the new product draw on the same core competence in the company, the chances are that consumers perceive the functional fit as good. Nike should be able to produce casual shoes, for example, which the company has tried. This is depicted in the next figure (see Figure 6.3), where the original product and the new product involve different functional risks.

The second question of fit involves the brand's ability to reduce psychological risks and enhance self-expression. This is a question of whether the brand itself fits the new product.

Figure 6.3 How the Brand Extension Reduces New Risk

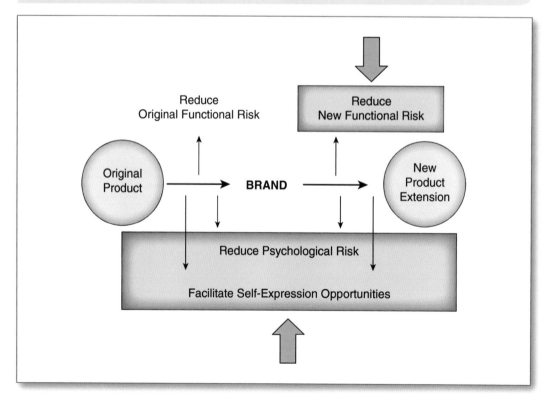

The issue is whether the brand identity, image, and personality are suitable for the new product. For example, while Mercedes-Benz clearly is technically capable of producing buses, one wonders if the brand associations for the automobiles are very useful for buses. As we will see later in the chapter, when the Japanese automakers decided to go into luxury cars, the problem was not technical or functional but rather a matter brand character and they decided to introduce a new brand.

In fact, one way to gauge the likely success of a brand extension is to examine it in light of Figure 6.3. If the extension credibly enables reduction of new and important functional risk, it has passed the first test. The second test is to make sure that the brand's basic character is not undermined but instead contributes to the new product's likelihood of success. When both tests are passed, the brand extensions will not only help the new product acceptance but can also potentially raise the brand's value and equity. Thus, to understand if a brand extension is likely to succeed in the marketplace, it is important to understand not only the functional risk it is designed to quell, but also the psychological risks and the self-expression opportunities that are provided by the brand and its current attachments. We will return to the discussion of fit and extension successes and failures later in this chapter.

BRAND EXTENSION PROS AND CONS

The benefits of brand extensions fall into two categories: (1) those that relate to the acceptance of the new product and (2) those that affect the extended parent brand's value (see Figure 6.4).

These benefits are not automatic. There are several pros and cons to brand extensions (e.g., Broniarczyk & Alba, 1994; Völckner & Sattler, 2006).

New product acceptance:
   Pros:

   1. A strong endorsing brand will reduce consumers' perceived risk.

   2. The product can piggyback on an established brand's distribution.

   3. An established brand will yield spillover effects in advertising.

   4. The introduction campaign will be less costly.

   Cons:

   1. There is less uniqueness compared with a new brand.

   2. The brand fit may not be good enough to create acceptance.

Parent brand value growth:
   Pros:

   1. It increases the brand value by expanding brand reach.

   2. It adds desirable associations of size to brand identity, image, and personality.

Figure 6.4   Benefits of Brand Extensions

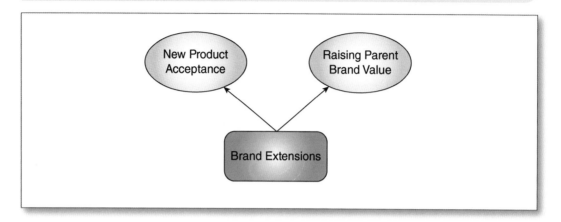

Cons:

1. A bad fit may dilute brand equity by creating negative associations.

2. New product failure will generate negative feedback to parent brand.

The pros and cons need to be analyzed carefully and balanced against one another before committing to an extension. Weighing heavily on the issue is how strong the alternative options are—what other brand(s) could be extended and what new brand could be used. We discuss the new product acceptance first and then the parent brand value growth.

NEW PRODUCT ACCEPTANCE

The basic product acceptance question for any new product involves company competence in the product category. The question is one such as the following: Can Apple produce a cell phone? This is a question of core competence of the company and goes beyond the brand, but the established brand identity and image can help increase the credibility of the company's product. The answer is like the following: If any computer company could do it, it would be Apple. It helps if the product technology for which the brand has become well known is similar to the technology in the new product. Honda's extension into airplanes is clearly stretching the brand identity very far—presumably its well-known engineering skills in moving vehicles can be transferred to aircraft.

Thus, an established brand can help lower *functional risk* when there is a match between the product category and the perceived brand identity. *Psychological risk* and *self-expressive benefits* can also be influenced by a well-known brand, when the customers of the new product are image-conscious and the image fits. "This brand will give the new product the right image." A Chanel watch will at least look good.

How important these risks and benefits are depends on the new product category. One can distinguish between utilitarian and hedonic product categories and also the level of involvement with the category.

Utilitarian Products

In utilitarian "think" products, functional risk reduction can be quite valuable. The many saturated markets for household products would seem to offer little incentive for a new-comer. The dominant brands of Procter & Gamble (P&G), Unilever, L'Oréal, Kellogg's, Heinz, and Johnson & Johnson are firmly established in many markets, and a new entrant has to ask loyal customers to switch. They are "red ocean" markets—very competitive. An established brand can help lower the perceived risk of a new product trial. Thus, the strength of Dove Soap has presumably made it possible to successfully introduce Dove Shampoo. Heinz, the ketchup maker, has also introduced baked beans and soups with some success. As we have seen, however, its foray into nonfood products—Heinz Cleaning Vinegar—did not succeed. The Heinz identity is as "a food company," not a detergent producer (http://brandfailures.blogspot.com/2006/12/heinz-all-natura-cleaning-vinegar.html).

These kinds of products also need access to distribution channels, and here, an established brand can help. For Dove, the Unilever parent has a strong channel presence, reassuring consumers that they will find the new product easily. This has been a problem for Beiersdorf, the German company behind Nivea, the skin cream, which has extended Nivea into bath care, lip care, aftershave, and other products. Its effort to penetrate the U.S. market has been slowed down because of strong competition and channel weakness, and instead, the company is increasingly targeting emerging markets, including Brazil and China where it is increasingly successful (http://www.beiersdorf.com/Press/Press_Releases_News/Beiersdorf_continues_on_its_growth_path.html).

Hedonic Products

In symbolic "feel" products, where psychological risks and self-expressive benefits can be important, brand extensions typically come from luxury brands and designer brands. In watches, for example, there is a vast proliferation of brands from other than watchmakers. As watches become accessories rather than functional timekeepers, the self-expressive use of brands becomes more common. Thus, it is that Chanel, Burberry, and Fendi offer watches in addition to the many luxury watchmakers. The manufacturing of the watches is often outsourced to Asian watchmakers, and functional risk can be high—but also relatively unimportant. These watches are not really used to tell time.

Involvement

The endorsement by an established brand will be less necessary in *low-involvement,* inexpensive items. Purchasing the new product is simply less risky, and impulse trials are more common. The established brand can attract more attention and stimulate trial, however. This is the principle behind Starbucks' use of in-store sales of music CDs. Customers will give the music a chance because of the Starbucks endorsement in playing and packaging the CDs.

In *high-involvement* product categories, the brand extension really serves as the guarantee one expects. When the fit between brand identity, image, and product is good, the likelihood of success is increased. The Harley-Davidson extension into bike apparel is clearly such an example. On the other hand, a Harley-Davidson Cafe is more of a stretch; although it is apparently successful. One would expect the coffee to be strong, the baristas to wear leather vests, and the customers to be rough. There are apparently a sufficient number of actual and wannabe bikers to provide a viable market. As an iconic brand, Harley-Davidson has a very distinct personality, scoring high on the "rugged" trait (Fournier, Sensiper, McAlexander, & Schouten, 2000).

PARENT BRAND VALUE

Ideally, the brand extension will increase the value of the parent brand. In the short run some of the parent's equity may be leveraged to support the extension. And the equity of one or more of the parent's sub-brands may be reduced by the extension. But a highly successful extension will not lower the overall value of the parent brand in the long run.

There is some evidence that successful brand extensions do boost the brand equity in the parent brand. One example is the way Apple has boosted its value with a string of successful new product introductions. According to Interbrand listings, Apple's brand value rose from about $5.0 billion in 2001 to $7.9 billion in 2005 and an astounding $76.6 billion in 2012. Not all was the result of brand extensions, but the large jump after 2005 was surely due to the success of the iPhone, which was released in 2007, and the iPad, which was released in 2010. Both the iPhone and the iPad are good examples of brand extensions, coming after the naming success of the iPod in 2001.

Another example of how brand extensions can raise brand value is Samsung. The Korean electronics manufacturer is a vertically integrated firm. It makes semiconductors and chips as well as televisions, mobile phones, and home appliances, and—since 2009—laptops and printers. The company possesses the leading market share for their principal products in a number of countries. Its brand value as measured by Interbrand rose from $6.3 billion in 2001 to $15.0 billion in 2005 and $32.9 billion in 2012 (http://www.interbrand .com/en/best-global-brands/2012/Best-Global-Brands-2012.aspx). It surpassed its Japanese rival Sony in 2005.

There is also evidence that shows how brand extension failures can lead to parent brand dilution (Roedder-John et al., 1998). Sony, for example, with its share of product failures and questionable diversification into movies, music, and entertainment is emblematic of brand extensions that are not successful. While Samsung stayed very close to its core identity, Sony became a conglomerate without sure footing. In 2000, its brand was the *parent brand* of what the company called five "pillars" of businesses, as shown in Figure 6.5.

The figure shows the relative unimportance of the electronics products (radio, televisions, stereos, and so on) that had originally been Sony's identity and helped create the Sony brand image and personality. Sony's extensions into the other businesses meant that it took the eye off the ball in electronics. According to Interbrand, Sony's brand value fell from $15.0 billion in 2001 to $10.7 billion in 2005, a dramatic decline. The company still has not recaptured the magic. Its 2012 brand value was estimated at $9.1 billion (http://www.interbrand.com/en/best-global-brands/2012/Best-Global-Brands-2012.aspx).

SUCCESSES AND FAILURES

Some brand extensions are successful; others are not. The following list offers some examples from the web (e.g., www.brandchannel.com and www.brandexpress.net):

Successes:

Colgate toothbrushes (from toothpaste)

Honda cars (from motorcycles)

Figure 6.5 Five Division "Pillars" of Sony

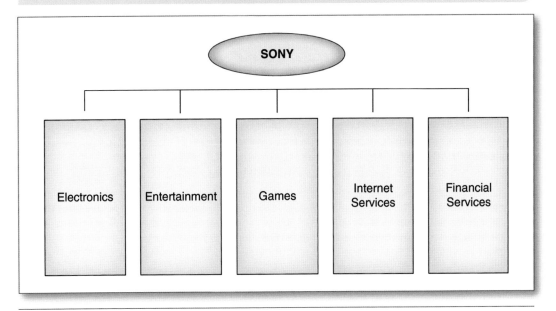

Source: Podorowsky (2001). Used by permission.

Dove shampoo (from soap)

iPod (from iMac)

iPhone (from iPod)

Google Gmail (from web portal)

Virgin Atlantic airline (from music business)

Mars ice cream (from candy)

Failures:

Marlboro clothing (from cigarettes)

Virgin Cola (from music business)

Nike casual shoes (from athletic shoes)

Coca-Cola apparel (from soft drinks)

Jury Not Yet In:

Montblanc watches (from fountain pens)

TAG Heuer mobile phones (from watches)

Virgin Mobile (from music business)

The reason for successes and failures is not always clear, but a common problem is that the extension is too far away from the company's core competence and thus brand identity. Branded Marlboro clothing might have the requisite image and personality. The leather vests it offered put a Western-themed urban swagger reminiscent of its iconic cowboy. But what does a tobacco company know about apparel? The same disconnect might have worked against Coca-Cola apparel.

The Nike failure reflects the limits that a narrowly focused brand identity can set. In the early 1980s, Nike, the iconic athletic shoemaker, extended into casual shoes and apparel. Despite being viewed by many as a natural extension, it was not very successful, and in 1985, founder Phil Knight discontinued the division. "Nike is a sports company," he stated, reaffirming the basic identity of the brand (Bartlett & Lightfoot, 1993, p. 7).

Brand extensions are attractive as value builders for the reason that they leverage the reach and allegiance of a well-established brand. Literally "everybody" would seem to recognize a brand such as Sony. This suggests that one of the obstacles to brand building is overcome—awareness and knowledge are already established. As we will see in the next chapter, this matters a great deal when expanding into new international markets. But in brand extensions the brand is extended into a new product category. This can easily confuse not only existing customers but also channel members and even company employees—as clearly happened at Sony and also at IBM when it introduced the personal computer. The identity of the corporate brand can easily get unmoored. What the failures and the successes in brand extensions teach is that brand extensions cannot go against the basic identity of the brand.

PARENT BRAND EXTENDABILITY

In managing brand extensions, it is important to carefully analyze the parent brand extendability.

Every brand has a boundary beyond which it should not be extended. As we have seen, the brand's character (identity, image, and personality) sets limits. In addition, the *extendability* of a brand depends on four product-related factors: (1) customer segment, (2) distribution channel, (3) price point (or quality level), and (4) technology (Hill & Lederer, 2001, p. 74). The more narrowly defined the company competence and product markets are, the less room there is for a brand extension. Brands with an identity not tied so closely to a narrow product market category tend to have greater extendability.

One instructive failure is the extension of IBM into the personal computer field. The IBM PC was introduced in 1981, quickly taking the lead from Apple. As a brand extension, the IBM PC business had several strong features. The clear brand image and personality—the ethical "Big Blue"—was tied to computers and there was a fit in technology. PC models were priced at a premium over competition, maintaining IBM's customary brand advantages. But IBM's business-to-business (B2B) competence did not link up well with the skills needed for consumer sales and distribution channels of the PCs. This made for internal organizational difficulties. With the rapid appearance of PC clones (Compaq, Gateway, Dell, and others), the dominance could not be turned into a profitable operation (www.inventors.about.com). The PC business was finally unloaded to Chinese Lenovo in 2005 (Quelch, 2006).

Brands that are built on one product category alone tend to have their identity tied closely to the product. Toyota makes cars and trucks. Honda, which makes motorcycles and cars, lawn mowers and off-road vehicles, robots and now airplanes, has an identity that is less tied to a specific product, but it is tied to technological products. Multiproduct Samsung and Apple have weaker ties to specific product categories than more narrowly focused Nokia and Dell. Volkswagen might be more closely identified with automobiles than even Mercedes-Benz, which also manufactures buses and trucks.

These examples show how past decisions about brand extensions have come to impact brand identity, image, and personality and therefore extendability. The lessening of the link to specific product categories, if successful, will therefore help further extensions. Brands such as Coca-Cola, whose brand extensions have largely been unsuccessful, have become increasingly identified with their core product. It is a vicious circle: Failure limits future opportunities while success opens up further extension possibilities.

THE BRAND–PRODUCT FIT

Assuming that the parent brand has some extendability, the degree to which the brand extension program should move forward depends on its fit with the new product. As we have already seen, the brand–product fit refers to the degree to which the new product category and product features are reflective of the parent brand identity, image, and personality. The brand extension will help the new product acceptance if the fit is good. By the same token, the brand itself will be helped further by being attached to a product that has the established features and characteristics that go with the identity, image, and personality.

To best show how the fit is established, we discuss the three brand components in reverse order.

Brand Personality

There are brand extensions based on brand personality alone. Since brand personality basically transcends the product category, a very strong brand personality can in principle be used for widely different products. If the new product's value proposition and target positioning can use the same brand personality, an extension is usually a logical step.

The Virgin example illustrates this. The Virgin brand, by virtue of its charismatic founder, basically stands for excitement, imagination, and daring. These are personality traits that extend to approximately 40 Virgin brands, including Virgin Atlantic Airways, Virgin Media, Virgin Books, and Virgin Mobile (www.virgin.com). Not all the extensions have been successful (see Figure 6.6). But the rationale behind the extensions is that the Virgin brand will attract customers—often younger—who value excitement and imagination (Branson, 2009).

But Virgin is an extreme case. In most cases, the personality may loom large, but some product category expertise and image factors also play a role. For example, with Apple and its foray into cell phones personality matters, but clearly also identity and image play a role.

Brand Image

Remember that brand image—as opposed to brand personality—usually involves a strong relationship to the underlying product. The images of Ford as well as Ferrari are inextricably linked to cars. Practically speaking, this means that a strong image of an established brand sets limits to how widely it can be extended. A consumer simply does not expect to see the Audi brand on a supermarket item—or a L'Oréal soft drink. We do find Harley-Davidson cafes, but you might hesitate to enter without your leather jacket. These kinds of extensions threaten to dilute the brand name.

When it comes to the role of brand image, the distinction (from the pyramid in Chapter 2) between tangible product-related and intangible nonproduct-related associations is useful. Apple's introduction of the iPad, Sony's introduction of PlayStation, and Arm & Hammer's toothpaste are usually examples of closely related products and brand images. Less closely related products need support from nonproduct associations including brand personality. Many luxury brand extensions fall in this category. Montblanc, the fountain pen company, has now also moved into men's and women's watches, not too far a stretch given the luxury brand image—and provided the watch design and price are luxurious enough (they run $3,000 to $8,000 and should fit the bill). As always in extensions, the value proposition and positioning needs to match the parent brand character.

A similar extension is the Swiss Army brand's extension into luggage. From its famous Swiss Army knives, the brand first moved into watches (slightly lower price point from Montblanc) and then luggage. Swiss Army's brand image would likely show as Swiss, good function, sturdy design, and useful with the more transcendent personality traits of rugged, outdoorsy, down-to-earth, and reliable. These are good characteristics for luggage, making suitcases a natural extension (see Figure 6.7).

Figure 6.6 Some of Branson's Missteps

Source: http://www.empowernetwork.com/geraldcyr1/blog/sir-branson-top-10-greatest-pr-stunts/; http://en.wikipedia
.org/wiki/Virgin_Cola ; http://www.youthnet.org/virgin-money/; http://www.bridalwave.tv/2008/02/virgin_brides_c.html;
http://360digest.com/2008/06/16/virgin-on-the-ridiculous/; http://www.taylorherring.com/blog/index.php/2009/02/
sir-richard-branson-king-of-the-publicity-stunt/publicity-stunt-4/

Brand Identity

As we have seen, the brand identity plays a fundamental role, since it helps define the competency of the company and thus the ability of the brand to reduce functional risk. But this also means the brand identity can act as a constraint. The brand identity can undermine an otherwise promising extension as the Nike failure in casual shoes demonstrates. A brand's country of origin can also jeopardize extensions. Swedish company Ericsson made an early attempt in the 1990s to establish itself as a global cell phone brand and foundered when it found that among consumers the Scandinavian heritage called up "cold and distant" (Kashani, 2003). The company ended up in a joint venture with Sony to mute its Swedish identity and help soften its image. Sony Ericsson (now Sony Mobile) has a "mixed" identity.

Figure 6.7   Swiss Army Luggage

Source: http://www.behance.net/gallery/Swiss-Army-Luggage/3403299

In general, the closer the fit, the higher the probability of success (see, e.g., Aaker & Keller, 1990; Fournier, 1998). In particular, if all three brand factors—identity, image and personality—come together in the product, the synergy will be strong. An example is Giorgio Armani, the Italian designer. The brand identity involves Italy with its art heritage, the brand image is built with beautiful models with designer suits from high-class cloth, and the brand personality is partly created by the designer himself. The logical extension into a slightly lower end brand, Armani Exchange (A/X), is a natural and has been deftly handled, with an explicit endorsement from the corporate brand. Armani Exchange may be lower priced, but is still in the luxury range.

For every rule, there are always exceptions (for some examples, see Klink & Smith, 2001). A paradoxical example of a durable and successful extension despite lack of fit is the Yamaha Corporation from Japan.

Established in 1887 to produce pianos, it has grown to become the world's leading producer of musical instruments, from pianos and electric guitars to trumpets and other brass instruments. Its logo shows the intersection of three tuning forks (see Figure 6.8).

The company also manufactures a range of consumer electronics products—mainly audio products such as radios and stereo equipment. These product extensions can be seen as organic and fitting with the basic brand identity in audio products. But Yamaha has also extended its brand into a separate division for motorcycles, snowmobiles, wave runners, and outboard motors, as well as tennis rackets and other sports equipment. The lack of fit between motorcycles and pianos would have suggested that the brand should not have been extended, and the motor division should get its own name.

The reason the unlikely extension has been kept is the historical heritage. The motor division came out of the forced conversion of the company's manufacturing plant in World War II. After the war, as the music instrument production restarted, the company's senior management decided to retain the wartime motor plant and continue building motorcycles. There was no real need to reconsider the branding issue. Yamaha was by that time well known for its motorbikes and simply kept the name (http://usa.yamaha.com/about_yamaha/history/). Without knowing the history, many customers may feel bewildered—and the image and personality of Yamaha are diluted. But for company employees there is no confusion about the brand identity.

Co-Branding

One way to leverage an existing brand and get more value out of its promotional expenses and brand equity is co-branding. Co-branding is the practice of combining two independent

Figure 6.8   Yamaha's Tuning Fork Brand Logo

Source: Yamaha Corporation. http://hqdesktop.com/2013/03/21/logo-yamaha-wallpaper-hd/

brands into a single product or promotion (Grossman, 1997). It can mean that both brand logos appear on a product, as when Jeep offered a special Eddie Bauer model. It can involve the advertising of the two separate brands jointly. For example, in Europe, Bacardi and Coca-Cola use a co-branding strategy of advertising together. It can mean that the brands share the same facilities. Starbucks and Barnes & Noble is also one such example (McKee, 2009).

The perhaps best known co-branding case is the Intel Inside campaign. This is an example of "ingredient branding," where Intel actually partners with most of the major computer manufacturers. The campaign launched a brand that few consumers had ever heard of into a major global brand by piggybacking on the equity of big computer makers such as IBM (IBM) and Compaq (Hewlett-Packard [HP]). Available to all computer makers, it offered to cooperatively share advertising costs for PC print ads that included the Intel logo. Adding the Intel logo not only made the original equipment manufacturer's (OEM's) advertising dollar stretch farther, but it also conveyed an assurance that their systems were powered by the latest technology. The program launched in July 1991. By the end of that year, 300 PC OEMs had signed on to support the program (http://www.intangiblebusiness.com/news/marketing/2005/11/ingredient-branding-case-study-intel).

Since the Intel products are essentially computer "chips" hidden inside PC processors, the logo was designed to show a cradled Intel name inside a circle. On the panel of a co-branded PC, it is affixed as a sticker no larger than a coin, usually in a blue color (see Figure 6.9).

Figure 6.9   Intel's Ubiquitous Co-Branding Logo

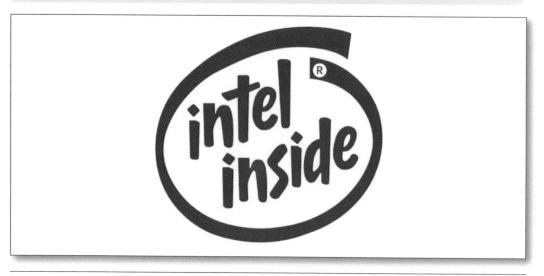

Source: http://www.androidauthority.com/chrome-android-arrives-devices-using-intel-x86-processors-118280/

Note: The Intel Inside logo is a trademark of Intel Corporation in the United States and other countries.

The benefits from co-branding are clear. Each of the two brands gain goodwill and potential customers from the partner. This means the two brands should have some complementarity and fit between the products (Park, Jun, & Shocker, 1996). When Kellogg's combines with Healthy Choice, it potentially adds customers to both brands. The arrangement typically involves a cooperative sharing of any promotional expenditures. The stronger brand will generally have the upper hand in determining the cost sharing, and for a very new brand, tying up with a well-known brand might be quite costly. In the Intel case, the weak original brand was helped by the fact that its technology was the best available.

Another benefit of co-branding is cost savings. P&G's Ariel and Whirlpool co-brand in India to reach the target more efficiently (Srejeesh, 2012). Yum!'s fast-food restaurants like Pizza Hut and Taco Bell often share the same building—and sometimes the same counter, menu boards, and staff (McKee, 2009). Co-branding can, in principle, also help a new and unknown brand piggyback on a better known brand and thus gain a quick and possibly less costly launch. The problem is getting a brand to partner with at a reasonable cost. One leading brand has the following formal rules for accepting a branding partner: First, they will co-brand only with companies that share complementary values. Second, they will co-brand only with products that (as they do) hold best-in-class status. Third, they will co-brand only in situations where they can retain full review and approval rights on all elements of communications (McKee, 2009). Not an easy partner . . .

There are risks involved in co-branding. If the fit between the brands is not clear, the strong partner's equity may suffer. This is something that could be avoided through prior testing with relevant customer groups. More important, and a greater risk, is that the co-branded product fails to live up to expectations, usually because one of the partners does not perform well. Co-branding can become a policy of falling between two chairs. The Eddie Bauer Jeep did not stay very long, and it sometimes seems that Starbucks is propping up a losing bookstore in Barnes & Noble. But these are clearly the kind of risks that businesses in very competitive markets need to take. Managing an established brand offers opportunities that not always succeed.

UMBRELLA BRANDS

Brand extensions into many different product categories lead naturally to the use of umbrella branding. Umbrella branding means one overarching name for a set of products, with sub-brands "under" the umbrella. In automobiles and food products, umbrella branding is common. Mercedes-Benz is an umbrella brand (the company "marquee") as is Goya in authentic Spanish, Mexican, and Hispanic specialty food products. By contrast, beer companies do not often use umbrella brands and neither do candy makers (Hershey is one exception), although these industries are consolidated under a few large corporations.

The umbrella brand is typically a corporate brand. The practice is most common when the customer decision is made on the basis of corporate identity in addition to specific product criteria. Corporations with strong reputations such as Johnson & Johnson and General Electric (GE) derive benefits from their corporate brands in several different product categories. Luxury brands such as Chanel and designer brands such as Ralph Lauren follow the same strategy, deriving benefits from their logos attached to a wide variety of products. Corporate umbrella brands are also used frequently in B2B situations where long-term relationships with suppliers are important. IBM, Boeing, and 3M are companies whose branding consistently emphasizes the corporate brand.

As in any brand extension, corporate umbrella branding serves two functions. The established corporate name endorses the sub-brands, lending its strength as support. Umbrella branding also helps to sustain and grow the corporate name, offering increased opportunities for exposure and economies of scale in advertising.

Umbrella brands are sometimes known as *master brands* or *family brands,* but the basic purpose is the same—endorsing a group of sub-brands and creating a more pervasive presence for the corporate name. Here is how Electrolux, the Sweden-based appliance maker, explains its approach:

Electrolux is working to generate a family of brands by having Electrolux (as a corporation) endorse its brands in those countries where the Group has more than one brand. Electrolux (as a product brand) will be the Master brand in the geographic areas where the Group is less developed or where the corporate brand is the primary reason for purchasing the Group's products. The function of Electrolux as a corporate brand is to endorse the promises of the product brands. (Hartmann, 2001)

Thus, the Electrolux name serves two functions—(1) as a product brand and (2) as an umbrella for other brands. According to the annual report, the corporation's overall vision stresses innovations that are thoughtfully designed, based on extensive consumer insight and sustainability (see http://annualreports.electrolux.com/2012/en/visionandstrategy/electroluxstrategy/innovation/innovatingforsustai/innovating-for-sust.html). Hence, when used as an umbrella name, the Electrolux name incorporates the tagline "Thinking of you," which is a user-focused endorsement of the product brand promises (see Figure 6.10).

There are exceptions to the use of corporate umbrella bands even when the product categories would seem to naturally belong to a "family." Two well-known examples are P&G and Unilever. Both are strong in a wide variety of consumer packaged goods (CPG) and would presumably benefit from the use of their corporate brand as endorsement. But their corporate names have long been conspicuously absent in their advertising, although the company's recent Olympics sponsorship does emphasize their corporate family of products (http://news.pg.com/category/tags/thank-you-mom). It is probably safe to assume that frequently their customers do not know whose product they are buying.

There are at least two explanations for why P&G and Unilever do not use umbrella brands. One reason is that the product portfolio often contains several competing brands in the same product category. For example, P&G has three major shampoo brands, all more or less global: (1) Pantene, (2) Head & Shoulders, and (3) Clairol (plus Rejoice and Vidal Sassoon in some markets). A common umbrella brand would make it more difficult to evaluate the performance of the individual brand managers and would likely hamper managerial initiatives by limiting independence. P&G has instituted "category management" to help coordination among the brands, but has not yet adopted an umbrella strategy, although after the practice in its Japanese subsidiary where corporate identification is important, the brands sometimes end commercials with its corporate logo (Capon, 2007, p. 306).

The second explanation is that the spillover of an accidental product failure can be contained. Both companies have a wide variety of products in many countries and need to be close to the market in order to limit transportation costs. This means manufacturing is widely diffused. Quality control at individual plants is therefore not always easy to

Figure 6.10   The Electrolux Umbrella Logo With Its Tagline

Source: http://www.goodmansparks.co.uk/article.php/62/approved-electrolux-partner

implement. In addition, the many personal products sold by the two companies means that consequences of product failure can be very serious. For example, P&G had trouble in 1980 when its Rely brand was a culprit in toxic shock syndrome (http://www.nytimes .com/1982/08/25/us/procter-gamble-settles-a-toxic-shock-suit.html). In 2006, its high-end skin cream SK-II was accused in China of containing traces of chromium, a possible cause of eczema (http://www.chinadaily.com.cn/china/2006-09/22/content_694757 .htm). The consequences of such product failures are less likely to spread to other products when no corporate umbrella brand is used.

SUB-BRAND OR NEW BRAND?

So far we have discussed brand extensions for cases where the company moves into different product categories—Sony from televisions to computers, Bic from pens to shavers, and so on. As we have seen, one major question is whether the brand can be stretched that far. In Chapter 5, we discussed product *line* extensions, such as adding liquid detergents to powder detergents, or a medium-sized sedan to a product line of small compact car, or light beer to a line of lagers and ales. When such line extensions veer further away from the original brand identity, that might also stretch the brand too far. Both cases raise the question of how the new line member should be branded.

The alternatives are basically two: (1) a sub-brand or (2) a new brand.

Using a Sub-Brand

A sub-brand could use the same name with an indication of the new product characteristics, such as Tide Liquid and Bud Light. Or the name could be kept with a new model designation, such as Honda Accord. Another slightly different case is Vaio, the PC from Sony. Sony downplays its name from both the Vaio and the PlayStation game controller, making the brands almost freestanding. At the most extreme, the new product might get a completely new name, such as the Acura from Honda (see the next section).

As the wide variety and proliferation of strategies attest, there are no hard and fast rules here. There are corporate names (Samsung), umbrella names (Pantene), model names (Prius), versions identified by a few numbers and letters (E320i, 300SL), new labels (Blue Moon) and type (Select). Generally, however, each industry tends to settle on an accepted approach. Automobiles have their system of corporate name, model, and specification (Toyota 4Runner SR5). In beer, the corporation is largely invisible; there are some limited versions of umbrella brands (SABMiller has Miller High Life and Miller Light), but labels are basically unique for each version. Stella Artois and Budweiser are positioned as just two different brands of beer even though they are now both part of Anheuser-Busch InBev.

New Brand

When the product line extension goes too far—when it breaks the limits set by the brand identity, image, and personality—a new brand is called for. The entry of Japanese cars into the luxury segment provides one illustration. Like many auto manufacturers, the three main Japanese manufacturers—Toyota, Nissan, and Honda—have extended product lines under their original corporate names. In Toyota, for example, the line includes the Corolla, the Camry, and the Avalon. But they have decided to use new names for their luxury car makes, Lexus, Infiniti, and Acura, respectively. This started with Honda (see the First Japanese Luxury Car box).

The First Japanese Luxury Car

In the early 1980s, Honda decided that its lineup of cars needed a more luxurious entry. Research had shown that while the Honda Civic provided a good entry car for new buyers, and the Honda Accord a natural next car, customers asked for another step-up. The quality, reliability, and driving ease of the Hondas with their front-wheel drive and fuel efficient engines had created brand loyalty. These loyal customers wanted another Honda but a larger and more prestigious model.

As explained by Dan Bonawitz (2001), vice president of Auto Corporate Planning & Logistics, American Honda Motor Co. Inc., the company faced a branding problem. Management was confident that a bigger and more luxurious car could be produced. The problem was that the Honda brand had been created by small, light, easy-to-drive, and fun cars. The original CVCC, the Civic, the Prelude all fit that bill. Furthermore, the company's founder, Mr. Honda, had started with motorcycles, and its brand identity and image derived partly from successes in TT and Formula 1 and 2 races.

After some soul-searching, management decided that what Honda the brand stood for and its identity, image, and personality were just not appropriate for a luxury automobile. Instead, a new name was decided on. Hiring an external search firm, the company decided on Acura as the best name. The name could signify a high quality car with vaguely European associations but also evoked accuracy, efficient engines, and precise steering characteristics, part of the Honda core competence. In addition, the choice mean that in any listing of car models, the Acura would be one of the first models listed—a feature that was expected to take on increased importance in the emerging Internet era.

Figure 6.11 shows a comparison between the brand characteristics of Honda and those planned for the Acura.

We see how the *unique DNA* (or brand identity) differ in that the Acura should take on a more European flavor. In terms of personality traits, it should be more individual as opposed to Honda's more family oriented and practical slant. The common DNA includes *advanced design* and *fun to drive*.

The Acura was first introduced in 1986 with two models: the Legend and the Integra. The initial reception was weak. Honda had to establish a whole new dealer network, and the need to provide first-class service was an early challenge. About a year after the introduction, the car was pronounced a possible "first Japanese stumble" by *Wall Street Journal* (Johansson & Nonaka, 1996, p. 77).

But the car started to take off, and a year later, with the dealer network more complete and more positive J.D. Power reviews of quality and reliability, the Acura Legend became successful. It was also a beneficiary of the introduction of two other Japanese luxury brands: the Lexus from Toyota and the Infiniti from Nissan. Their implicit endorsement helped Acura overcome the drawback of its Japanese identity in the luxury segment.

Figure 6.11 Honda and Acura Distinctions

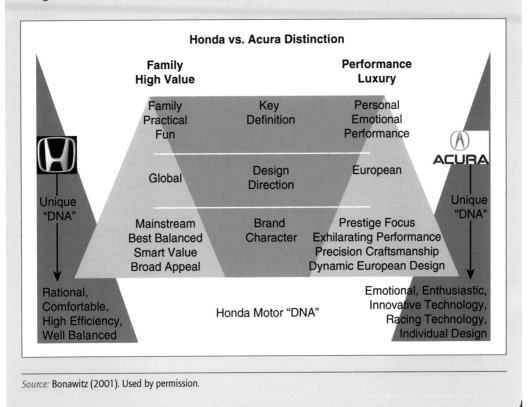

Source: Bonawitz (2001). Used by permission.

RESEARCH FOR BRAND EXTENSIONS

The typical marketing research necessary before a contemplated extension is implemented consists typically of two types of studies. The first involves qualitative research to identify more precisely the parent brand character and extendability (essentially double-checking on how consumers perceive brand identity, image, and personality). The second involves a more quantitative assessment of the degree of acceptance of the extension in the target market.

Qualitative Research

The first step is to try to find out more precisely what kind of associations the existing brand elicits. Here projective techniques are common. They include in-depth interviews with consumers, asking what comes to mind when they view brand stimuli, and recording the answers via video. Focus groups are also common, when participants are asked to freely exchange ideas and top-of-mind reactions to generate attributes. Some of this work can be done quite inexpensively and fast via online panels, chat boxes, or simple invitations to respond online. As always with focus groups, there is a need for some control over the process to avoid having certain individuals dominate the process. In addition, management needs to approach the process without their preconceived notions biasing what they hear.

It is important in the focus group sessions that the participants are comfortable with more abstract thinking, in particular when asked to project personality or style of an existing brand or a suggested name. To capture the brand's consumer-defined style, manner matters more than expertise. For example, the researcher may ask, "Is BMW a brand that wears jeans or suits?" Is the New Balance brand more like Kevin Costner or Jack Nicholson? Similarly, one might ask whether a brand such as Sony is more like Fred Astaire or Rudolf Nureyev—*both* being great dancers (Schwartz McDonald, 1990).

It is also important to emphasize that the qualitative research is not meant to generate new product ideas. It is mainly to gain insight into how consumers view the brand—their perceptions of brand identity, image, and personality.

Quantitative Analysis

The quantitative research involves standard surveys of representative samples of target audience members. There are several tasks to accomplish in the quantitative phase of the extension research:

1. The first is a confirmation of the brand identity, image, and personality that the qualitative research has suggested. Do people in general seem to agree about the brand's character?

2. Second, the quantitative research needs to check whether the brand is extendable to the new product category. Do the tangible functional aspects align well with what the salient attributes are in the intended product category? Do the more intangible factors and perceived image and personality of the brand go with the kind of buyers in the target market? For example, Microsoft might well have the right competence and brand identity for extension into an Android-based cell phone, but its lack of exciting personality may not be appropriate.

3. The third task is to assess the pros and cons of the extension for the parent brand's equity. Remember that an extension does not simply have a one-way effect. How does the success or failure of the extension feed back into the original brand equity? A failure will almost always be a negative, but even a success might not be so beneficial for the parent brand (Milberg et al., 1997). When Levi's

extended into khakis and targeted older men (and women), the risk for dilution led to the introduction of the Dockers brand. Levi's rebellious brand image was deemed to likely suffer if seen on khakis.

The typical questionnaire falls into four parts (Schwartz McDonald, 1990):

1. What kinds of attributes are important for these users, including the more personality-related questions about style?

2. How do they think our extended brand would perform in the category? Here it is important to match the extended brand against the existing competition. For example, "You usually prefer Goya's salsa dip. How would you feel about a Ragu salsa dip?"

3. The research has to elicit some kind of intention to trial and purchase at different price points.

4. Finally, the research also has to ask about the potential feedback to the extended brand. So, for example, a question might be whether a Ragu salsa sauce would make the respondent feel better (same or worse) about Ragu.

Although the questions asked are relatively standard and well tested in practice, these questions are necessarily quite hypothetical and the researcher has to take the answers with a good deal of caution. As always, what people say they will do is not always what they end up doing.

SUMMARY

Brand extensions have become a very popular way to leverage the value of an established brand. Their traditional purpose is to help the acceptance of a new product in a category where the company has not competed before. With the more recent recognition of brands as valuable firm assets, however, corporate-level management has also focused attention on brand extensions as a way to grow stronger brands. This has always been the strategic reason for extensions of luxury brands and has now been adopted for strong brands generally.

The basic role of the parent brand is to facilitate the acceptance of the new product. A well-established brand's identity can help raise the credibility of the new product entry, reducing the functional risks for the consumers. The brand's image and personality can also help reduce psychological risk and increase self-expressive benefits but only when there is a fit with the new product. Where the fit is bad in one way or the other, the brand extension may fail, and the negative spillover can dilute the parent brand equity.

Co-branding with another brand is also one way to extend and grow the brand. Co-branding has been successful where the complementary fit between the two brands enhances both—a win-win situation that lowers the promotional costs. It can also help the brand to stretch further than otherwise, becoming a viable partner in a new product category and reaching new customers. The downside is related to a lack of fit—for example, a leader in one category should avoid diluting the brand by tying up with a midlevel competitor in another category.

In the end, brand extensions are attractive as a way of building brand value mainly when the extensions reaffirm the existing brand. When brand identity is threatened, confusion among customers, among channel members, and among company employees is likely to dilute the brand equity sooner or later. As for the function of brand extensions to endorse a new product, risk reduction is most important for high-involvement products. When the stakes for the consumers are high, an established brand can reduce functional risk for many utilitarian products and can reduce psychological risks for symbolic products. And for self-expressive categories such as luxury products, a well-established endorsement brand is often a prerequisite for a successful introduction. And as always, prior to launching a brand extension, both qualitative and quantitative consumer research is strongly advised, so the proper fit can be assessed.

KEY TERMS

Brand extendability, Brand extension, Brand–Product fit, Co-branding, Family brands, Master brands, New product acceptance, Parent brand equity, Product development, Sub-brands, Umbrella brands

DISCUSSION QUESTIONS

1. For what kind of products (Hedonic or utilitarian? Low involvement? Convenience items?) would you expect the brand–product fit to be based mostly on functional characteristics? For which products on image or personality? Please give examples.

2. As you know, Dockers khakis were introduced by Levi Strauss so as not to dilute the jeans brand name. Discuss the pros and cons of this move. Was this a correct decision? (Try the same discussion of the Acura make from Honda.)

3. McDonald's and Dunkin' Donuts are two chains that have introduced premium coffee to ward off the Starbucks attraction. What would the benefits have been to work with Starbucks as a co-branding operation?

4. For an umbrella brand of your own choice (e.g., L'Oréal or GE), discuss the pros and cons of the umbrella. There is some evidence in the press that P&G is moving closer to umbrella branding; do some research and find the reasons for why this may (or may not) be a good idea.

MINICASE: MR. BEZOS BUYS THE WASHINGTON POST

Jeff Bezos is the founder and CEO of Amazon.com, the on-line bookseller established in 1994. The company has grown into the largest online retail operation in the world, successively extending its product line from books to CDs to consumer electronics to apparel and shoes and recently into consumer packaged goods, appliances, and furniture. In 2013 Bezos was estimated to be worth $26 billion, thanks to the value of his Amazon shares.

In August 2013, Mr. Bezos surprised many by announcing he was acquiring a newspaper, *The Washington Post*. This is the newspaper made famous by the Watergate break-in and the subsequent resignation of President Nixon in 1974. The newspaper business in the United States has been weak for several years, and the renowned paper had been losing money for the last 5 years. Mr. Bezos paid $250 million for the paper, considered a generous sum and financed entirely from his own money. While most other extensions of the Amazon.com business involved extending the brand to new product categories, this one would be different. The plan was to keep the existing brand and to attempt to revitalize the news business.

Most outsiders were perplexed about the purchase, and many of the existing employees feared the worst. What could possibly be done to save the newspaper business except eliminating, cutting down, and pruning? Young people no longer read newspapers or even books or magazines for that matter, and even older veterans increasingly turned to online news or simply stayed with television. Newspaper reading had more or less disappeared from people's lives.

But Bezos had a different idea. He was not going to close down the paper, and he was not going to change the brand or the name. He argued that the brand was very valuable. He was going to continue the strong news reporting and many other features in the newspaper, drawing on the existing staff and on the well-deserved reputation of the paper. But he had a new business model in mind.

He argued that it was time to bring the paper away from print and into electronic media. But this was not to be simply an on-line edition. He argued that people won't pay for on-line news, an experience well recognized by many failing efforts by other media. Instead, the news would be produced for tablets, the iPad and its many clones and imitators of this world. His argument was that on a tablet, the reading experience can be tailored to mimic the positive aspects of a newspaper reading, mixing focused search with more happenstance but interesting notices. What would be required is that the news and information is "bundled" together and sold as a unit to subscribers. While people would be unlikely to pay for news, they would be more likely to subscribe to a bundle with attractive extras, stories, offers and newsworthy items (Farhi & Timberg, 2013).

Many observers are not so sure that this business model makes sense. One writer in Forbes magazine says that the *Washington Post* brand will not be enough (Bovim, 2013). The writer continues: "Very rich people sometimes do what one might deem odd things with their fortunes, though there's perhaps reason to at least hope this commercial visionary sees something we don't."

(Continued)

(Continued)

Would it not be for the impressive track-record that Mr. Bezos can claim, one would be tempted to dismiss this new business model as just another failing attempt to invigorate a dying business. Back in the year 2000, Amazon.com was widely expected to become another victim in the "dot.com bubble." Even though its stock market rating continued reasonably strong, the company had hardly shown any profit in its first 5 years. The strength of the company lay in the founder's firm focus on customer service, secure transactions and faultless shipment routines. Combined with lower prices, over time Amazon.com has changed the way Americans bought books, CDs, and now other products, in the process destroying whole retail businesses. As we saw in Chapter 2, by 2012 its brand equity score was the highest among all EquiTrend brands.

Discussion Questions

1. How could the Amazon.com brand name be tied in and used to boost the sales of the *Washington Post*?

2. How important do you think the endorsement by Jeff Bezos is to the Washington Post brand? How could the Post capitalize on it?

3. What exactly determines the brand equity of a highly reputable newspaper? What difference would it make to a potential customer?

4. What would you recommend to Mr. Bezos? How likely is it that he will succeed?

Sources

Bovim, E. (2013, August 19). For Amazon's Jeff Bezos, the *Washington Post* brand won't be enough. *Forbes*. Retrieved from http://www.forbes.com/sites/realspin/2013/08/19/for-amazons-jeff-bezos-the-washington-post-brand-wont-be-enough/)

Launder, W., Stewart, C. S., & Lublin, J. S. (2013, August 5). Bezos buys *Washington Post* for $250 million. *The Wall Street Journal*. Retrieved from http://online.wsj.com/article/SB10001424127887324653004578650390338

Paul Farhi, P. & Timberg, C. (2013, September 04). Jeff Bezos to his future *Washington Post* journalists: Put the readers first. *The Washington Post*.

SUGGESTED PROJECT

Extension Exercise: Select a brand of interest. Identify an extension that would serve a completely different function than the products the brand currently offers but would maintain the personality of the brand. Identify an extension that would serve the same function as that served by the products the brand currently offers but with a different personality. What unique challenges would a brand manager face when supporting each of these two extensions? Which extension would you prefer to support? Why?

Branding Strategies

C H A P T E R   7

International Brand Expansion

A global brand isn't a brand which comes from nowhere . . . it is a brand which may be sold everywhere, but it comes from somewhere quite definite.

—Simon Anholt[1]

LEARNING OBJECTIVES

In this chapter, you will learn the following:

- How the Internet has made almost all brands "global"
- How companies have tried to adapt brand names and logos to foreign markets
- About the risks and benefits of foreign licensing (including **franchising**) the brand
- Why the strongest brands are almost all **global brands**
- Why consumers in advanced economies tend to prefer **local brands**
- How **counterfeits** can dilute the equity of the top global brands
- Why success abroad may or may not mean increased brand equity at home

Expanding an established brand into a foreign market is in some ways no different from expanding into any new market ("market development" in Ansoff's matrix). There are new customers to persuade, and their preferences may or may not be the same as those of current customers. There are logistical and communication problems in transferring the brand

---

[1]Simon Anholt is chairman of Earthspeak Consultancy in London and independent policy adviser to governments. The quote is from Anholt (2003, p. 149).

character via advertising, promotions, and event sponsorships. Getting the attention in the stores and other touch points can be problematic and requires some diligent work in the field and local agencies. These obstacles will arise in any market expansion.

But there are also significant differences with international expansion. The new market is foreign. The language might be different, threatening the brand name. The cultures might be different, jeopardizing the logo and slogan. The communication network offers different and sometimes limited possibilities for advertising. Promotional efforts face different constraints and regulations. The retail network might be less open, with different channel members in control.

Still, many established brands find that the foreign markets offer the best opportunities for leveraging the equity in their domestic brand. The first half of the chapter will discuss why this is and what it takes for the brand to succeed in foreign markets.

The second half of the chapter focuses more directly on global brands. After entry into several foreign markets, many international brands will turn into truly global brands. When this happens—more on that later in this chapter—this changes the strategic calculation for the brand. While a novice brand entering a foreign market only succeeds if it adapts, a global brand often has the power to challenge existing norms and set new standards. The second half of the chapter discusses the pros and cons of global brands and how they can be successfully managed.

THE GLOBAL WEB

It is important in brand management to recognize that expansion abroad is not just an add-on to the more regular task of managing the brand. Contemporary brand management is intrinsically tied to managing the brand internationally. Today's brands are all, more or less, international. The reason is the Internet. The web is global.

As we know and have seen in this text throughout, presence on the Internet—with a home page displaying brand names and products, with online direct sales, and with ads uploaded on YouTube, etc.—is a must even for the most local of brands and markets. This effectively puts local brands out on the global marketplace, to be seen and bought by consumers anywhere. To illustrate, if you really want something local from far away—such as having your Lebanese mezze dinner with As Samir Arak from Bekaa Valley, you can get it on the global web (www.bekaawines.com).

As a result, in contemporary branding, every brand, however local, is in a fashion already international. Of course, for many brand managers the international markets might seem hard to navigate without language proficiency, cultural knowledge, and foreign experience. But the first step to recognize is that international expansion no longer means traveling abroad. With the Internet, international management of the brand starts at home.

Expanding into international markets used to be complicated and risky. It is still more complicated than expanding at home, but with the Internet the risks can be managed more easily. A presence on the web with brand and product descriptions can be done in several different languages with photo illustrations of the merchandise. What is needed

Figure 7.1 As Samir Arak From Lebanon

Source: As Samir. http://www.bekaawines
.com/chatonakad/9.html

is the creation of an online ordering system, not necessarily easy but there are several standard software solutions available. Tariffs and customs barriers complicate shipping, but independent carriers—including FedEx and UPS and DHL—offer importing and exporting services between many countries. Payment can be by credit card, eliminating most of the credit risk.

Of course, international marketing by the large companies is a much more involved affair than this and the management of an established global brand is not simple. But many companies, even small businesses, find the web a natural platform for first presenting their brands and selling their products. This is one reason why many new brand names are from the beginning picked for global acceptance, as we saw in Chapter 4.

Many brands can in this way "go global" from the beginning. That is one thing that has changed with the emergence of the Internet. Another change is that consumers around the world are much better informed than before. They have learned about brands and products from other countries to an extent previously impossible. Using a search engine like Google, all of us can learn about Chinese beer brands, Nordic ice hotels, New Zealand merino wool, and the best tempura restaurants in Tokyo. Even from a distance we learn about what brands consumers buy in some foreign market. Many companies are surprised to find that the consumers in the new markets have already been exposed to the brand name and know about their products and services.

This also means that many companies start selling abroad before they even think about expanding their brand internationally. Orders come in, seemingly out of nowhere. But as foreign sales start accounting for a larger share of revenues, more deliberate brand management becomes increasingly important. One reason can be that counterfeits and knockoffs of a new popular brand begin to appear in local markets and online. Brand name jeans are one popular target. Another reason is that without local middlemen, local resellers will get in on the new action, raise prices with no merchandising or service, and dilute the brand name. Women's brand name shoes provide several candidates to be found on the Internet.

The upshot is that the international expansion is no longer a choice. Just staying home is not an option. An established strong brand has to venture out and go "across the river and into the trees," to paraphrase Hemingway.

BRAND ADAPTATION

There are three main areas where some brand adaptation may be needed when going international. They are as follows:

- Adapting brand name and logo
- Adapting the product
- Adapting advertising and communications

We will cover these areas in order before discussing brand licensing and then global brands.

Adapting Brand Name and Logo

The first issue that arises when a brand crosses borders is how suitable the brand name, logo, and slogans are in a different language. The cases where expansion has been slowed or even foiled by badly translated names are legion. The reason is usually that the name and logo suggest something inappropriate in a foreign language.

When McDonald's began opening outlets in France, it translated its Big Mac as *Gros Mec.* In French slang, it means "big pimp." The name is now *Le Big Mac.* (www.myburger.fr).

Figure 7.2   The French Big Mac From McDonald's

Nike offended Muslims in June 1997 when the "flaming air" logo for its Nike Air sneakers looked too similar to the Arabic form of God's name, Allah. Nike pulled more than 38,000 pairs of sneakers from the market (Toren, 2012). The brand *Bich* (French pronunciation: *bik*) changed its name to Bic to prevent it from being mispronounced in English-speaking countries as "bitch." Hunt-Wesson had a problem while introducing its Big John line into Canada. It translated as *Gros Jos,* a slang expression for large breasts. However, since the Big John's Pizza name had already been appropriated by a small single pizza outlet, the *Gros Jos* name has been kept to no obvious loss.

Slogans can also misfire. "Nothing sucks like an Electrolux" makes for a nice rhyming slogan but forgets the double meaning of "sucks." In Chinese, the KFC slogan "finger-lickin' good" means something like "eat your fingers off." During its 1994 launch campaign, the French telecom company Orange had to change its slogan in Northern Ireland: "The future's bright . . . the future's Orange," the slogan already discussed in Chapter 4 (see Figure 4.6). However, in Northern Ireland the term *orange* suggests the Orange Order. The implied message that the future is bright, the future is Protestant, loyalist . . . didn't sit well with the Irish Catholic population. The Orange logo does not help the company either. After a 2010 merger in the United Kingdom with T-Mobile, the new joint venture has muted the orange logo color and a more neutral slogan: "everything everywhere" (see Figure 7.3).

The fit of the name and logo and slogan to the local market is one issue that usually is manageable once the problems are detected. Minor adjustments can often be made, still

Figure 7.3   The Adapted Orange Telecom Logo

Source: The Knowledge Engineers Network Ltd. http://blog.gadgethelpline.com/ee-4g-uk-what-does-it-mean-for-orange-and-t-mobile-customers/

conveying the basic brand identity, image, and personality. Toyota makes the sporty MR2 model, which in France is pronounced *merdé,* or spelled *merdeux,* and means "crappy." It is sold simply as MR there. Unilever's household cleaner Jif is sold as Cif in some countries. In other cases, the brand name is changed to convey the same impression but in a different language. One example is the Snuggle fabric softener in the United States, which has different names in different countries (for example, *Mimosin* in France, *Kuschelweich* in Germany, and *Coconino* in Italy), all using a cuddly teddy bear icon (Yip, 2002).

Adapting the Product

In many cases, there will be a need for product changes when going international. Differences in incomes, preferences, infrastructure, and other factors will force adaptation to the local market. Europeans need smaller cars than the Americans and homologation requirements are different. In electronic products, electric power varies across countries and system compatibility is not always guaranteed. Food and drink products need to offer different sugar and salt levels to accommodate palate norms.

Some of these changes have no real bearing on the brand. They involve localization requirements for proper functioning and usually do not involve consumer preferences. Nobody really cares if there are three or two brake lights on their car—but many countries now require three. Consumers want to simply plug in their new flat screen TV and not worry about power voltage. Such changes do not threaten the brand.

Others changes may challenge the brand. A compact Cadillac car can change the brand's luxury image and upper class personality. A "light" Guinness could change its staunch Irish identity. But again there are exceptions. Coca-Cola reportedly varies the sweetness across countries with apparently no loss of brand character. It keeps the red-and-white logo and cursive name in most countries, even using it in China as an endorsement brand (see Figure 7.4).

Generally speaking, the threat to the brand character from product changes depends on how closely the brand character is tied to the product and brand positioning. The Cadillac identity is not just tied to automobiles; it is tied to luxury cars. The Mercedes-Benz identity was similarly identified with high-end luxury until its downsizing with its more economical cars, including the 190E. In other cases, the positioning does not change even if there are changes to products and services. McDonald's adapts the menu to local tastes, but the yellow arches stay the same in most countries, and its brand character still has a value and fun-for-the-family focus, with its worldwide slogan "I'm loving it."

In some cases, the entry is best made without any product changes. One reason is the lower cost—product, packaging, and promotional changes can be costly. Another is that there is often pent-up demand in the new market for the foreign brand as it is. This often happens in markets that were previously closed, such as when McDonald's entered Russia, in China when Starbucks entered, and in India when Western cars were allowed access. Often such entries come at the top of the market because a skimming strategy requires less capacity and can provide plenty of profit—and exploits the exclusivity that comes with the perceived scarcity of the brand. Mercedes-Benz has used this approach with its entry into India with the top-of-the-line models, targeting the rich. General Motors (GM) started its

Figure 7.4   Coca-Cola in China

Source: IPCN News (2011).

Chinese joint venture with Buick, a model with strong pre-Communist history in China. Coca-Cola started producing in Russia after the opening of the wall, with its flagship main brand because of its pent-up demand.

After gaining experience in the country market, many firms have developed more mainstream products adapted to each country. Producers of consumer-packaged goods in particular have developed products adapted for the lower income segments in many countries. Unilever sells small and inexpensive packets of its leading Sunsilk shampoo in India that works well in cold water. Procter & Gamble (P&G) has sold small packets of a purifying water powder named PUR at cost also in India. The effort to provide products to those struggling to make ends meet has become a point of pride for many firms and helped increase trust in the brand (Prahalad, 2005).

Adapting Advertising and Communications

Because of language and cultural differences between countries, the advertising and other marketing communications need typically to be adapted. It is common to appoint foreign nationals to handle marketing communications, including sales. This does not mean that the brand identity, image, and personality necessarily change, but they may. Marketing messages in leading markets tend to spill over to other markets, including home countries. In fact, some strong brands derive more of their character from advertising abroad than at home. Some successful brands such as Absolut vodka, Heineken, Corona, and Samsung derive their global positioning as much from the efforts of foreign ad agencies as from their original ads. Part of the reason is simply that the multinational firm—and global ad agency—will use good creative ideas from wherever they come. The Absolut Vodka iconic "Absolut Perfection" advertising focusing on the unique bottle was suggested by the Swedish owner but ultimately created by the TBWA agency in the United States, for example (www.absolutad.com).

Today, local adaptation is becoming less imperative. Because of the increase in global communications, locally designed ads can be uploaded on the web and seen everywhere. Using *pattern standardization,* the basic brand message can often be transferred intact to new markets. Pattern standardization is the practice of using the same story line or appeal but making the context and actors locally relevant. MasterCard's "Priceless" campaign is a pattern-standardized campaign with execution that varies across foreign markets (www.mastercard.us/ads). Coca-Cola has long used its "Always" meme in different countries. Nike's World Cup commercials are global ads and its "Just do it" slogan is common also abroad sometimes with (in France "*Juste fait le'*") and often without translation (Pfeiffer, 2011).

Many brands use their country of origin appeal in markets abroad, emphasizing their brand identity. But since citizens in different countries can view the same country differently, attachment to the country-of-origin can give a brand a different image in different countries. The slogan "Foster's: Australian for beer" plays quite differently at home than abroad. Same with Volkswagen's "Das Auto" and Audi's "Vorsprung durch technik." In the opposite case, Budweiser's 2012 "Made in America" tour is designed to assure its home market that despite the Belgian brewer InBev's takeover of Anheuser-Busch, Budweiser is still American (www.madeinamericafest.com). Many American brands—McDonald's, Nike, Coca-Cola, Pizza Hut—tend to be viewed abroad as just that, "American," with the epithet conjuring up either positive or negative imagery. Because of the different images evoked, using the same country of origin appeal at home and abroad is rare, but "Das Auto" is used also in VW's German advertising (www.volkswagen.de).

Levi's jeans are standardized products with basically the same brand name and logo everywhere. But at home in the United States its image and personality are firmly grounded in an active lifestyle and rugged outdoors appeal. In other countries, they are seen as fashionable slacks to underscore a freewheeling and daring self-expression. This affects their communications. Cars are typically very standardized, using the same name and logo abroad and protective of the brand character. BMW is "The Ultimate Driving Machine" in most countries, but at home in Germany "Fahrfreude" ("Driving pleasure") is used, softening the image and making the brand appealing to a broader base (http://www.bmw.de/de/home.html). In some countries, including Germany, Mercedes-Benz cars are used as taxis, lessening the brand's exclusivity.

Multinational companies tend to allot a fair share of their communications budget to local subsidiaries and allow them creative and operational freedom to execute local campaigns. But they also keep a significant share (typically between 25% and 35%) for global campaigns in order to maintain consistency for their main brands across countries. Most large global companies have clear guidelines for precisely how their main brands and logos should be shown—what font, what color, how the slogan should be inserted, and where on the page or in the commercial the logo should appear. It is also common to keep creative control over the global or flagship brands at home and let local subsidiaries manage smaller local brands.

BRAND LICENSING

Licensing the brand is an attractive option for many established brands expanding internationally. For example, many designer brands—Ralph Lauren, Calvin Klein, Nine West—license their brands for a fee and royalty to independent manufacturers of accessories and certain products. In many cases, the designer or brand owner only does the design, outsourcing all production.

The amount of fees and royalties taken vary widely. The rule is that the stronger the brand, the higher the fees and the royalties. As an example, Tokyo Disneyland is a licensed operation. The final contract, which was signed in 1979, gave Walt Disney 5% of the gross revenue on all food and merchandise, 10% of the gross revenue on admissions, and 10% of any corporate sponsorship agreement in exchange for a token $2.5 million investment in the park (www.legco.gov.hk). The royalty rates are often uncertain because revenues are only estimated. Although not the case in Tokyo, in some cases the initial contracts will specify conditions for renegotiations, taking into account the actual sales and profits. With the runaway success of the Tokyo park, Disney later decided not to license its brand for the EuroDisney project, wanting to keep more of the revenues for itself.

One form of licensing is franchising, common in the fast-food industry but also used in other categories. As in a typical licensing deal, the brand owner—the franchisor—offers an independent entrepreneur—the franchisee—the use of the brand name against a fee and royalty. To protect the brand, the franchisor also offers a blueprint for how to manage the business and promises to support the brand by sharing local advertising costs.

The Subway formula offers a good illustration. Its franchise fee is $15,000. The ongoing royalty fee is 8%. The term of agreement is 20 years and is renewable. The total investment is $84,300 to $258,300. These estimated costs include real property, leasehold improvements, equipment lease security deposit, freight charges, opening inventory, insurance, supplies, legal and accounting expenses, training expenses, opening advertising expenses, outside signs, business licenses, and utility deposits (www.subway.com). The parent company provides promotional materials, including visuals and copy advice (see Figure 7.5, with copy that reads approximately "Excellent delicacy that you will not regret," a bit longer than the "Eat fresh" slogan in the United States).

A wide variety of firms have utilized franchising to penetrate new markets by leveraging their brand name and the local market awareness and familiarity with it. Support activities are designed to ensure the success of each franchise so that the brand name is protected. They also serve to ensure some level of standardization in operations that are essential to ensuring a high degree of brand consistency so that consumers have a similar experience in any franchise location. Some franchisers operate firm-owned franchises in certain markets as a means of ensuring that standards are followed and that the brand name is

Figure 7.5   A Subway Ad in the Czech Republic

Source: http://world.subway.com/Countries/frmMainPage.aspx?CC=CZR&LC=ENG

not adversely affected. When the McDonald's restaurant on Champs Elysees in Paris gave mediocre service in unclean premises, the McDonald's corporation stepped in and took over.

The key issue for the brand owner in licensing is keeping the product and service at a uniform quality level. The brand promise should not be jeopardized. Luxury brands, in particular, do not usually do licensing except for accessories and marginal items. Even production away from their country of origin raises some problems (Kapferer, 2013). When the rumor spread that certain luxury brands had moved some production to China, Chinese consumers were outraged. The companies have urgently denied this, claiming that their products come from Western Europe. In order to make good on this brand promise, however, some have moved their Chinese workers into Europe. A number of luxury brand factories around Florence employ a significant share of Chinese women as guest workers in Italy.

GLOBAL BRANDING

For many large multinationals, global branding has taken on an aura of a holy grail. Companies from Adidas and BMW to Xerox and Yahoo! in products from antacids and beer to washing machines and water all aim to establish global brands by focusing resources on a few main brands. The emphasis on global branding is found not only in mature economies but also in countries like Brazil, China, India, and Turkey. If you have not yet heard of Natura cosmetics from Brazil, Haier appliances from China, Bisleri water from India, or Efes Beer from Turkey, chances are you soon will.

What Is a Global Brand?

The exact definition of what is a global brand differs between observers. In marketing, a standard definition is that global brands are brands that have widespread recognition, availability, and significant market shares in several major world markets and are found under the same name and logo in major markets and managed centrally through coordinated marketing strategies and programs (see, e.g., Özsomer & Altaras, 2008). Another example comes from the criteria used by Interbrand to select brands for its Top 100 Global Brands rankings (http://www.interbrand.com/en/best-global-brands/2012/):

- At least 30% of revenues must come from outside the brand's home country.
- The brand must have a significant presence on at least three major continents.
- The brand must have broad geographic coverage in emerging markets.

For us here, it is important to see that availability and recognition alone do not make for a true "global" brand. The brand needs to have a certain size in important parts of the world (Hollis, 2008). A true global brand should be a brand that has taken a significant market share in several major markets. Gaining significant market share is a sign that it sells to native consumers and has risen beyond recognition to liking, preference, and perhaps even loyalty.

Even though there is still some disagreement about what exactly a global brand is (see the What Is a Global Brand? box), many of the brands we have discussed so far in this book are in fact global. For example, all the high value brands from Interbrand and BrandZ in Chapter 2 are considered global. This is also a clue as to why companies have come to champion global brands. There are, in fact, several reasons why companies have grown interested in focusing their branding efforts on a few global brands. Global brands offer the following benefits to the firm:

- Increased brand reach that raises brand value

- Easier penetration of new emerging markets

- Economies of scale in advertising and communications

- Cost efficiencies in standardized products

- Bragging rights to corporate owners

- Favorable reviews by stock analysts

The drawbacks and company risks center on lack of adaptation to local markets. Global brands are not usually:

- Adapted to local consumer preferences

- Sensitive to local cultural norms

- Allowing local management to maximize brand performance

- Flexible enough to meet local competition

- As acceptable as domestic brands

All of these factors are important, and the brand manager needs to make sure that the drawbacks do not outweigh the positives. In many emerging markets, global brands are perceived as better than local brands. But in advanced markets domestic brands might well be stronger than global brands. When corporate executives want to champion a standardized global brand to appeal to investors, the brand manager of a globalized brand may well lose customers to more adapted domestic brands.

We will go into the consumer pros and cons of global versus local brands in more depth soon, but let's first try to explain the success of global brands.

THE SUCCESS OF GLOBAL BRANDS

As we saw in Chapter 2, a majority of the brands with high value are all global brands. They may not score the highest on brand allegiance, but when combined with their reach, the global brands have been very successful. They do claim, if not complete loyalty, at least a large market share in many markets around the world. How come they have been so successful in so many local markets?

We know that global brands have the same name and logo around the world and are managed centrally with coordinated marketing strategies, often with standardized products and services to captures economies of scale. Is this the kind of "good" branding practice that would explain the success?

The basic answer is no. Name and logo and other brand elements should be adapted to local language, norms, and culture. Local tweaking of marketing strategies is necessary to move local customers up the brand loyalty pyramid in Chapter 2. Products and services need adaptation to match to local customer preferences and desires. Without these adaptations, global brands should not be successful.

So how come they have been successful in local markets? The answer comes in two parts.

Emerging Markets

Many markets are still emerging. After years of neglect, consumers are finally able to buy good things. Their preferences and desires have not been met by existing products and services for many years, and the new global brands are greeted with welcoming arms. This is one explanation for the success of global brands; they are filling pent-up aspirational demand for their products. Furthermore, in the growth stage of a market, consumers are still trying to decide exactly what their preferences are. The good branding notion of adapting to consumer preferences is not particularly useful when preferences are still in flux—as they tend to be in emerging markets.

As research shows, these consumers tend also to show much greater emphasis on getting a certain brand rather than looking for a better price. For example, a 2008 study showed that close to 80% of consumers in Russia, India and China looked for a specific brand rather than price. The corresponding figure for consumers in the United States, the United Kingdom and Germany was 65% (Hollis, 2008, p. 97).

Mature Markets

In saturated advanced markets, global brands succeed because they offer something new. New products and services tend to come from brands in leading countries, markets with high levels of innovation. Luxury goods from Italy and France, computer hardware and software from the United States, automobiles from Germany and Japan, electronics from South Korea, and other new innovative products disrupt existing markets and create new ones. The new products re-create consumer preferences, where the new brand is the new thing. These new brands are global, as the leading firms quickly expand into foreign markets

In these cases, the new products effectively create "blue oceans" and the "good" branding notion of adapting to consumer preferences is not needed. This is the explanation for the success of global brands in advanced markets; their new products create the preferences.

If global branding is not good but still successful, who needs to use good branding practices? The answer is that in the end, also global brands do. Over time and in fact very quickly, emerging market consumers also develop the kind of finicky preferences that you find in mature markets. Even emerging market customers will soon want the "best" brand on the market. And in saturated advanced markets, the "new" thing does not stay "new" for very long, as competitors and "me-too" versions quickly crop up. Even the global brand soon finds that while it is focused on developing the next new thing, it also has to adapt to local differences for its existing product line.

Figure 7.6 shows what research has uncovered about consumer expectations from local and global brands. We will discuss global brands first, then local brands.

THE GLOBAL ADVANTAGE

A number of studies have emphasized the advantages of global brands. For example, one large cross-cultural study found that global brands were associated with three distinctive characteristics: (1) they have higher quality, (2) offer a "global myth," and (3) have greater social responsibility (Holt, Quelch, & Taylor, 2004). Other studies have identified aspirations as a key factor in the attraction of global brands.

Higher Quality

A global brand is perceived to have higher quality than other brands. Global brands are successful in many major markets around the world, impressive to many consumers and an indication of reduced functional risk. The perception that global brands have higher quality is particularly evident in emerging countries (Batra, Ramaswamy, Alden, Steenkamp, & Ramachander, 2000). The evidence is less clear in advanced countries; some research finds little evidence that consumers in advanced countries attribute quality to a global brand (Dimofte, Johansson, & Ronkainen, 2008).

Figure 7.6   What Global and Local Brands Promise the Consumer

Global Brands	Local Brands
Superior quality	Adapted to local culture
Global myth	Unique
Prestige, esteem	Local pride
Ethical burden	Respect
Aspiration	Community

Consumers also believe that multinationals compete by developing new products and breakthrough technologies faster than rivals. Global brands offer more up-to-date products with state-of-the-art features. Global brands are also expected to be faster with new products to the market and to make sure that their products incorporate the latest technology (Holt et al., 2004).

Global Myth

The study also found that global brands create in the consumer a sense of belonging to the world at large. Global brands help consumers transcend their narrow provincial circumstances and be part of a greater whole. Consumers become part of a mystical global myth. This is akin to the "aspirational" aspect of global brands, which has been confirmed in other studies. Again, in some more mature markets the evidence on this is less strong; U.S. consumers seem to be less entranced by the global prospects than perhaps others (Dimofte, Johansson, & Bagozzi, 2010).

Greater Social Responsibility

As a result perhaps of the anti-globalization rhetoric in books such as Klein's (2000), consumers around the world also view global brands as having more of a social responsibility. Global brands are seen to have a greater impact on society's well-being than other brands and must therefore do more good. Many companies have accepted this burden that comes with large presence and power, and when they do, consumers seem to develop allegiance toward them. But the same sentiment can be a negative when the perception is that the global brands do not shoulder the responsibility, as has happened to companies from Coca-Cola to McDonald's to Shell and BP.

Aspirations

It is clear that many global brands are acquired for self-expressive aspirational purposes. This has always been true for luxury brands but is now true for many other global brands. For example, in one study of a representative sample of American consumers, global brands were shown to be associated with excitement, unique aura, and saying something special about the buyer (Dimofte et al., 2008). Users of global brands were also seen to be more self-conscious. This shows the important role of self-expressive benefits in global brands. The same study found no support for an association of global brands with higher quality but with a lack of customization to local tastes.

We also know from research in emerging countries that the aspirations among their consumers are clearly directed toward global brands, largely for self-expressive reasons. "Local brands are what we are, global brands show what we want to be," according to a Costa Rican interviewed (Holt et al., 2004), and in Korea, there is a strong association of global brands with prestige (Steenkamp, Batra, & Alden, 2003). Global brands represent aspirational goals for many consumers in emerging markets (see Figure 7.7).

The positive gains from a global brand status involve developing a prestige image of cosmopolitanism, attractive among many consumers for self-expressive purposes (Alden, Steenkamp, & Batra, 1999). Global brands are not really preferred because of functional superiority but because of the aura they confer on the user.

THE LOCAL ADVANTAGE

Local brands are actually more numerous than global brands. In most mature markets, the list of the top consumer brands can typically include about 75% local brands (Schuiling & Kapferer, 2004). Even if the big global brands have prominent presence in many markets, there are also a number of local brands that score high on affinity and attract consumer patronage. This means that local brands, although less well known in other countries, can be strong too. Examples include Jever Pilsener in Germany, Selfridge's in the United Kingdom, A&W Root Beer in the United States, and Pocari Sweat in Japan. These brands also have identity, image, and personality. Selfridge's claims to

Figure 7.7   In 2013 Chanel was the no.1 fashion luxury brand in China

Source: Istock

have been voted "the best department store in the world," combining tradition and modernity (see Figure 7.8).

Research shows that a local brand often evokes more affinity because they tend to be seen as helping the local community. They are part of "who we are." They also serve as cultural icons, signifying ethnic, religious, and national belongingness, and the act of acquiring them can take on a ritual significance. Supporting the unique local "culture" plays a significant role for many people, and local "icon-ness" has become an important attribute of local brands (Özsomer, 2012). Even though not all consumption acts are so endowed with significance, at certain times the national pride and allegiance will surface strongly, as when the Chinese attacked Japanese automakers in 2011.

In advanced markets, research finds that local brands are often preferred. The quality differences between global and local brands are minimal, and the aspiration to be part of the greater world is either nonexistent or already fulfilled. Of course, for some consumers many "local" brands will actually be global—Americans will see Coke as theirs, the French probably think of Perrier as local, and the Japanese "own" Sony. Research attempting to corner a real advantage of "being global" has shown some advantages among minority subcultures but not among the general population in mature markets (Dimofte et al., 2010). And as emerging markets become increasingly similar to advanced markets, the special attraction of global brands may soon disappear.

But just as global brand advantages can be temporary and sustained only with continuous effort, local brands need to nurture and support their local constituents. In the longer run, not even the most patriotic consumer will continue to patronize an inferior

Figure 7.8   Selfridge's Stores in London and Birmingham

Source: www.selfridges.com; http://en.wikipedia.org/wiki/File:Selfridges_Oxford_Street.jpg.

brand when better brands appear on the market. Local brands will also have to update its products, start innovating, and adapt to the evolving consumer preferences.

FROM GLOBAL TOWARD LOCAL

Over time, as emerging markets grow and mature, there has been a decided shift from global toward local. One reason has been difficulties with managing the global brand. More importantly, the market growth has forced global brands to adapt to local differences.

Managing the coordination and balance between global uniformity and local adaptation becomes a continuing problem in most global companies. A major benefit of a global brand is the scale economies that allow lower cost and higher profit margins. What makes global brands cost efficient is the standardization of product design, wide distribution, and large promotional budgets, which all yield scale economies (Yip, 2002). As a first step toward local adaptation, some firms have tried "mass customization." Mass customization is the middle ground between standardization and complete local adaptation. Mass customization is the ability to offer a customized version to any one individual customer in the market, made possible by computer-aided manufacturing, online access, e-commerce, and global transportation; it makes it possible to gain the advantages for a consistent global brand while still offering some adaptation.

An increasing number of global brands now adapt products and services to local needs and wants, and new brands are developed specifically for some larger emerging markets, especially India and China. For example, P&G's Rejoice is a shampoo developed specifically for China, and the company has developed a lower price Pampers diaper for the Brazilian market (P&G, 2011).

In fact, many strong brands have had to scale back their global expansion efforts. This includes major brands such as Benetton, Starbucks, Marks & Spencer, Pepsi-Cola, and Walmart. Although the reasons for the problems vary, the general problem is that what works in one country may not work in another country and the company gets too extended trying to adapt. Customers at home will feel ignored, as efforts to reach more consumers weaken efforts to deepen allegiance.

Of course, local brands can suffer from their lack of scale economies. But in the big markets, this is not in itself a problem. In the large emerging economies—aka BRICS, or Brazil, Russia, India, China, and South Africa—the "local" population is often large enough to provide scale economies. Not surprisingly, as the leading local brands gain confidence and resources, they also start exploring options abroad, starting with neighboring countries. Haier's small refrigerators from China can now be found in many countries around the world. Natura, the cosmetics maker from Brazil, is now making a push for foreign markets as well. It's transparent and leaf-like logo suggests fresh air and health, and the Portuguese slogan "Bem Estar Bem" translates as "Well Being Well," making the logo easily communicated in many languages (see Figure 7.9).

One problem looming for the direct sales company is the fact that (as a Google search readily uncovers) the Natura name is already in use by several other companies in a variety of categories, including health care products and pet care products in the United States. This may be one reason why the company has so far stayed away from North America, although it has entered Mexico.

Figure 7.9   Brazil's Natura Brand

Over time, the global brand will have to deliver value the same as any other brands—global or local. In fact, that time might already have arrived. Even for the most prestigious and iconic global brands such as Apple's iPhone and Hugo Boss's suits, service, functional, and other benefits have to be on par or superior with local brands. Very soon consumers could not care less if their brand is global or not.

THREATS TO GLOBAL BRANDS

There are external threats to global brands due to the spillover from the global presence. Global brands are targets of attacks from anti-globalization and other activist organizations. A focus on the practices of large global brands makes for more attractive media coverage and is likely to affect more people and thus makes the activists' efforts more productive. Global brands are also very attractive to counterfeiters. Their worldwide recognition ensures that any fake product with the brand name attached can find an eager buyer somewhere.

Counterfeits

Global brands are favorite targets for counterfeiting, fake products embossed with the brand logo. Asian markets in particular tend to be flooded with counterfeits produced in China. Companies may also find that their brand names have been slightly amended, tricking customers into believing the brands are the original (see Figure 7.10). Still further, it may find that the brand is on the market through gray or parallel trade, shipped in from the

Figure 7.10   Chinese Knockoffs of Adidas and Pizza Hut

Sources: The Street, www.mainstreet.com; Joe Crazy.com

home country or another foreign location. Much of this activity can be explained by the cachet that is often attached to a foreign global brand in the local market. In either case, the brand name might already have been diluted by less than satisfactory products and poor service.

In these cases, the first job for the multinational is to reestablish the authenticity of its brands. The company has to request local enforcement of illegal activities. While gray trade is not strictly illegal, counterfeiting is. The companies can usually enlist the help of home country governments to ask for more vigilant enforcement. If the piracy and counterfeit problems are severe, the company will typically employ private security outfits that can help remedy illegal infractions. Of course, in a country as a large as China, effective enforcement is a challenge. Customers—and counterfeiters—know this. Even though luxury brands have opened their own outlets in many big Asian cities, customers in Hong Kong and Singapore and even Tokyo are still known to travel to Paris and London for the express purpose of acquiring the authentic products for leading luxury brands. A Chanel purse bought on Rue Cambon in Paris is somehow worth so much more than a guaranteed authentic one bought at the Chanel boutique in the Ginza Mitsukoshi in Tokyo. Psychological risks are lower and self-expressive benefits greater.

Anti-Globalization Threats

Global brands, as emblematic of globalization, have typically been accused of dominating local brands, eliminating local varieties, and creating a uniform global culture through cultural imperialism. The early efforts of completely standardized global campaigns did seem to bear out the criticism. Levitt's well-known 1983 article, "Globalization of Markets," seemed to suggest that one size fits all. Saatchi & Saatchi developed the early British Airways global commercial "Manhattan Landing," coining a slogan that quite arrogantly asserted "The World's Favorite Airline." McDonaldization and McWorld became well known concepts in the 1990s, as American brands went global (Barber, 1995; Ritzer, 1993).

The backlash to globalization soon surfaced. The anti-globalization movement rose rapidly through the 1990s and crested with World Trade Organization (WTO) protests in Seattle in 1999; a McDonald's in France was thrashed the same year. Naomi Klein's 2000 book *No Logo* set up a blueprint for how to defeat global brands (Klein, 2000). But the 9/11 terrorist attack changed the global landscape dramatically in 2001. Since the attack, anti-globalizers as well as pro-globalizers have muted their invectives in favor of a more mature dialogue. Companies are still using global brands, but complete uniformity is no longer the norm. And anti-globalizers in the various countries have been more concerned with the existential threats from terrorism. According to Holt et al. (2004), consumers do not seem to act on their anti-global sentiment. Even anti-globalizers wear Levi's, run in Nikes, and have lunch at McDonald's. It is probably safe to say that global brands as such are no longer the lightning rods they once were.

BRAND EQUITY AT HOME

Success in markets abroad is also supposed to boost the brand equity at home. There is no systematic evidence that this happens. Nor is it clear that failure abroad hurts equity at home. Does Starbucks' brand equity in the United States rise because the brand enters China? Or gain because they have entered France? Does brand equity rise when it is successful in China? Does it lose brand equity because it failed in Israel? There is no evidence that Coca-Cola's poisoning problems in Belgium 1999 hurt its business in the United States (Beale, 1999).

What is clear is that brand *value* rises with market expansion—simply more countries where there are revenues from. In a sense, the same is true for brand extensions—more product categories where the revenues come from. And as was discussed in Chapter 2, a firm can get significant revenues and profits from established brands even without necessarily asking consumers to be bonded and loyal.

It is also certainly the case that as the brand expands abroad, there will be more consumers who have at least some awareness and familiarity with the brand. They may not climb very high in the brand equity pyramid, but they do add to the sum of aware and familiar consumers. But the average "depth" of allegiance among the brands customers at home and abroad may well go down. If equity is seen as the multiplication of the number of consumers reached times the average level of allegiance—similar to EquiTrend's calculation in Chapter 2—the result for the overall brand equity is not clear. In some cases, the increased reach will make up for a lower average depth of allegiance and other times it may not.

One equity problem is that with expansion abroad, the attention to the home market might go down. Loyal customers at home might feel neglected, and local competitors might step up. This seems to have happened with Starbucks in its postmillennial fast expansion abroad, forcing it to retreat and close some stores in the United States

(Linn, 2008). Similarly, when Lenovo, the leading Chinese computer maker, made a global push by acquiring IBM's PC business in 2004, its strategic focus turned away from home. Soon customers began to complain about lackluster service. Domestic competitors like Great Wall and foreign entrants Hewlett-Packard (HP) and Dell seized the opportunity to step up its efforts in China. By 2008, Lenovo had to shift its focus back on to the Asian market and used a Beijing Olympics sponsorship to showcase its renewed focus on China (Xing, 2009).

Among top executives, it is common to think that the "challenge" of succeeding in a competitive foreign market yields other benefits. It is true that managerial experience in a competitive foreign environment builds skills, but the spillover to the company's brands is not obvious. Peugeot, the French automaker, failed and withdrew from the American auto market, but the brand is still strong in Europe and elsewhere (www.peugeot.mainspot .net). The Tata group's takeover of the Jaguar and Rover auto brands will help to test whether an Indian company can manage a global brand, but it also will help to show whether the brand equity will suffer. Mindful of the threat to the brand identity, the initial advertising campaign (see Figure 7.11) has focused on Jaguar's roots and long tradition with no reference to Tata and India (Levere, 2012).

Figure 7.11   Jaguar Print Ad 2012

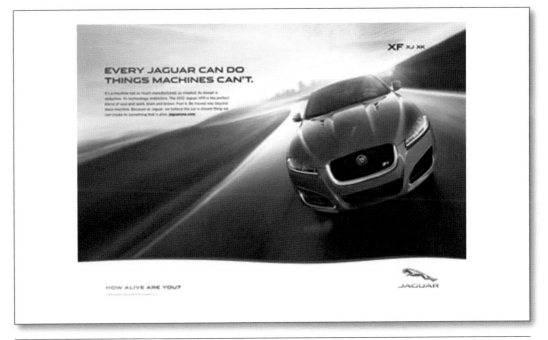

Source: Jaguar Land Rover North America, LLC. http://www.luxurydaily.com/jaguar-resets-image-with-multi-billion-multichannel-campaign/

The fact is that as a brand grows bigger, brand value will typically rise, but as we have seen throughout this book, brand equity, the individual consumer's allegiance to the brand, may suffer.

GROWING BRAND VALUE

In the end, growing the brand through brand extension and, in particular, through international market expansion, should be seen as a strategy to grow brand *value*—but not necessarily growing brand *equity* in the original home market. It is a strategy of leveraging the brand equity asset—at the risk of lowering it. Growing the brand value should be done while also maintaining and defending the established brand equity. Figure 7.12 shows how the brand value can grow once the brand is established.

To maintain brand value, loyalty programs and upgraded products are necessary. They will help maintain and possibly grow equity among current customer but will not necessarily grow the dollar brand value. To grow brand value, the brand needs to be leveraged into new products and new markets. This may or may not grow the brand equity with current customers, but it should raise the value of the brand by the increased awareness and familiarity from new customers.

Figure 7.12   Growing Brand Value

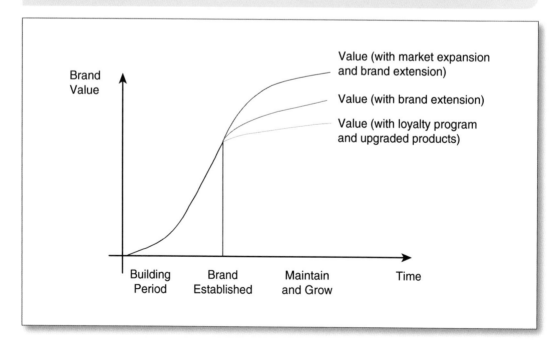

SUMMARY

Market development by going into international markets presents both opportunity and risks. The web is intrinsically global, and most well-established brands find it very attractive to expand abroad. Growth is usually higher in foreign markets where an established brand can leverage its equity and increase its brand value. For the expansion, however, care has to be exercised so as not ignore loyal customers at home.

To be successful in a new foreign market, an established brand has to recognize the likely need for adaptation. One concern is the appropriateness of brand name, logo, and slogan. Although adaptation is often recommended, in many cases the basic brand elements can usually be used "as is" or only slightly adapted. The main changes are typically in the product and the positioning. Products usually need to be adapted to the requirements and preferences in the foreign market. Unadapted products may find acceptance with a short-term "skimming" policy to capture pent-up demand, but as the market evolves, the early excitement fades and customers start demanding better functionality and adaptation.

A product change does not necessarily mean a different positioning, however. The positioning is determined by the value proposition and this may or may not change with product changes. By the same token, an unadapted product might still require a new positioning, because its value proposition might be different in the foreign market. Here, there are no hard-and-fast rules, and even within the same product category, one can find examples of each combination.

Increasingly, with the rise in global communications, the advertising and promotional effort needs to be consistent across countries. Communications need to be in the local language and adapt to the local culture, but the brand message can increasingly be the same across countries, allowing creative campaigns to be extended into other countries.

Global brands have taken on a certain aura mainly because of their immense asset value that firms have come to recognize. Corporations try hard to establish global brands, partly with an eye to their company stock price. There are both demand and supply side advantages to global brands. On the demand side, global brands can exploit the already existing awareness in foreign markets and the pent-up demand that might exist for their products. Also, the global brands are consistently rated higher in self-expressive benefits, offering the buyer a means of acquiring prestige and a sense of cosmopolitanism. In addition, the cost advantages on the supply side can be great. Still, the brand equity of local brands can be great enough to offset the potential dominance of a big global brand.

Global brands face other threats as well, including counterfeits and anti-globalization. The upshot is that the global brands today have to stress local adaptation more, including new products and brands developed for the "bottom of the pyramid" consumers. Furthermore, there is no guarantee that success abroad will spill over to increased brand equity at home. The attractiveness of international growth and the potential rise in brand value will have to be counterbalanced against the threat of neglecting loyal customers at home.

KEY TERMS

Brand adaptation, Brand licensing, Brand value, Counterfeits, Franchising, Global brands, Global web, Local brands, Localization, Market expansion

DISCUSSION QUESTIONS

1. The Chinese electronics company Huawei is a new player in Western business-to-business (see the minicase above for details about Huawei) markets but also introducing consumer products, including cell phones. Would you recommend the company to adapt its brand name to make it less Chinese and easier to pronounce? Why or why not?

2. Subway is a franchising operation that is very successful internationally. Access its web-available franchising guidelines and other Internet sources to learn about their efforts to ensure consistent quality abroad.

3. Try to identify a strong local brand whose positioning and equity at home has changed as it has ventured abroad (compare, e.g., Corona and Budweiser). Has the large American home market made a difference in the degree to which Budweiser is adjusting compared of Corona?

4. Discuss what luxury brands can do to protect themselves against counterfeits.

5. Think of some local brand that you prefer to a bigger global brand and explain why.

MINICASE: HUAWEI–WHAT'S IN A NAME?

The biggest telecom-producer in China is Huawei (pronounced "wah-way" for those without Chinese fluency). The company is second to Ericsson in the world's telecom equipment market, a B2B business, and, on the basis of its strength at home and other emerging markets, third in global consumer cell phones sales, after Samsung and Apple. It is, in other words, a very serious competitor—one that is now attempting to move into the major Western consumer markets.

The first issue has been whether the brand name needed to be change. A quick and informal survey showed how difficult the name was to pronounce for westerners. You can find the survey on-line at (http://blogs.wsj.com/tech-europe/2013/09/04/huawei-mulled-changing-its-name-as-foreigners-found-it-too-hard/). A first attempt was made to change the name to something similar to its meaning in Chinese. Since Huawei in Chinese means something like "splendid act," a play on "wei" as "way" offered possibilities such as a "better way" and "future way." In the end, however, the company decided not to create a new brand but instead to rely on its original name, arguing that it was a well-established brand, with a strong reputation at least in the B2B telecom-equipment sector.

Also playing a role in the decision to keep the original was the Japanese and Korean example. These countries' companies had kept their own names. And some patriotism played in as well. If China was ever going to establish its own global brands, the country of origin will sooner or later not matter, or even turn favorable. As companies like Lenovo and Haier establish China as a credible manufacturer of computers and appliances, the image of the country as a manufacturer of electronics would likely improve as well. A name such as Huawei, which clearly signals the country of origin, could then become an asset.

The next question was then to find a way to build the brand in Western markets. First and foremost, the products had to be up-to-date and technologically advanced. Huawei felt strong on that count. Because of its B2B roots, the technology was state-of-the-art and considered on par with Samsung, including ultra-fast 4G speed. The experiences in the consumer markets in the Asian countries had been put to good use in developing stylish designs with some of the lighter and thinner phones on the market.

After a wide-ranging competitive search, Huawei hired the giant WPP group to lead its global branding campaign, with the Ogilvy and Burson-Marsteller agencies taking lead roles (Beattie, 2012). The agencies decided not to try to take on the name itself, but simply work with a voice-over pronouncing the name at the end of a commercial as the logo was shown. The introductory campaign, kicked off at a convention in Barcelona in February 2013, used the slogan "Make it possible," with an emphasis on how the technological capabilities enhanced individual performance (http://www.youtube.com/watch?v=VNY6sP9mLGw). There was no indication of the country-of-origin of the brand. As a kind of endorsement of the new slogan, Korean competitor LG soon introduced its own new slogan, "It's all possible." Huawei later introduced a secondary emphasis using the slogan "Green Huawei, Green Telecom, Green World," stressing the role of Huawei in protecting the environment.

The avoidance of referring to China was partly a result of the negative reaction among U.S. legislators toward the company's penetration of the American B2B market. China was not welcome (Constantinescu, 2011). Maybe even more interesting, there was no reference in the new campaign to the difficulty for Westerners in pronouncing the name. The creative minds at WPP probably assumed that the voiceover's pronunciation of the name when the brand name and logo were shown at the end of the commercial as a sufficient means of making the name comfortably familiar.

Discussion Questions

1. How important is the fluency of the brand name for cell phones that you might buy? Any problems in social media, word-of-mouth?

2. Would you favor using more fun advertising to attack the pronunciation issue?

3. Is the Chinese country-of-origin a factor in product acceptance—good or bad or not at all?

(Continued)

(Continued)

4. Like other Chinese companies, Huawei sometimes uses women, sometimes men as spokespersons in official meetings and product launches. Should the company stay with one person as American companies tend to do? A woman or a man?

Sources

Chang Beattie, A. (2012, December 3). WPP set to pick up global branding work for China's Huawei. *Advertising Age.* Retrieved from http://adage.com/article/news/wpp-set-pick-global-branding-work-china-s-huawei/238590/

Constantinescu, S. (2011, May 13). Huawei to launch advertising campaign in the US, hire 500 workers, all in an effort to look legit. *IntoMobile.* Retrieved from http://www.intomobile.com/2011/05/13/huawei-launch-advertising-campaign-us-hire-500-workers-all-effort-look-legit/

Kan, M. (2011,October 13). China's Huawei aims to build an iconic phone brand. (http://www.pcworld.com/article/241821/chinas_huawei_aims_to_build_an_iconic_phone_brand.html)

SUGGESTED PROJECT

International Expansion Exercise: Identify a country you have not lived in previously but that you could imagine yourself living in for an extended time (3 months or longer). In preparation for your stay, you should learn a bit about the culture of this new country. Using resources on the web (e.g., www.everyculture.com/) give yourself a crash course in the culture of your new country. Knowing that you are a brand (see the project in Chapter 9 for more detail) and that many brands need to be modified to be successful in a new country, identify three things you should do to prepare your brand for your move to the new country.

PART II

Branding Strategies

191

Brand Acquisition and Portfolios

A brand portfolio strategy defines the position, role and relationship of each brand in the portfolio. The trick is harnessing their power without allowing their power to limit a company's perspective.

—Erich Joachimsthaler[1]

LEARNING OBJECTIVES

In this chapter, you will learn the following:

- Why brand acquisitions are common even if expensive
- When to change, and when to keep, the acquired brand name
- Why sometimes even weak brands are acquired
- How firms structure their portfolio of brands
- How to decide which brands are most important strategically
- When to rebrand or divest a failing brand

Many large companies have diversified and have more than one brand. At inception, the company may have started with a signature brand like Ford's Model T, Procter & Gamble's

---

[1]Erich Joachimsthaler is the founder and CEO of Vivaldi Partners, a strategy, innovation, and marketing consulting company. The quote is from Joachimsthaler (2007, p. 154).

(P&G's) Ivory soap, and Sony's transistor radio. Over time, through product line extensions, new products, and acquisitions of other brands, the brands multiply.

To be competitive, companies increasingly try to establish dominant positions in their product markets. This strategy is easier to execute when a company owns multiple strong brands. Since building a brand takes time, effort, and resources, firms often look to brand acquisition as opposed to brand development to grow.

Today brands can be bought and sold quite routinely. Acquiring a global brand is one way for emerging market companies to gain instant credibility—provided, of course, financing can be arranged. Chapter 2 documented some of the stratospheric dollar values of well-known brands. These dollar values are like price tags and show that brand acquisition can be very expensive. Showing the financial strength of emerging market companies, Jaguar and Land Rover were bought by Tata Motors of India in 2008 for about $2 billion, and Volvo was acquired for 1.5 billion by China's Geely Motors in 2010 (Bajaj, 2012).

The collection of brands that a firm owns is its brand portfolio. The management of the portfolio can be complicated, since there is often a need for coordination among the different brands. There can be "cannibalization" problems when there are several brands from the same product category (as for Nestle's water brands, including Perrier, S. Pellegrino, and Deer Park). There is a coordination problem when brands share basic parts and components (as for General Motors [GM] and Saab). There is an issue of whether an acquisition of a competing brand really makes sense for the corporate identity (as when Volkswagen acquired ultra-luxury Rolls-Royce).

We deal with brand acquisitions first and the brand portfolio later.

ACQUIRING BRANDS

The fundamental reason why a company acquires other brands is the desire to grow. But there are also several other more specific reasons for brand acquisitions. They include the following:

- To capture a brand's loyal customers and avoid having to build a new brand
- To eliminate a competitor and introduce one's own brand instead
- To get access to distribution channels and consolidate operations to get economies of scale

Adding a New Brand

In the most typical case, the acquiring firm simply wants to add a brand to its lineup and capture the brand's loyal customers. To decide on the offer price, the company needs to estimate its ability to retain the brand's customers. To accomplish this, three questions need to be answered:

1. Can the firm maintain or improve product quality?
2. Can the firm maintain or improve customer service and channel support?
3. Can the firm maintain or improve brand identity and image?

The answers to these questions depend a great deal on managerial judgment. When the acquiring firm has a great deal of experience in the industry, the answers are easier and more positive. The acquisition of IBM's consumer computer division by Lenovo and the efforts of various companies to acquire the French soft drink brand Orangina illustrate these three issues in action.

A good example of affirmative answers to the first two questions can be found in the 2004 acquisition of IBM's PC business by Lenovo, which we discussed briefly in Chapter 7. The acquisition price was $1.75 billion, with Lenovo taking over the whole PC division from IBM. Lenovo acquired the use of the valuable ThinkPad name for its laptops and gained the right to use the IBM name and logo for 5 years. Lenovo kept the angled position of the logo from its IBM days (see Figure 8.1).

In this case, the Lenovo management clearly judged that it could run the operation better than the Americans. IBM, basically a business-to-business (B2B) company, had had a difficult time competing in the very competitive PC business. To reassure IBM's existing customers, many loyal to the IBM ThinkPad, Lenovo promised continued technological and service excellence on its website's FAQ menu:

Q2. What changes for me, the customer? Before the transaction closes in the second quarter of 2005, nothing changes. And after the transaction closes, your experience as an IBM customer should be the same. Your IBM sales teams should include the

Figure 8.1   The Lenovo ThinkPad Logo, Emphasizing ThinkPad

Source: Lenovo. http://forums.lenovo.com/t5/General-Discussion/New-Brand-Logos-for-ThinkPad/td-p/6016

same PC specialists, only they will be Lenovo specialists who will continue working closely together with their IBM colleagues. IBM customers will still have access to the world's finest PCs, integrated into end-to-end, on demand solutions. And IBM has contracted to support the new Lenovo with the PC service support, and financing—and the long-term relationships you expect.

An example of a case where many firms believed a particular brand would help improve their distribution, product quality, and (perhaps most importantly) their image can be found in the fervor around the Orangina brand, which has a very strong positive image that is tied to a very popular soft drink made from orange, lemon, mandarin, and grapefruit juice and is very popular in Europe. It is a strong brand with loyal customers built partly with an attractive bottle design and imaginative and quirky advertising. In colorful ads, the pear-shaped bottle is shown with anthropomorphic animals, often in sexually provocative situations (see Figure 8.2). Especially successful at home in France, the campaigns have created furor in other places, something that has only enhanced the allegiance toward the brand among its young target markets (Nudd, 2013; Salter, 2008).

At the beginning of the end of the last millennium, Orangina's robust annual revenues were about $190 million. The product filled a void in Coca-Cola's product lineup, and Coca-Cola made a bid of $844 million for the brand. This bid of 4.44 times the annual sales showed a strong belief on the part of Coca-Cola's management in the future of the brand—even under Coca-Cola stewardship. However, the deal was rejected by France's Competition Council in 1999 on the grounds that it would give Coca-Cola too great of a market dominance (Hays, 1999).

Figure 8.2   Orangina's Provocative Advertising

Source: Orangina. http://www.coloribus.com/adsarchive/prints/orangina-drink-lilas-10757805/

Instead, British Cadbury bought Orangina at a price of $643 million. The lower price reflects partly the fact that the purchase was 100% cash, an unusual feature, but also shows the lower estimate a chocolate maker like Cadbury might have of its effectiveness to maintain Orangina's success. Cadbury did not hold the brand for long. Orangina was unloaded together with Cadbury's other international drink brands to two private equity firms in 2006 for $2.1 billion. They, in turn, sold the brands to Suntory of Japan in 2009 for $2.3 billion. Suntory, with experience in soft drinks and alcoholic drinks, paid about $920 million for Orangina (Hayashi & Fujimura, 2009). The brand is now owned by the Dr. Pepper-Snapple group in North America and by Suntory in the rest of the world.

Eliminating a Brand

There are cases where the objective is to gain market access and gradually eliminate the acquired brand. Anecdotal evidence suggests this is not unusual in consumer packaged goods (CPG) and cigarettes, where global giants simply move the acquired brand off the shelf and substitute their global brands. Of course, the desired outcome is never certain. This seems to have been the case of Thums Up in India.

Family-owned Thums Up was a leading soft drink brand in India when market barriers came down in 1990. Pepsi-Cola entered quickly, and Pepsi and Thums Up fought for leadership. In 1993, Coca-Cola entered and managed to buy Thums Up for a relatively low amount of $60 million. Thums Up had fought Pepsi to a standstill, and the two shared the lead in a large and growing cola market (Kurien & Nanji, 2009).

Coke's strategic intent was to gradually eliminate Thums Up and replace the brand with Coca-Cola. But despite reduced marketing expenditures, Thums Up still claimed considerable loyalty among consumers, especially young men who were attracted to its macho image. In the end, Coca-Cola was forced to reinstate marketing expenditures for Thums Up and has repositioned its own brand further toward the younger market segments (see Figure 8.3). At least Coca-Cola did gain access to distribution channels.

Scale Economies

To achieve scale efficiencies, the acquisition typically involves consolidation of supplier networks, production facilities, and distribution channels. The international beer industry provides several illustrations. For example, Carlsberg, the Danish beer brewer, controls about 35% of the Russian beer market after its 2008 acquisitions of Baltika Breweries with its leading Baltika brand (Johansson, 2012). Similarly, as of 2011, Heineken owns or controls several strong national beer brands including Kaiser (Brazil), Moretti (Italy), Dos Equis (Mexico), Bintang (Indonesia), and Lapin Kulta (Finland). Many of these acquired brands have loyal customers. By and large, the beer brewers have decided to keep the local brands. The acquisition is mainly to gain scale economies in supplies and raw materials and also to get access to local distributors.

In other consolidations, the change in ownership has been announced more openly, however. For example, in home appliances, a more global product—a global brand—does carry some weight. As we saw in Chapter 6, the policy of Electrolux has been to use the corporate name as an endorsement, keeping the local name for loyal customers but offering a global guarantee that the products are state of the art. The corporate brand is added as a master brand.

Figure 8.3   Thums Up Ads in India

Source: Brand Channel (2004). http://www.brandchannel.com/features_profile.asp?pr_id=211

The success of an endorsement strategy hinges on two factors:

1. The degree to which the corporate brand is familiar to the market. Higher familiarity naturally increases attractiveness.

2. The degree to which the corporate brand provides additional product quality information. If there is a fit between the corporate brand and the local brand, functional risk is reduced and attractiveness rises.

In international acquisitions, the endorsement is particularly useful when the acquiring corporation is known for strong CSR, or corporate social responsibility. This tends to alleviate any local concerns and helps retain loyal customers.

CHANGING NAMES

In some cases, an acquired brand cannot be kept in the market, either because of the sales contract (Lenovo could use ThinkPad but not IBM on the acquired PCs) or because the consumers are likely to be confused (as when Cingular acquired AT&T). In some cases, company changes an existing brand's name to get scale economies in advertising (as when Mars changed the Marathon candy bar to Snickers).

Companies use two alternative strategies to change names.

1. A fade in and fade out gradual option is the more common strategy (as in IBM and Lenovo)

2. Summary axing—just drop one brand name and introduce the new brand (P&G dropped the Pert shampoo after Vidal Sassoon was acquired)

Fade In and Fade Out

The fade in and fade out option usually consists a period with dual branding, where the new brand name is featured together with the old name. It is common to support the brand with public announcements and advertising, showing both names together. After some time—usually some months—the old name may get a smaller font, with the new name featured more prominently. Finally, the old name disappears.

One illustration of the fade in and fade out process is the way Black & Decker changed the brand name when it acquired the small appliance business of General Electric (GE) (Saporito, 1985).

In the early 1980s, Black & Decker was well known for its tools and home care equipment sold mainly through hardware stores. To grow further, the company entered the small home appliance business (irons, toaster ovens, portable mixers, coffeemakers, and hair dryers) dominated by GE. In 1984, Black & Decker bought GE's small appliance business for $300 million. The sales contract stipulated that the GE brand could be used for 3 years.

The company broke the changeover process for each product into several sequential steps to be completed over 2 years. It decided to sequentially relaunch all products as if they were new and make alterations ranging from color changes to major overhauls. It also doubled the warranty period for every product to 2 years. In some cases, Black & Decker's changes added new features. It remodeled GE's under-the-cabinet Spacemaker line into sleeker units.

However, the company avoided using both names on the products. Some were kept under the GE brand for a time; after 2 years, the GE brand was dropped on all the products. The Spacemaker was reintroduced with nary a reference to GE. TV commercials played up the Spacemaker name, with a postscript: "Now by Black & Decker."

Cingular and AT&T is a curious example of fade in and fade out. Cingular Wireless acquired AT&T wireless in 2004, using a temporary dual branding phase for the changeover to Cingular. But in 2006 after AT&T acquired Bell South, Cingular's parent, Cingular announced that it would change its brand to AT&T starting in 2007. The justification was the strong tradition of AT&T as a telephone company. Again, a transition period of dual branding was used, ending in June, just before the Apple iPhone was introduced on the AT&T network.

Summary Axing

In summary axing, the old brand is simply replaced on the market by the new brand. After the Berlin Wall fell in 1989, Mars, the family-owned confectionery multinational headquartered in the United States, decided to take Snickers into Eastern Europe. While Snickers had been its leading brand in the Americas and Asia, Europe had kept the old name Marathon for basically the same candy bar.

Once Eastern Europe opened up, the company saw the need to use the one name for global advertising: Snickers had long been associated with team sports events. Since the purchase of a candy bar is usually does not involve a very long consideration phase, the company decided that simply changing the brand would be sufficient. Bolstered by a strong advertising and event promotional push, the 1990 changeover was quite successful, and Snickers is now a leading confectionery brand worldwide (www.justmisc.com/history/snickers).

But Marathon has been resurrected as a good name for an energy bar, endorsed by Snickers (see Figure 8.4). As can be seen in the figure, the Snickers name is prominently displayed. The obvious intent is to piggyback on Snicker's brand equity, a classic brand extension. Marathon, with its allusion to endurance, stamina, and resilience, surely seems a natural name for an energy bar.

Summary axing can backfire. Brand loyalty to the original can be so strong that even the original owner cannot introduce changes. The ill-fated "New Coke" example discussed in Chapter 1 provides an example. Another example is Radio Shack's renaming itself "The Shack" in an apparent effort to "hip and cool." The move has been ridiculed by branding experts who lamented the loss of the intangible assets lodged in the established "Radio Shack" name, however old-fashioned (www.businessinsider.com). The same branding experts have also doubted the shift of AOL.com to simply AOL. But on this change the loss of the old image seems less significant. As always with brand names, in retrospect some brand names can be safely dismissed, but even seeming mistakes such as Accenture can gradually be invested with meaningful associations.

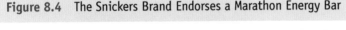

Figure 8.4   The Snickers Brand Endorses a Marathon Energy Bar

Source: Taquitos.net. (2013). http://www.taquitos.net/energy_bars/Snickers_Marathon_Energy_Bar_Chewy_Peanut_Butter

WHAT TO ACQUIRE?

What kind of brand should a company acquire? A number of considerations have to be taken into account.

Brand Strength

One key issue is brand strength. Most brand acquisitions involve strong established brands. The established brand gives the entry immediate credibility and access. If a local brand is weak, there might be no particular reason to acquire it. A weak brand might have some market recognition and access to distribution, but it will also likely have a negative image. If entry into the market is the issue, the company might as well introduce its own brand rather than starting from behind.

Still, when external circumstances change, some old and weak brands have been turned into successful contenders. Volkswagen acquired the Skoda works in the Czech Republic in 1991 after the Berlin Wall fell. The strategic calculation was that the Czech manufacturing plant could be restored and upgraded with German components and technology, the skilled worker wages would be relatively competitive, and there would be some lingering nostalgia attached to the brand in the newly opened Eastern European markets. The calculation proved correct. Competing not simply on price but with up-to-date modern cars, Skoda has thrived. Sales and awards have been sometimes stronger than VWs own cars. In 2005, Italian car magazine *Automobilia* pronounced the Octavia Skoda the "Most Beautiful Mid-sized Car," and in 2007, J.D. Power awarded the Octavia its "Family Car of the Year" prize (Edmondson, 2007; see Figure 8.5).

Figure 8.5 The Award-Winning Skoda Octavia

Source: Skoda Auto a.s. www.new.skoda-auto.com

Ability to Manage

A skill issue centers on the capability of the buyer to manage the brand. Does the firm have the required managerial resources?

A foreign takeover often means that the acquired brand has to be managed by a foreign individual who can understand the foreign customers better. Many of the employees may in fact have to come from the acquired brand. The existing managers may not find it so easy to get used to working with the new owners. Organizational cultures may clash.

When Lenovo took over IBM's PC business in 2004, many existing IBM employees were asked to stay on. Deepak Advani, an IBM veteran, was one of them. He became the chief marketing officer. Others also stayed on, and the Chinese leaders at Lenovo made sure that they were not going to constrain the marketing effort unduly. Still, after a couple of less than successful years, by 2008 and 2009 several American executives were replaced as the Chinese top executives reasserted their authority. Weak performance will of course always be a problem, but especially so when there are cultural differences in an organization.

Product Quality

Another issue to be considered is whether the quality of the acquired product can be sustained or even improved. This depends intimately on the core competence and technology of the acquiring company. This is one reason why most acquisitions tend to be in the area in which the company currently operates. Even when the acquired brand is to be replaced, it is important that quality can be sustained. As we know, an established brand functions as a quality signal. When they know a brand has been acquired and replaced, loyal customers will be looking for undesirable changes in product quality.

When GM acquired Swedish Saab, customers suspected that the uniqueness of the "quirky" Saab would be compromised. GM's announcement that scale economies dictated that new models share platform and components with other GM cars did little to calm their fears. It became increasingly difficult to feel "special" to belong to the Saab community, and sales plummeted.

Sustaining Loyalty

The most relevant question is often the ability of the acquirer to sustain the acquired brand's loyalty base. It is a moot issue if the brand is to be replaced, but in many cases it is the most important issue.

Acquired brands that are well established have brand identity, and image, and perhaps even a definite personality. They also have strong brand loyalty. Orangina, discussed earlier, would be a good example. In these cases, the new brand owner will have to start by maintaining everything as is and only introduce innovations gradually.

A good example is how Belgian brewer InBev integrated American Anheuser-Busch and its Budweiser brand after acquiring the company for $50 billion in 2008. The primary rationale was scale economies. The companies said the deal would yield cost synergies of at least $1.5 billion annually by 2011 phased in equally over 3 years.

InBev announced immediately that nothing will change. Carlos Brito, InBev's chief executive officer, said the following:

> What consumers care is that their Bud will always be their Bud, and that's what we're committed to, not only the product, the quality, the beer . . . but also the heritage, the breweries, who brews the beers, and everything that's connected to the breweries" (Leonard & Fredrix, 2008). Also, InBev retained key managers from Anheuser for marketing and distribution.

Still, the initial reaction from Budweiser consumers was negative. Irate customers pronounced Budweiser a great piece of American history and were no longer proud to drink it. Songwriter Phil McClary put his thoughts in a song posted on the web: "America is not for sale and neither is her beer." But more realistic observers suggested that brand loyalty would return after a few months. "Unless it affects the product or the pocketbook, we are likely to forget about it," was a typical comment (Lendon & Simon, 2008).

The InBev company seems to assume that the waiting period is over. In 2011, the company announced that the cans were going to be changed to a "bolder and cleaner" look with more red (see Figure 8.6). It remains to be seen whether the new owner's legitimacy is established well enough for such a move. The company does not intend to change what is in the cans, but it is a risky move since research has repeatedly shown that consumers use the package to judge taste.

Figure 8.6 The Classic and the Redesigned Budweiser Cans

Source: Anheuser-Busch Companies (2013). 1312499488-budweisercanredesign_280

Brand loyalty does not usually mean that innovations should be avoided. But a new owner will not have the same legitimacy to make changes as the original owner has.

THE PORTFOLIO PROBLEM

The portfolio management problem involves coordinating branding strategies for the various brands and sub-brands to capitalize on positive spillover effects and minimize negative spillovers. Positive synergy means that the total is more than the sum of the individual parts. Negative synergy—through cannibalization, for example—means that total is less than the sum of the individual parts.

It is important to understand the situation facing a manager trying to coordinate a portfolio of brands. First, each separate brand and sub-brand has to be managed properly. This is the responsibility of the individual brand manager. He or she is in charge of identifying the best brand positioning, the brand appeals to be used, the spokesperson for the brand, the distribution channels to be used, the in-store promotions to implement, and so on.

Figure 8.7 shows how the Hugo Boss company, clothiers for men (and women), tries to differentiate its portfolio sub-brands (www.hugoboss.com).

The legacy brand, the original brand that started the business, is Boss Black. Its target segment is the upscale business market. The "selection" sub-brand goes further upmarket, into the luxurious level. Boss Orange is targeting a more youthful and active market, still upscale but now definitely closer to the women's wear market. Boss Green aims, in particular, toward the golfing market and offers upscale sport attire. The Hugo sub-brand is aimed more toward the professional creative submarket. As the personality items show, there are crossover products and styling similarities between the collections, but the market segments are well defined. The models and actors used in Hugo Boss' advertising also helps define what market is targeted (see www.fashionadexplorer.com). It is easy to see that portfolio management involves potential conflicts between the individual brand's needs and the portfolio requirements. The management of the portfolio will typically place some constraints on what the individual brands can do. The positioning may have to shift to accommodate another brand in the portfolio, necessitating a shift in price. The appeals used may have to include some that reflect the overall company image, and the spokesperson may have to be chosen to represent all the brands in the portfolio. Since retail shelf space is typically assigned on a company, not brand, basis, shelf space has to be shared with other brands in the portfolio.

It is also understandable why some companies have avoided the use of umbrella brands and simply given the individual brand managers sole authority over a brand. As a result, of course, the potential positive synergies in the portfolio may easily turn into negative synergies as brands from the same company battle each other.

Differentiating Brands

A portfolio manager trying to convince the individual brand managers to change their strategies needs to answer one question. How large are the gains and losses associated with this repositioning?

Figure 8.7 The Hugo Boss Brand Portfolio

Source: Adapted from Hugo Boss (2013).

The first step is to try to identify exactly how large the overlap and potential cannibalization is. This is typically done with the help of scanner records and consumer panel data where repeat purchases and brand switching rates are readily available (Lomax, Hammond, East, & Clemente, 1997). Customers shown to switch between brands in the same portfolio provide evidence of cannibalization. However, care has to be taken so that a household's purchases for different members of the family are taken into account. The mother might well buy Pantene shampoo for herself, Head & Shoulders for her husband, and Herbal Essences for the teenage daughter (see Figure 8.8). This "overlap" does not mean these three P&G brands cannibalize each other. This can be positive synergy, one purchaser buying from the same company.

For less frequently purchased products, consumer surveys can help show what the possible overlap is. For example, it is common for companies selling consumer durables to ask a customer what alternative brands were considered before the choice was made. This helps identify what brands are in the consideration set. If two brands from a company's portfolio are consistently part of the consideration set the brands are probably not sufficiently differentiated (Srinivasan, Ramakrishnan, & Grasman, 2005). Again, care has to be exercised to draw conclusions too quickly; it may be that the decision involved two or more individuals, each with a separate set of criteria. The husband wants a sporty muscle car while the wife wants a smaller fuel-efficient car (or, today, of course, it could be the other way around).

The differentiation strategy is particularly important where the original legacy brand spawns other sub-brands that potentially can cannibalize on the original sales. According to one study of some 22 pharmaceutical firms, the most promising differentiation strategy involves two parts (Best Practices, 2012). To gain synergies, the new brands should be

Figure 8.8   Three P&G Shampoo Brands

Source: www.pg.com; http://www.pakswholesale.com/brand/clairol/herbal-essences/herbal-essences-fruit-fusions-fresh-balance-shampoo.html

clearly promoted as belonging to the same franchise as the legacy brand. Under that franchise umbrella, however, the differentiation should clear both in terms of customer segment targeted and in terms of product differences (the drugs' efficacy, delivery method and strength). This dual approach ensures positive synergy but still maximizes the individual sub-brand's performance.

Armed with the data on the apparent overlap of customers the portfolio manager is better able to engage the individual brand managers. The gains to the company as a whole have to be weighed against the potential losses for individual brands. More clear differentiation of the brands will lead to more positive synergy, even though any on brand may lose some of its current customers.

STRATEGIC BRAND ROLES

One way to coordinate branding decisions in the portfolio is to assign brands different strategic roles. Following a team analogy, one brand is designated the "lead" brand (the team captain), other brands are "strategic" brands (on the field), and a third level are "support" brands (substitutes, on the bench).

This approach works well when the brand portfolio is made up of master brands, sub-brands, and smaller local brands. Then the brand roles fit logically in a hierarchical fashion (see Figure 8.9).

Figure 8.9 Typical Brand Architecture

Typical Brand Architecture

Master BRAND	Sub-BRAND	Specific MODEL or PRODUCT
• Often the company name • The umbrella or company reputation resides here • The core identify of the brand exists here • Acts as an *endorsement* for the sub-brand • Consistently applied with sub-brands	• A product or line that derives strategic advantage through association with the master brand • The value proposition and positioning reside here	• A defined model or product under a sub-brand • Drives customer satisfaction and loyalty

Source: Adapted from Tait (2001).

As can be seen, this kind of structure assigns the brands' different strategic roles, clarifying what promotional messages should aim for. The global L'Oréal cosmetics company from France offers a good example of how the structure works in practice.

The large brand portfolio of L'Oréal is first organized into four divisions according to the distribution channels used (see Figure 8.10).

As can be seen, in addition to its primary brands, the L'Oréal company has a large number of secondary and supporting brands in the portfolio with stronger or weaker ties to the main cosmetics brands. The Body Shop is one secondary brand, and others include Lancome, Shu Uemura, and Diesel fragrances.

The different strategic roles of the brands are clearest in the primary Consumer Products division (Chailan, 2008). Within this division, the lead brand is L'Oréal Paris. It is described as a brand that is involved in all facets of beauty care, from skin care, hair care and hair coloring to makeup and styling products (www.loreal.com/brands). Products are marketed under names such as Elsève, Studio Line, Dermo-Expertise, Men Expert, and others. The spokespersons are some of the world's most glamorous women, including Laetitia Casta, Eva Longoria, Doutzen Kroes, and Claudia Schiffer. The core competence of the brand involves the expertise of top beauty specialists, makeup artists, hair colorists, and dermatologists, including James Kaliardos for makeup and Christophe Robin for coloring. Above all,

---

Figure 8.10   L'Oréal's Corporate Brand Portfolio

- **L'Oreal Luxe**
  (sold in department stores,
  cosmetics stores,
  own boutiques)

- **Consumer products**
  (sold in retail stores)

- **Professional products**
  (sold in salons)

- **Active cosmetics**
  (sold in healthcare and
  drugstores)

- Lancome, Biotherm, Kiehi's, YSL Beauté, Diesel,
  Giorgio Armani et.al.

- L'Oreal Paris, Garnier, Maybelline, Softsheen Carson,
  Createurs de Beaute.com, Essie

- L'Oreal Professionel, Redken, Shu Uemura et al.

- Vichy, The Body Shop et.al.

the lead brand features the latest innovations from L'Oréal Laboratories, for beauty products tailored to your specific needs.

While L'Oréal Paris represents the basic French identity and upscale positioning of L'Oréal, the company's **strategic brands** are targeted to more specific consumer segments. Garnier is such a strategic brand, offering value-based skin and hair products, with active natural ingredients. Garnier Fructis shampoo and Garnier Nutritionist for skin care are the main sub-brands. Maybelline is another strategic brand, with cosmetics products targeting a younger segment. SoftSheen-Carson is a world leader in hair care products for people of African descent.

SABMiller, the beer giant from South Africa, follows a similar model (www.sabmiller.com/brands). Four brands have been designated *global* brands: (1) Grolsch, (2) Peroni, (3) Pilsner Urquell, and (4) Miller Genuine Draft. A second level is designated *flagship* brands with 21 brands. The flagship bands include local favorites such as Blue Moon (United States), Castle Lager (South Africa), Haywards 5000 (India), Snow (China), Aguila (Colombia), and Gambrinus (Czech Republic). The support brands are the local brands, extending the product line in one or two countries. SABMiller has 53 brands in all.

SABMiller first makes sure the global brands are available in all countries. They are not necessarily the largest seller in any one location but "represent" the company. The strategic brands tend to be the leading brands in its home market and receive the most promotional resources there. The other local brands support the effort and are kept in the market to fill out the product line and keep local loyalties.

THE CONGLOMERATE PORTFOLIO

Many multibrand companies are conglomerates, in that their brands cover a wide variety of different product categories. For example, Philips from the Netherlands has brands in consumer electronics, appliances, health care, and personal care as well as lighting. The Walt Disney Company is slightly less diversified but still owns the ABC television network, several cable channels including ESPN and the Disney Channel, in addition to its theme parks and a large Hollywood film studio. While some of these firms tend to manage their brands independently, as in the Disney case, others have devised an explicit hierarchy of brands for their conglomerate portfolio.

Swiss Nestle is one of the pioneers in developing the logic of conglomerate brand hierarchies. For Swiss Nestle, the **brand hierarchy** is intimately tied to product division and geography. With about 8,500 brands, most of the Nestle products fall in six global product divisions, from baby food and juices, dairy milk, to pet food, coffee, and chocolates. The leading strategic brands are Nestle, Nescafe, Nestea, Maggi (instant soup and seasoning), Buitoni (pasta), and Purina (pet food). The geographical distinction means that three levels of brands are considered: (1) global, (2) regional, and (3) local.

The strategy used by Nestle is basically umbrella branding (called "family branding" by the company) in which the Nestle stylized name (see Figure 8.11) endorses the brands in each category (www.nestle.com/brands). The overarching positioning of Nestle is that the company serves consumers who want quality products without compromise on price.

Figure 8.11 The Nestle® Brand Logo

Source: http://www.nestle.com/info/contactus/contactus. NESTLE are registered trademarks of Société des Produits Nestlé S.A., Vevey, Switzerland.

Accordingly, the Nestle brand serves three different roles.

1. It is a corporate brand, endorsing all the other brands.
2. It is one of six strategic brands, with the status of a family brand.
3. It is simply a product brand, as in "Nestle chocolate."

The allocation of resources starts at the division level where profit and loss responsibility is located. Each brand within the division is then allocated funds in relation to its strategic importance in the division. Complicating the equation is the multinational dimension. A strategically important country such as China will receive increased allocations, and product divisions will coordinate all supply and distribution activities within the country. Acquired local brands will have to be considered as well. Like many other Western companies, Nestle simply manages its China operation separately, as a freestanding operation.

As we have already seen in Chapter 6, the P&G and Unilever portfolio strategy is different from Nestle. It avoids using a corporate umbrella. This has the advantage that decision making can be decentralized and brand management is pushed closer to the market and customers. The brand management system was invented by P&G precisely to allow each individual brand—and its manager—to stand on its own. This organizational structure works well when the company has only one brand in a category or when brands are clearly differentiated. But this is not always the case, as we have already seen in the shampoo example that was given earlier. In fact, to coordinate better between competing brands in shampoos and other categories, the company has returned to what is called "category management," making sure that cannibalization is limited (Dumaine, 1989).

In the case of Unilever, the company offers several ice cream brands, including Breyers, Magnum, and Ben & Jerry's (as well as Popsicle and Klondike bars). To maintain some differentiation despite the obvious overlap, the company uses different distribution channels for the brands. Furthermore, the Ben & Jerry's unit operates completely independently. Still, there is undoubtedly some competition and some cannibalization between these brands.

REBRANDING

Changing the name of an established brand is not common but sometimes necessary. Rebranding can become crucial when the current brand associations are too negative or derogatory. Philip Morris, the cigarette maker, changed its name to Altria to avoid the poisonous tobacco aura. The Accenture brand, mentioned in Chapter 4, is another example. In 2001, the consulting arm of Arthur Andersen, the giant accounting firm, broke off from its parent and created the Accenture brand to signal its independence from traditional audits and bookkeeping. The Accenture name was widely ridiculed in the media as "one of the worst brand names ever" but gradually gained acceptance and a strong identity, using Tiger Woods as a spokesperson (www.time.com). It was a fortuitous rebranding since Accenture survived the Enron crisis fallout that destroyed the Andersen accounting firm.

The fall 2008 financial crisis claimed as victims many bank brands, and some names disappeared from view. Wachovia was absorbed and buried within Wells Fargo. The Bear Stearns investment bank was acquired by J.P. Morgan and also disappeared. By contrast, Merrill Lynch was acquired by Bank of America, but its name survived. It might have been that its famous bull logo was deemed too valuable to drop the name altogether. However, the financial crisis took its toll on the Merrill Lynch image as is evident from association maps that were generated by two different groups of our students before and after the financial crisis (see Figure 8.12).

Rebranding can also involve changing the positioning and brand character—but keeping the name and logo—of an established but weakening brand. Some of the best-known brands today have been involved in this kind of "brand upgrade" through their history. The return of Steve Jobs to Apple in 1997 was the start of a rejuvenation of the Apple brand. The image changed from a quirky niche player targeting a small market of tech-savvy nerds who could get help to fix all the quality problems through their own brand community to today's aspirational high-end and high design brand. Harley-Davidson, the motorcycle brand, went through a similar transformation in the 1980s when the company applied Japanese-style quality controls to back up their brand prestige with worthwhile products.

A less obvious example of rebranding includes the 2001 creation of a dynamic and powerful new image for UPS, the worldwide express mail and package firm. Undertaken to counter the increasing strength of FedEx, the rebranding involved not only a communication emphasis on the company's international reach and integrated shipping capabilities but also a modernized logo with increased visibility and recognition on the street

Figure 8.12   Merrill Lynch Brand Associations Before and After the 2008 Crisis

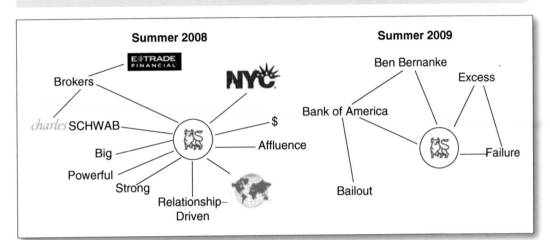

(see Figure 8.13). As the figure shows, two less than ideal but longstanding logo features were kept to reassure loyal customers. One was the brown color, which was turned into a new slogan, "What can brown do for you?" (In 2010, it changed to "We love logistics.") The other feature was the three-initials brand name: UPS comes uncomfortably close to the abbreviation for a close competitor, the United States Postal Service, or USPS (Brady, 2010; Niemann, 2007).

Target, a relatively undistinguished discount store similar to Kmart, started introducing higher quality designer apparel—at still low prices—in the 1990s and transformed itself to an acceptable destination store for even upscale urban housewives with a flair for a good deal. Another example is Corona, the favorite of the college break beer-guzzling crowd, which has morphed from a Mexican low-end light beer to the coolest serving at the Hard Rock Cafes around the world—complete with the omnipresent lime slice stuck in the unfashionably long neck of the transparent bottle.

Figure 8.13   The Revamped UPS Logo

Source: www.ups.com

How should a company approach a rebranding effort? When the change involves changing an established name, the answer is to do it very carefully. The negatives are clear:

- Potential loss of existing customers
- Potential loss of credibility—need for public relations (PR) to justify the shift
- Internal confusion and uncertainty
- Costly investment in new campaign, new advertising and other promotional material

On the pro side, the new brand hopefully casts off the negative associations but can only hope to get established over time:

- No more associated with old negatives
- New brand will become an established strong brand

On the other hand, rebranding by keeping the brand and logo but shifting positioning and brand character can have many pros:

- Reaching a new segment
- Revitalizing the brand character by changing image and personality—with name and logo unchanged, brand identity should typically stay the same
- Refreshing the brand and keeping it up to date
- Energizing the internal workforce

The negatives are few:

- Possible alienation of existing customers
- Cost of money and resources

Companies can protect against possible alienation where it might happen; Corona still presents itself as a Mexican beer, for example, to keep the home market happy. So the negatives mainly involve saving money and resources. It is in fact possible to argue that most successful established brand are those that continually keep updating and recreating themselves, maintaining relevance as their customers' needs and wants keep changing.

BRAND DIVESTMENT

Portfolio management also has implications for when to delete or sell a brand.

In fact, portfolio reasons may be the main justification for dropping a brand. When streamlining the portfolio, overlapping brands and lack of clear differentiation can be used as motivations for simply selling off a brand, rather than trying to modifying and repositioning all brands.

Reasons for selling a brand can include need for funds (as when Ford sells its upscale marquees Jaguar and Volvo), weak customer demand, retreat from a market segment, and so on. These are not all necessarily portfolio reasons. But when the portfolio as a whole is evaluated and synergistic gains are targeted, quite often companies find that their various businesses are too diverse. P&G has gradually exited the food business in recent years. It finally sold its Pringle's snack brand to Diamond Foods in 2011 (Martin, 2011). In fact, brand divestments occur frequently because of a need to refocus a company's business. As we saw in Chapter 7, IBM sold its PC business and ThinkPad brand to Lenovo with a proviso that the IBM logo itself be eliminated after 5 years. Cisco tried to diversify its B2B by acquiring the Flip video camera in March 2009 for close to $600 million. Flip, the most popular video camera in 2010 in the U.S. market, sold nearly 2 million units. Still, Cisco closed down the operation in April 2011, as smartphones have now added HD-video capability (Reardon, 2011).

For companies with many brands, the effort to establish less overlap between brands and increase differentiation is clearly an impetus for some divestment of brands. For individual brand managers, it often means that their brands will have to change or be marginalized by targeting a minor local market or niche, sold—or disappear. There are plenty of examples of well known but now eliminated brands. In autos, Saturn, Hummer, Plymouth; Pan Am and TWA in airlines; and Chemical Bank, E. F. Hutton, and Lehman Brothers in financial markets. Most eliminated brands are not actually eliminated but sold to other firms. Even when discontinued, some entrepreneurial risk taker might buy the brand up for use at some later date. For example, the Pan Am airline brand is today in use on a popular handbag (see Figure 8.14) with the original blue-on-white color and logo (Mooney, 2012).

The reasons for discontinuing a brand vary but are often a result of some version of a streamlining of the brand portfolio. A good example is the GM press release on dropping its Oldsmobile brand in 2000 (see the GM Drops Oldsmobile box):

GM Drops Oldsmobile

DETROIT—General Motors today announced a series of actions intended to strengthen the company's competitiveness in a rapidly changing business landscape and better focus its resources on key growth activities.

In making the announcement, GM President and Chief Executive Officer Rick Wagoner said GM will phase out its Oldsmobile marketing division and brand over the next several years—a measure that will accelerate GM's effort to focus resources on strengthening its market position and growth opportunities.

(Continued)

(Continued)

"This is a very difficult decision for us," said Wagoner. In recent years, major investments have been made in new Oldsmobile products expending significant capital and engineering resources to reposition the brand. Even with the introduction of highly regarded new products, and with the great efforts of the Oldsmobile dealer and marketing team, the brand's sales and profit performance have remained under pressure" (http://cnnfn.cnn.com/2000/12/12/companies/oldsmobile/charge.htm).

As we saw in Chapter 5, Oldsmobile was one of the original five divisions designed by GM's Alfred P. Sloan in the 1920s to offer "a ladder of success." Commentators were quick to point out that GM had long failed to keep Oldsmobile uniquely differentiated from the other brands in the company portfolio. As one blogger said: "If it is the job of branding to distinguish one product from the next in the mind of the customer, the Oldsmobile brand failed decades ago" (http://brandfailures .blogspot.com/2006/11/tired-brands-oldsmobile.html).

Figure 8.14   The Retro Pan Am Flight Bag

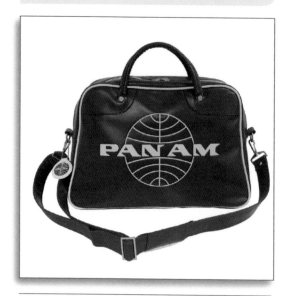

Source: pan-am-airlines-logo-orion-blue-vintage-travel-bag__38812_1290209869_1280_1280

In the end, portfolio management should only be pushed so far. Research shows that the biggest difficulty in managing a portfolio is insufficient buy-in from the individual brand marketing team and sales force (Best Practices, 2012). Independent creativity is important for innovation, and even though an uncoordinated portfolio may exhibit some inefficiency, it is better to allow freedom of expression in branding than to make all ideas accountable to the bottom line. Brand management is fun an exciting and creative—or it is nothing.

SUMMARY

Diversification through brand acquisitions have become commonplace in recent years. The recognition of the value of brands and the strategic value of belonging to the top one or two players have made companies willing to acquire several brands in the same product category and also expand into new market niches. As a consequence, how to manage a large brand portfolio has become an important issue.

Brand acquisitions can be expensive, but with economic growth even emerging market companies have started to acquire global brands, helping them to enter foreign markets. The most common objective in acquisitions is the increased access to new markets and new products, but acquisitions also help to gain scale economies and sometimes to eliminate competitors. Whether the acquired brand name will be retained or dropped depends mainly on the degree to which it can still attract loyal customers. Since many of the acquired brands are strong brands with a loyal following, acquisitions typically do not reduce the number of brands in the market. And changing a name can be risky, as New Coke found out.

Brand portfolio management involves typically coordinating the various brands' strategies. The individual brand manager is no longer solely responsible for his or her brand but is constrained by the need for some coordination with related brands in the portfolio. When such constraints become too limiting or difficult to implement, firms usually end up letting each individual brand be freestanding and largely self-sufficient. This is one reason companies such as Unilever and P&G avoid the use of corporate umbrella branding

The typical brand portfolio is structured as a hierarchy. The largest brands, often global, are at the top, managed centrally. At the next level come regional or country brands, managed by regional or country managers. A third level has more local brands, often specific to some countries of metropolitan areas of a country. Resource allocation for promotional purposes typically involves a major portion for the larger brands in volume, and less for the local brands.

Rebranding and brand divestment are sometimes necessary when the brand associations become negative. It is typically the image of a brand that suffers when negative news or accidents happen. Where the basic identity and personality of the brand are unharmed, a repositioning may be called for rather than a new name. It has the advantage of potentially keeping more of the existing customers, and the repositioning can be presented as the kind of improvement it actually should be. Dropping a brand completely is sometimes done for financial reasons, but, as history shows, even failing old brands can have a second life after death.

KEY TERMS

Brand acquisition, Brand divestments, Brand hierarchy, Brand portfolio, Fade in and fade out, Legacy brand, Rebranding, Strategic brands, Summary axing

DISCUSSION QUESTIONS

1. Discuss the pros and cons of the name change of Marathon to Snickers example in the chapter. (Do some research on Google to find out why the Marathon name still appears.)

2. What could be the strategic rationale behind InBev's acquisition of Budweiser (or some other major acquisition that you can do some research on)? Do you think the price tag is warranted?

3. The Pan Am brand is still active; discuss what possible product categories could be usefully explored under that brand name and logo. Justify your argument with value proposition and positioning statements based on brand identity and image.

4. The financial crisis of 2008 eliminated some brands from the financial industry, including Wachovia, Lehman Brothers, and AIG. Some, like AIG, have come back. Merrill Lynch still survives as a division in Bank of America. Against this background, how important do you think brands are in the financial industry? Is rebranding the best option for a faling institution? (Remember the risk-reducing roles of brands).

5. For the Hugo Boss or L'Oréal portfolios, how separate do you think the target segments are for the different brands? Any cannibalization?

MINICASE: GOOGLE—MANAGING A TECHNOLOGY PORTFOLIO

Google, the well-known Web search engine, is one of the most valuable brands in the world. In 2013, it was valued at about $52 billion by BrandFinance.com, making it either the 2nd or 3rd ranked global brand. It has for several years been by far the most popular search engine, accumulating vast revenues and profits that have been used to acquire other technology firms and starting up new businesses. The company still retains a $54 billion cash stockpile, more than enough to cover the annual budget for the National Aeronautics and Space Administration (about $20 billion in 2013). Its share price hovered above $900 through the summer 2013.

Google still receives more than 50% of its revenues from search and search-related advertising online (Crawford & Chau, 2013). But because of the ambitions of the founders, Larry Page and Sergei Brin, and because in the technology business the only way to stay in front is to keep moving, the company has made a number of big efforts at innovation. One invention, the development of the Android mobile operating system is said to bring in about $6.8 billion annually from use on smartphones. Google has also bought a number of businesses. It acquired YouTube in 2006, and the video-sharing website now contributes about $4 billion in revenues each year.

A glance at Wikipedia shows the number of Google mergers or acquisitions at 129 as of September 2013. Whether this is true diversification or not is not clear—some observers point to the narrow focus on technology, and the fact that most revenues comes from advertising generated by search or the Android operating system. Others see the collection of businesses as an unorganized and irrational collection of separate activities. Here is one example from *Time* magazine:

"Google is, of course, in the search business, and more important for its profitability, it is in the online-advertising business. But it's also in

the mobile-operating-system business,
the Web-browser business,
the free-e-mail business,

the driverless-car business,

the wearable-computing business,

the online-map business,

the renewable-energy business and

the business of providing Internet access to remote areas via high-altitude balloons, among countless others." (McCracken and Grossman, 2013, p 24)

Bloggers routinely complain that Google is fragmenting itself by operating in so many different businesses. Here is a typical refrain:

"They innovate, refine and deliver some of the best services out there. At other times, I can't help but wonder if there's anyone with a clear vision for the company and the various product groups operating within." (http://simonjthomas.com/business-of-tech/googles-baffling-product-line-up.html)

Co-founder Larry Page served as chief executive of Google for the first 3 years until 2001 when Eric Schmidt was brought in from software giant Novell to bring some management expertise. It was the troika of Page, Brin and Schmidt that led Google's M&A-fueled fast growth through the first decade of the new millennium. In April 2011, Page reclaimed the CEO title, and Schmidt became executive chairman. The management change is intended to allow Page to take on the task of coordinating, streamlining and managing the Google portfolio of businesses, not an easy task.

Page's leadership quickly made a difference. He closed down two failing efforts, a Wikipedia knockoff Knol and Google Buzz, a Twitter clone. He reduced the number of new-product introductions and axed existing projects in periodic "spring cleanings." He reshaped Google's management structure, creating a team of top managers to better coordinate, consolidate and streamline the difference businesses. But he also expanded, acquiring handset maker Motorola Mobility in a $12.5 billion acquisition, in order to start Google manufacturing its own hardware in the mobile search field.

The overall philosophy draws from Google's original strategy. Early on, Google beat search competitors like AltaVista by being much more accurate. Other early successes like Gmail, with abundant free storage, and Google Maps succeeded for similar reasons, because what they offered was far beyond what competition had. According to Johanna Wright, a vice president, "Larry wants innovation that is 10 times greater than what we have in the market today" (McCracken & Grossman, 2013, p.28).

Discussion Questions

1. Briefly characterize Google's brand identity, image and personality.

2. As an umbrella brand, what commonality can the brand bring to its portfolio of businesses?

(Continued)

(Continued)

3. How would you characterize the management of the portfolio—more like P&G or more like SAB Miller or just unique? Explain.

4. Any recommendations for Larry Page?

Sources

Crawford, A.,& Chau, L. (2013, June 25). Why Google's business model works. *U.S. News and World Report.* Retrieved from (http://www.usnews.com/opinion/blogs/economic-intelligence/2013/06/25/why-googles-business-model-works

http://www.infoworld.com/t/technology-business/googles-next-act-diversify-and-conquer-218839

McCracken, H., & Grossman, L. (2013, September 30). The audacity of Google: Larry Page and the art of the moonshot. *Time Magazine,* pp. 22[en]30.

http://en.wikipedia.org/wiki/List_of_mergers_and_acquisitions_by_Google

SUGGESTED PROJECTS

Acquisition Exercise: Yum! Brands is a fast-food company that has acquired three major brands: (1) KFC, (2) Pizza Hut, and (3) Taco Bell (see Figure 8.15). It has a slogan "Alone we're Delicious. Together we're Yum!" But the corporate brand is not very visible, and the individual brands are typically managed separately. Do research on the Web, and analyze the history of Yum!'s acquisitions. Then identify to the extent possible the rationale behind each acquisition. What synergies, if any, were expected? Suggest one other acquisition that would seem logical given the existing three. Why has this not been accomplished?

Figure 8.15   The Yum! Fast-Food Portfolio

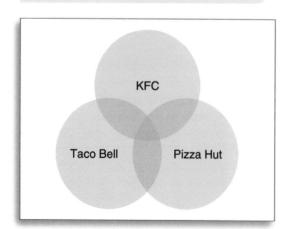

Portfolio Exercise: Follow up on the Yum! case, analyzing to what extent Yum! Brands is actually used as an umbrella in promotion. How does the company attempt to create spillover from one brand to the other—or does it? Why should Yum! Brands not be treated as a master brand—or is it? Sample fellow students to determine how many of them frequent all three restaurants and whether there are target segment overlaps. Then do a Venn diagram that shows the degree to which these three brands' market segments overlap. What is the respective size of the overlaps? Analyze and discuss possible cannibalization and synergies and how they can be managed.

(This exercise can be done for other portfolio brands of your choice).

New Branding Applications

CHAPTER 9

Summary and Extensions

Brands are first and foremost providers of experiences.

—Bernd Schmitt[1]

LEARNING OBJECTIVES

In this chapter, you will learn the following:

- The components of a nation brand
- How personal branding can help individuals set goals for themselves
- How experiential branding grew out of service branding
- How consumers have come to love their favorite brands
- Why social media might be enough as a sales channel
- How simplicity and design come together in today's leading brands

---

What have we learned so far about brand management? In the early chapters, we covered what brands actually do from a consumer and company perspective. For the consumer, brands help to reduce functional and psychological risks and also provide self-expressive benefits. The brand equity helps the consumer trust that the brand functions well and is viewed positively by peer groups and others. Trusting the brand means that the consumer can make faster and more accurate decisions, and eliminating

---

[1]Bernd H. Schmitt is the founder and director of Columbia Business School's Center on Global Brand Management. He also directs the Institute on Asian Consumer Insight in Singapore. The quote is from Schmitt (1999, p. 30).

psychological risk reduces cognitive dissonance and offers emotional support. Self-expressive benefits go beyond the product itself and allow the consumer to shape his or her own personality and individual self.

For the company, the chapters have shown how to build a new brand and what it takes to develop a well-known brand. An established brand has a well-defined identity, image, and personality. The chapters have shown how these features of a strong brand are created, drawing equally on company core capabilities, product and service features, and promotional campaigns. Strong brands with high brand equity are not simply created by advertising. They depend on imaginative market segmentation, a credible value proposition and a positioning that highlights competitive advantages. To the extent there is a science in brand management, that science derives much from traditional marketing know-how.

Later chapters focused on growth strategies for the established brand. They covered market penetration, brand extensions, and growth by using the brand in new product categories. We also covered extensions into new foreign markets. These growth opportunities not only increase total revenues to the firm but also increase brand equity and value. We made a crucial distinction between growing brand equity by increasing loyalty among existing customers versus increasing brand value by extending the reach of the brand. For brand management, the balance between depth and reach strategies is always a critical. It is simply not true that it is always better to focus on retaining and building loyalty with current customers. Reaching into new markets with an established brand can be a more profitable strategy, even though the new customers are not going to increase loyalty levels.

We also covered brand acquisition and brand portfolios, dealing with the issues of how companies diversify and manage multiple brands. The main takeaway here is that acquisitions should carefully assess the fit with the existing brands in the portfolio, clearly specifying what the new brand's role in the portfolio will be. When the brands in the portfolio form a unified group—by, for example, belonging to the same product category—the use of umbrella branding is often helpful in coordinating individual brand strategies and deriving synergies. The exception is where clear distinctions exist—between target segments or price position, for example—in which case independent strategies can be advantageous because the separate brands can be more precisely adapted to each segment.

In covering these topics, the text has drawn on existing marketing tools and techniques. This means it has emphasized features and benefits, recognized that both rational and emotional factors influence consumers, and emphasized the role of the brand as both a trusted name and a warm friend. This basic branding paradigm can be—and has been—extended into new areas of application. The rest of this chapter discusses several of these new applications.

PLACE BRANDING

Place branding refers to the notion that places can be brands too. It started with nation branding.

Nation branding comes from the idea that country names are like brands and their flags are brand logos. The competitive advantages of a brand's country of origin have long been recognized. French wines, Italian fashion, German cars, and Japanese electronics possess an edge over competition because of their origin (e.g., Peterson & Jolibert, 1995). But the effect can also go the opposite way—from strong products to the country image. For example, the image of "brand Germany" is partly created by its great automobiles. Among the first writers to recognize this were Papadopoulos and Heslop (1993), who showed the correspondence between brand images and country images. Government agencies eager to attract foreign investments and tourists started to pay attention, and soon, a comprehensive model of how national brand images come to be was developed by Anholt (2003).

The national "product" that is branded by the country name consists of the features that make the country attractive to the various consumers or audiences—potential tourists, investors, expatriates, former emigrants returning home, and so on. Anholt's model suggests that there are six major factors that define a country's brand. They are as follows:

1. Exports: The higher the exports from a country, the more it is able to produce goods and services desired elsewhere. This means that other people will find something positive to like about the country.

2. Governance: As the country scores higher on governance, it will be more stable and peaceful, again raising its attractiveness level.

3. Culture: Culture is an obvious factor, including both high culture and popular culture.

4. People: People's friendliness and openness likewise contribute to attractiveness.

5. Tourism: High levels of tourism are direct evidence of attractiveness and accessibility.

6. Immigration: A high level of immigration is similarly evidence of attractiveness and accessibility.

Basically, as a country scores higher on these six factors, it is able to "market" a more attractive product. Anholt has combined the scores on these six attributes into a Nation Brands Index (NBI). The overall NBI ranking is based on the average of these six scores. The 2012 top 10 countries can be found in Table 9.1.

The NBI rankings have become national goals in several cases, leading to sustained effort by governments to improve their rankings. One example is South Korea where in 2009 then President Lee Myung-bak formed a Presidential Council on Nation Branding to combat negative stereotypes (Glionna, 2009). The ambitious goal was to move the country from 33rd place in Anholt's rankings in 2009 to 15th by 2013.

Nation branding is practiced by many states including Canada, the United States, France, the United Kingdom, Japan, China, Scotland, South Korea, South Africa, and New Zealand. There is also interest among less affluent states to practice nation branding to improve their image abroad and promote trade, tourism, and direct investment. A good example of what country campaigns involve is Finland's Nation Brand Initiative (see the Branding Finland box).

Table 9.1 Nation Brands Rankings 2012

Top 10 of 50 Nations	
1. United States	69.09
2. Germany	67.72
3. United Kingdom	67.14
4. France	66.58
5. Canada	65.90
6. Japan	65.87
7. Italy	65.08
8. Switzerland	64.61
9. Australia	64.36
10. Sweden	63.49

Source: http://www.simonanholt.com/Research/research-the-anholt-gfk-roper-nation-brands-index-sm.aspx

Branding Finland

Finland is a country that scores well on most international rankings. By 2008, it ranked among the best in education, health care, press freedom, global competitiveness, corruption, and environmental protection (Moilanen, 2008). But as a brand it had low awareness and low relevance in the world. The government decided to launch a nation brand initiative in 2009, with the objective of building a nation brand commensurate with its superior product ratings (Finland, 2010).

Involving more than 200 thought leaders, branding consultancies and crowdsourcing ideas, the massive effort was spearheaded by two ministries. Funding was allocated for a massive effort following quite closely standard marketing campaigns. First specific ideas about what constituted a true Finnish identity were collected via seminars, summits, and social media. Then the target countries and audiences were determined, and market research was conducted to find out how Finland was perceived among these target audiences. The results were compared to what would be specifically Finnish and constitute the core of the brand identity.

This identity formed the basis for a wide-ranging communications campaign that started in 2010 and is still ongoing. The 5- to 10-year-long campaign attempts first of all to make sure that people are not only aware of the brand but also know something about the country's impressive

(Continued)

(Continued)

Figure 9.1 The Logo of Finland's Cleantech

Source: http://www.cleantechfinland
.com/?q=content/job-opening-cleantech-finland-
marketing-and-communications-director

achievements. After this largely educational campaign, the objective is to position the nation brand by 2030 as "the problem solver of the world," a very ambitious goal. To accomplish this, the task force has assigned specific tasks to various government and official agencies. For example, considering how well Finnish society functions, one task is for Finland to be present itself as a "Silicon Valley of social innovations." Its excellent environmental record is to be used as a platform for ensuring drinkable water and organic food everywhere (see Figure 9.1).

The outstanding education system is to be exported with the notion that education is a protection force for peace (Finland, 2010). Its inspirational and ambitious branding mantra can be stated as "Finland: The World's Problem Solver."

As Anholt (2011) emphasized, a nation brand—as all brands—need to be able to deliver on its promises. High aspirations are useful as mission statements for internal motivation, but as brand promises, they should have some credible grounding to be effective as consumer appeals.

Place branding has been extended to include cities and regions. What was once referred to as "city marketing" has now evolved into city branding. Most of the principles for nation branding extend to city branding, with the *product* and target segments defined to be smaller and narrower. For tourists of a city, for example, the *value proposition* typically includes its cultural artifacts, events, its people, its security, and governance. To attract inhabitants, features such as housing costs, green spaces, health care, and social services play a bigger role. To get an *overall* ranking of a city, these different indicators are typically averaged across all market segments.

While there are some attempts to rank cities on the basis of their appeal (e.g., Best City rankings published by *The Economist* and *Money Magazine*), such rankings are generally based on available published data combined with survey data. This produces rankings that are closer to product ratings than direct measures of brand equity, and it is misleading to interpret them as "best city brands." For most branding purposes, it is desirable to base ratings on consumer perceptions rather than secondary sources. But a strong product will of course be the proper foundation for any branding effort, and for most practical purposes, these scores can be treated as brand values, if not exactly brand equity.

PERSONAL BRANDING

In recent years, personal branding has become a new watchword. Celebrities and movies stars have long been their own *brands* (see Figure 9.2), but now all of us are in the game as well. Your name is your personal brand—and your brand identity is who you are or whom you wish to portray yourself to be.

Especially with the rise of social media, the need to groom your personal brand has become more or less mandatory. Even without meaning to—and often without wanting to—all of us are projecting ourselves in our daily behavior and how we look. That is, we live our brand.

With the rise of Facebook, in particular, the personal branding business has become huge. There are now several guides available on the web for how to create your own online personal brand. They do apply principles quite similar to our branding text. Here is one example of the sequence of steps one should take (adapted from Marrs, 2012; Weber, 2013):

Figure 9.2 Paris Hilton, A Personal Branding Practitioner

Source: © Glenn Francis, www.PacificProDigital.com

Creating Your Online Personal Brand

Step 1: Personal Brand Pillars

- Select four or five special personality traits and skills that make you stand out from everyone else. These are your brand elements.

Step 2: The "Elevator Statement"

- Condense the elements into three sentences that could communicate your brand identity if you happen to meet someone in an elevator.

Step 3: Your "Brand Mantra"

- Look at your three sentences, and see how you can combine them into your brand mantra: three to five words, memorable and inspiring.

Step 4: Audit Your Online Profile

- Audit your online profiles, and adjust things to reflect the elements of your personal brand.

Step 5: Live Your Personal Brand

- Remember: Your personal brand should reflect your traits and skills authentically.

As should be clear, one's personal online brand is not always a true profile of who you are. The brand tries naturally to put the best spin on what you are really like. Remember also that the way you think you are viewed does not necessarily correspond with what others think.

The personal branding efforts draw much from the large literature on self-help and self-improvement. As such, it is important to see that a personal branding effort can help the person to behave more in accordance with the pillars of their personal brand. Even though the online personal brand profile is more or less an advertisement for an idealized "me" and thus probably contains a lot of "puffery," it can also help an individual to become more cognizant of how he or she ought to act. As one personal branding advocate puts it, "Are you going to live accidentally or are you are going to live purposefully?" (Weber, 2013).

SERVICE BRANDING

Throughout the book, we have treated services as part of *products*. This is a standard approach, since in most cases the branding tools apply equally to services as to goods. However, the intangibility of many services—hotels, restaurants, banks, entertainment, and so on—makes the product more elusive for branding purposes. The solution is to brand *the experience* of receiving the service. This is service branding.

The importance of offering consumers emotional experiences rather than mere physical products was recognized early in what is usually called store "atmospherics" research (Kotler, 1973). To enhance the shopping experience, store design, color and carpeting, background music, temperature, and even smell were delicately calibrated to maximize customer pleasure. The aim was to make the store an attractive destination, as a place to be, and thus win the first half of the battle for customer share of mind, that of actually coming to the store.

The customer's interaction with the service provider was then recognized as the "moment of truth" in service quality assessment and customer satisfaction (Bitner, 1992; Normann, 1991). In intangible services like restaurants, health care, and educational institutions (including universities), that interaction often *is* the product. Yes, the food matters, the quality of care matters, the educational content matters, but quality judgments are very subjective, and overall customer satisfaction depends on many intangible factors and the emotional state induced by them. The physical premises of the service provider, the music and decor, attentive employees, and so on all help produce a positive experience. A well-known brand clearly can influence—even bias—these judgments, whether it is a store (Barney's, H&M), a hotel (W Hotels, Ritz-Carlton), or airline (Singapore). Service providers benefit from a strong brand as much as goods manufacturers.

For service managers, it quickly became natural to use slogans and mantras to capture core brand experiences. "Singapore Girl—You're a great way to fly" (Singapore Airlines), "Fly the friendly skies" (United Airlines), "Feel the Power" (National Football League [NFL]), "It's everywhere you want to be" (Visa), and "You're in good hands" (Allstate Insurance) are some well-known examples. Place branding goes particularly well with experience branding. One illustrative example is the efforts by different countries to attract tourism. The standard appeal is for the advertising to promise "once-in-a-lifetime experiences" for the visitor to the particular country, whether it be bungee jumping in New Zealand, safaris in Kenya, or scuba diving on the Great Barrier Reef in Australia.

In one study, we queried individuals about the minimum they would expect from the experience when going to watch a favorite team play. Their responses are tallied in Figure 9.3. The sport itself seems secondary to the excitement of a live event. But remember also from the research presented in Chapter 3 (Figure 3.8) people's preferred team image revolves around competing hard and winning.

EXPERIENTIAL BRANDING

Marketers have now taken the experience thinking in services and moved it into goods marketing. The basic approach involves a mind-set shift from the purchase situation to the consumer experience when using the brand (Schmitt, 1999). Most traditional marketing efforts focus on getting the "sale," getting the consumer to "prefer our brand," and treating the consumer choice as the critical unit of analysis. Customer after-sales service, warranties, and guarantees of satisfaction are viewed mainly as sales tactics to get customers to "buy now" and become loyal. The new focus on the user experience involves a more holistic view of the consumer, one that involves not only choices and purchases but more

Figure 9.3 What Fans Expect When Watching Their Favorite Team

Fun	15%
Excitement	13%
Energy	13%
Good Crowd	9%
Effort by my Team	9%
Good time with Friends	7%
Competitive Game	7%
Good Sightlines	7%
Be Safe	5%
Drink Beer	5%
Fair Referees	4%
Good Service	4%
Freedom of Expression	2%

This is what game experience is for a fan at a game.

Source: B. Sandman.

generally the way the products and brands enhance the life of the consumer. True allegiance and lifelong dedication can even involve self-expressive tattoos.

The new view has spread gradually. As product differentiation becomes increasingly difficult to sustain because of benchmarking, reverse engineering and me-too products, the focus on product superiority shifted from tangible features and product quality to more intangible benefits. Initially this view led to an emphasis on after-sales service and customer loyalty programs. As this effort progressed, some marketers began to realize that the bottom line of marketing should be the "user experience." Market research, product development, and design should be focused on the usage and consumption situations (Joachimsthaler, 2007). Designing and delivering a pleasurable user experience has become the driving mandate for product marketers as well.

Here is how the Marketing Science Institute (MSI) formulated the new thinking in a call for a 2013 conference:

> People buy experiences, not products. While service experience design has a long history of scholarly research, product experience research has tended to focus on discrete features and benefits rather than the holistic experience of purchase, usage, and re-purchase. MSI members have asked if there are generalizations from the mature field of retail and service design that can help managers in all categories

enhance customers' experience and create brand value. Specifically, what accounts for experiences that are remembered, interesting, repeated and valued—and shared with others? What management and organizational structures, cultures, or practices are needed to successfully design positive product experiences?

What is the role of the brand in experiential marketing? Since we know that a strong brand reduces functional and psychological risks and also provides self-expressive benefits, the brand naturally assumes a central role in ensuring a positive customer experience. In fact, positive experience effects are often predicated on a strong brand. This is most easily seen on the negative side. In the absence of a well-established brand, the assumption that traditional features and benefits are taken for granted by the consumer no longer holds. An unknown brand cannot offer such guarantees. Experience marketing without a well-established brand is like advertising a steak that has no sizzle.

But experience marketing can certainly help in solidifying and cementing the brand–customer relationship. In fact, many proponents experience marketing view this bonding effect to be the major contribution of experience marketing. The emphasis on emotions serves precisely to raise the brand allegiance from liking and esteem to loyalty (Schmitt, 1999, pp. 21, 34). Some of the best known slogans and taglines for brands emphasizing the user experiences are the following: "Just do it" (Nike), "Sheer driving pleasure" (BMW), "Don't dream it. Drive it." (Jaguar cars), "The pause that refreshes (Coca-Cola), "For people who share a taste for excitement" (Martini & Rossi vermouth), and "We bring good things to life" (General Electric [GE]).

BRAND LOVE

The positive user experiences that result from using a favorite brand can dramatically enhance consumer well-being. It is not uncommon to find that consumers express feelings of "love" for their iPhone or Starbucks, treating the brands as irreplaceable totems in their lives. As we have seen throughout this book, brands are often used for consumer self-expression. Thus, it is not surprising to find that a brand can become an intimate "friend" of the consumer. One of the first experts to recognize this was Fournier (1998). In the same vein, some experts suggest that products and brands should aim to create consumer "happiness" (e.g., Schmitt, 2012). From there, it is but a small step to start considering the idea that there is something one might call brand love.

Several academic authors as well as practitioners and bloggers have recently proposed that brand love can be seen as the ultimate essence of brand equity. In Chapter 2, we discussed "Hello Kitty" as an example of a brand that evokes tender and heartfelt emotions among its loyal adherents. Also in that chapter, we introduced the Lovemarks championed by Roberts (2005) that supposedly induce a passionate "loyalty beyond reason." In fact, the well-known "I love NY" logo represents an early example of combining a brand (a "place brand" at that) with the love emotion. Beginning as an advertising effort in 1977 to attract tourism to New York, the success of the campaign owed much to the striking design of the now ubiquitous—and often imitated—advertising logo (see Figure 9.4).

Figure 9.4 An Iconic Logo

Source: © iStockphoto.com/jbk_photography

Note: The design by Milton Glaser is recognized as a modern art masterpiece, and the original sketch is now in the Museum of Modern Art in New York City.

Brand love, as with love between individuals, is not always easy to define and can have several meanings. The love of a brand would typically involve some passion, some loyalty and some affinity, but the overall commitment might not be as strong as that of interpersonal love. A recent article by Batra, Ahuvia, and Bagozzi (2012) attempted bravely to nail down the brand love concept. Drawing on personal and telephone interviews with consumers as well as responses to survey questionnaires, the authors derived several factors that together define brand love. These factors can be grouped into categories that reflect the similarities between brand love and (married) interpersonal love (see Table 9.2):

Table 9.2 Brand Love and Marriage

1. Passion: Desire and satisfaction

2. Natural comfort and fit with consumer self

3. Commitment: emotional connectedness, long-term use

4. Fear of loss

Source: Adapted from Batra et al. (2012).

Throughout this text we have emphasized the need to always keep the brand relevant, up to date, and dynamic, so as to maintain, defend, and deserve the consumer allegiance and commitment. With the extension of brand thinking into the realm of love and its parallel with married love, the difficult challenge of maintaining the loyalty of consumers is clearly put in sharp relief. As we all know, divorces are not uncommon.

BRANDS AS SOCIAL CURRENCY

How to build brands through social media has been a "hot topic" among brand practitioners in the last couple of years. One new approach is called social currency. The idea has been pioneered by a consulting company called Vivaldi Partners whose founder, Erich Joachimsthaler, has long been active in professional branding. His basic message can be summarized in the headline of one of his speeches: "Love is Not Enough: How to build brands and connect with consumers through Social Currency" (http://www.youtube.com/watch?v = drA-LBs4-Wk). Social currency is defined as the degree to which customers share information about a brand with others and act on it. The concept differs from other social media measures of "buzz" in that it does not simply stop at the level of sharing information but tracks how effectively social media brings ultimate purchase and loyalty (http://www.vivaldipartners.com/vpsocialcurrency/sc2012). It is a similar distinction to the one we drew in Chapter 2 between brand equity (in terms of brand allegiance) and brand value (in dollar terms). Does the social media buzz translate into a positive bottom line for the company?

The social media "conversion effect" on brands comes from the way the brand plays into a consumer's daily behavior. The model distinguishes between six pathways for a company to influence this behavior and thus raise a brand's social currency. In rough order of increasing social currency, social media provides the following benefits to the consumer:

1. Information (receiving worthwhile info about the brand and sharing it)

2. Conversation (talking about a brand with others)

3. Utility (deriving value from using a brand socially)

4. Advocacy (actively promoting a brand to others)

5. Affiliation (connecting to a wider community around a brand)

6. Identity (describing oneself via the relationship to the brand)

A firm with can build social currency by being active in all of these pathways. Offering useful information on the web clearly is a first step. Initiating conversations and providing fresh updates and news help the utility of interacting with the brand and help induce advocacy. These steps help both conversion from awareness to active consideration and also conversion to trial and purchase. Supporting the creation of a brand community and increasing the self-expressive potential of the brand via a strong identity helps convert the consumer even closer to a loyal brand user.

As one might expect, the brands with the highest social currency tend to be brands that require more involvement by the consumer. In the social currency rankings, Subway, the "make your own" sandwich restaurant, ranks highest, followed by Google, Target, and Heineken. As the company says, there is great variety in the way different brands score on the six characteristics (Vivaldi Partners, 2013, p. 3).

For example, while Apple scores high on the items of conversation and utility, the company has made surprisingly little use of social media to drive the conversion to use. Coca-Cola social media scores show the opposite: weak as a conversation item but strong on the bottom line conversion.

The social currency model represents an early attempt to show how brands can be built entirely through social media. Where most of the analysis of social media—including our coverage in Chapter 3, for example—has basically treated social media as just another communication channel to reach consumers, the social currency model attempts to treat social media as a self-sufficient interactive platform reaching all the way to purchase. Only the future will decide whether the social media will be resilient enough to serve without help from other media.

BRAND SIMPLICITY

In another new development, the emphasis on the user experience in experiential branding has led to the emergence of simplicity among branding experts. Here, simplicity is to be interpreted as more than just "simple to use." Simplicity refers to the notion that many consumers feel the need to simplify their lives. As technological advances provide us with ever more products and features, many consumers feel overwhelmed. Even if the new products are successful in the marketplace, many of their features are forgotten or ignored by consumers who do not use all options available (Thompson, Hamilton, & Rust, 2005). As new product introductions speed up, the consumers have to learn of new products and features ever faster. The complexity of their lives increases. If marketers really focus on the user experience, the design of the new products should avoid technological myopia and focus instead on ease of use and how their brands help consumers get the most out of their lives.

The result is a broad concept of brand simplicity. In addition to the product's ease of use, simplicity to operate, and clear design, brand simplicity involves issues such as the pleasure and/or pain of interacting with the company, how easy to understand the brand communication is, and the transparency and honesty of the company.

The Siegel + Gale ad agency has developed a Brand Simplicity Index used for annual assessments of the simplicity of major brands (Siegel + Gale, 2012). Their 2012 annual survey covered seven countries: United States, United Kingdom, Germany, China, India, and the Middle East (United Arab Emirates and Saudi Arabia), with approximately 1,000 respondents in each country representative of the demographics of the country. The respondents answered questions about a total of 500 brands. The questions included the brand touch points within specific industries, loyalty programs, the workplace, and generally how simple or complex they perceive their life to be.

The brand's Simplicity Score is calculated with the following inputs:

- *Simplicity/complexity.* Ratings of the brand's products and services, relative to their industry peers. The measures include *ease of understanding, transparency/honesty, innovation/freshness,* and *usefulness.*

- *Consistency.* The consistency of the brand experience and communications across respondents (the standard deviation of the ratings).

- *User/Nonuser.* Adjusting for the difference between user and non-user ratings (user ratings are weighted more heavily than non-users).

- *Industry/Category.* The simplicity score is finally adjusted for the product category, because certain product categories are intrinsically more complex to navigate than others. (Siegel + Gale, 2012, p. 94)

The list of top simplicity brands differs across countries. By averaging over all seven countries, the global top 10 brands are shown in Table 9.3.

It is interesting to note the wide dispersion of countries; brand simplicity is not confined to one or two countries. The lack of entries from Japan and South Korea is intriguing, but partly a function of where the samples were drawn. Honda was actually number 13 and Samsung number 14. Amazon placed 12th and Starbucks 17th. Google

Table 9.3   Global Top 10 Simplicity Brands 2012

Rank	Brand Score	Simplicity	Industry/ Category	Country
1	Google	891	Media	United States
2	McDonald's	812	Restaurants	United States
3	IKEA	789	Retail	Sweden/The Netherlands
4	C&A	782	Retail	The Netherlands/Belgium
5	Apple	779	Technology	United States
6	Pizza Hut	778	Restaurants	United States
7	Nokia	772	Telecom	Finland
8	Yahoo!	768	Media	United States
9	Carrefour	767	Retail	France
10	ALDI	761	Retail	Germany

Source: Siegel + Gale (2012).

at number 1 is well known for its effort to keep its search home page uncluttered (http://news.ebrandz.com).

BRANDING AND DESIGN

As Steve Jobs adherents know, simplicity has had a strong impact on Apple product design. The emphasis on user experiences in experiential branding naturally involves an emphasis on product design as well.

At the most fundamental level, the main determinant of the value proposition and the brand's position is often the look and feel of the product itself. Media advertising, promotional slogans, and spokespersons can only do so much—what the consumers see and feel depends ultimately on what the thing looks like. For many well-known brands, their competitive advantage lies partly in superior design. A prominent example is Apple, with its iMac, iPod, iPhone, and iPad. It is at least partly the superior designs of these products that generate the high brand affinity of its users. The loyal consumers delight in the aesthetically pleasing minimalist design, avoiding any extra embellishments or seductive ornamentation. It gives the brand and its users an uncompromising, sophisticated, and slightly arrogant personality. The emphasis on "insanely great" product design offers powerful ammunition for the company in the costly promotional campaigns against competitors, and Apple's efforts to protect any design innovations make me-too products less of a threat.

Product design involves not only aesthetically pleasing designs but also functionality and ease of use. For physical, tangible products, "design" is easy to understand. But design is also involved in intangible services. The manner in which personal service is provided, the look and dress of the service provider, the style of the service premises, and so on, are all results of conscious "design." The positioning of a brand sets the promises of the brand, which in turn form the expectations of the consumers. For both physical products and intangible services, the product design will either confirm or negate those expectations.

Some of the new thinking is inspired by the success of the Apple products and Steve Jobs' emphasis on design. The minimalist design philosophy exemplified by Apple has undoubtedly helped lead the move toward simplicity. According to Jobs, "Design is not just what it looks like and feels like. Design is how it works" (Walker, 2003). It's how the product works that create the user experience.

As the listing of the simplest global brands demonstrates, simplicity can be found in many countries. One famous product designer who stresses simplicity is Dieter Rams, head designer for Braun appliances in Germany (see Figure 9.6).

Rams' list of 10 essential principles of what good design is starts with "innovative" and "making the product useful." The tenth and bottom-line minimalist principle is "Good design is as little design as possible." He explained, "Good design is less but better—because it concentrates on the essential aspects, and the products are not burdened with non-essentials. Back to purity, back to simplicity" (www.vitsoe.com/us/about/good-design).

Figure 9.5   Dieter Rams, Vitsoe's Designer; the German Progenitor of Apple Designs

Braun radio, 1961

Source: Photograph by Abisag Tüllmann ©Vitsoe

The Apple head designer, Jony Ive claims to be very much influenced by Mr. Rams (Warman, 2013). Other brands designed with the same simplicity and minimalist spirit include Bang & Olufsen's consumer electronics products from Denmark and Honda cars from Japan whose design principle is "Man Maximum, Machine Minimum" (Johansson & Nonaka, 1996, p. 41). Paradoxically, simpler designs tend to lead to more expensive products. One reason is that good designs add value to the product, and the brand owner can charge premium prices. A more important reason is that simple designs are actually quite hard to achieve and therefore increase costs. The standard practice in many companies is to develop a new product and not think about design until the end—asking the design group to just come up with a suitable and not too expensive package. By contrast, good designers need to be involved early in the new product development, and brands known for their designs are often practicing what is called "design-driven innovation."

Two examples of design-driven innovations are the iPhone and Nintendo Wii (Verganti, 2009). In both cases, the new products involved technological advances in established *red ocean* markets. The standard mode of competition in each industry was to compete with new features and capabilities, driven by technology. New products could be expected to add further complexity. But with designers involved at the early stages of the product development, a focus on ease of use and simplicity combined to push the innovations in radical new directions. The iPhone offered the touchscreen display, a whole new user experience, and the Nintendo Wii allowed motion-controlled active play, opening gameplay to the family market. Both brands changed red oceans to blue oceans—until, of course, competitors were able to create me-too products. By that time, the pioneering brands had established strong and defensible positions.

CONCLUDING COMMENTS

The traditional perspective of marketing is that the marketing effort has to start with the consumers' wants and needs. However, consumers in many markets—mature markets, in particular—have few real unmet needs. This means that the underlying desire for more products or services is relatively weak. Asking consumers to please state what exactly they want or need, most consumers are stumped. Every consumer can articulate a "need" for a great new dress or car or cell phone they see. But without seeing it, consumers cannot say what they need. It is the new products that generate the needs and wants, not the other way around.

This means that in the recent past, the tables have been turned. Instead of satisfying customers' needs and wants, marketing has had to do double duty of creating new needs and wants and satisfying them. Advances in technology led to the introduction of new products, which both created new needs and offered new solutions to existing needs. The role of marketing then was to inform and educate consumers about the new products and services. Since technology was the driving force, much of this marketing was not consumer-centric but rather product-centric, selling products that came from engineering.

Today's brand marketing has reclaimed its consumer focus. The new marketing emphasizes the user experience and the way consumers actually engage with the products, services, and brands. Staying close to the customers and thinking about users, marketers are able to spot not only where new products and services may be needed but also how to design and communicate their offerings. Marketers help consumers expand their horizons; they offer the pleasures of beautiful designs, surprising new capabilities and new ways to simplify and enjoy their lives.

On the upside, the new thinking has led to virtually unimaginable new products and services that have not emerged from formal market research or consumer focus groups. As Steve Jobs, Apple's very successful leader, stated, "It is not the consumers' role to say what they want" (Lohr, 2011). Or, a feature on Barney's upscale clothing store in New York put it this way: "Don't give people what they want—because they don't know what they want" (Horyn, 2012).

On the downside, this slightly patronizing approach has opened up what might be called a Pandora's box of product variety and me-too proliferation, extravagant brand promises, and ever more intrusive brand communications.

From a branding perspective, the important point to remember is that brand promises should be fulfilled. Whether it is the promise of "insanely great products" or the appeal of "brand love," the brand should deliver. Leaving aside the issue of how today's omnipresent and powerful brands affect the social fabric of the society at large, from a management perspective the crucial issue is the actual performance. A strong brand must keep its promises.

KEY TERMS

Brand love, Brand simplicity, City branding, Experiential branding, Minimalist design, Nation branding, Personal branding, Place branding, Service branding, Social currency

DISCUSSION QUESTIONS

1. For your own home country (or some other country you are familiar with), please discuss how it might score on Anholt's six components used for nation branding. How might a brand manager from the country use the nation score for promotional support?

2. What would say your own ideal personal brand should be? Can you deliver on that promise? Why or why not?

3. Try to identify a brand with an identity (or image or personality) that is primarily experiential. Then identify another brand with an identity that is not experiential but basically functional and rational. What are the differences?

4. Brand simplicity goes well with what is called "minimalist" product design. Try to find brand examples where the simplicity and minimalist principle does not seem appropriate. What kind of product categories are those—cosmetics, automobiles, leisure wear, and so on? (Remember hedonic vs. utilitarian categories, high vs. low involvement, emotional vs. rational equity drivers, and so on).

5. China is now starting to export automobiles. Given your knowledge of branding, what will it take for China's automaker brands to be accepted in the West? How long do you think it will take?

MINICASE: IS THE EGYPT BRAND DAMAGED?

Egypt is a country with 80 million people, the largest Arab country in the Middle East and Northern Africa. It is predominantly Sunni Muslim. In 2012, after the "Arab Spring" revolution, a democratic election placed the Muslim Brotherhood party in a governing position. However, as the party moved to expand the religious influence, secular forces moved in opposition and a military coup in 2013 deposed the president and installed an interim government.

The economy of Egypt is more diversified than that of most Middle East countries, with strong sectors in tourism, agriculture, industry and services. Egypt is famous for its high quality cotton, and has a well developed energy market based on coal, oil, natural gas, and hydro-electric power. The cultural heritage from Egypt's glorious early history is underpinning a vibrant tourist economy. It is estimated that the tourism sector involves close to 10 million people directly or indirectly, and according to independent studies, about 20% of total foreign earnings come from tourism receipts. Tourism makes up 11.3% of Egypt's gross domestic product. (http://geographyfieldwork.com/TourismDependency.htm).

The Egypt brand has clearly been threatened by the recent political and military upheavals. In 2010, before the revolution, an estimated 14.7 million tourists brought $12.5 billion in revenue. In 2012, Egypt had 11 million tourists bringing $10.5 billion in revenue. Perhaps equally troublesome

(Continued)

(Continued)

for the brand strength, however, is the damage done over the last few years by terrorist groups. After November 1997, when a terrorist group attacked and killed 62 tourists at the famous Luxor temple on the Nile, a peaceful 7-year period followed, restoring tourism. But then, gradually over a 5-year period, terrorists opposing then President Mubarak attacked foreign tourists and others at tourist sites, including kidnappings, hostage-taking and bombings. The turmoil was eventually followed by the Arab Spring pro-democracy revolution.

A recent World Economic Forum report ranked Egypt below countries such as Pakistan, Yemen and Chad for "safety and security." Many travelers are still hesitant about traveling to Egypt, and many travel agents find that the Egypt destination business is very slow. Egypt tourism officials have naturally been very upset about the negative fallout and sometimes unwarranted rumors that has kept foreign visitors away. Pointing out that many other reports consider Egypt relatively safe—"avoid a few areas" is a typical warning—the officials also disseminate endorsements from travelers to minimize the negative fallout.

An NBC report quoted satisfied European tourists. "I can say to anybody, go to Egypt! It's a nice country. There [are] so many things to see," said Dirk Posner, of Leipzig, Germany, while visiting the Egyptian Museum in Cairo. Jaffar and Francoise Bentchikou, from Paris, France, encouraged foreigners to visit. "We saw that the problems were limited to some places so we just try to avoid them," Jaffar said. "[Tourists] have to be conscious of the situation, but for the time being we have seen nothing against tourists especially."

Even though the reality on the ground is more positive than some media reports, what matters is what people believe. As one observer put, it "A brand is nothing more—and nothing less—than the market's perception and the market now equates the Egypt brand with demonstrations and political upheaval" (Nelson, 2011). One certainly would hope that as the reality on the ground becomes more stable, the nation "brand" will be restored to its former glory.

Discussion Questions

1. In terms of Anholt's six characteristics of nation brands (Exports, Governance, Culture, People, Tourism, Immigration), how would you rate the Egypt brand?

2. To what extent is the Egypt brand equity dependent on its neighboring nations and therefore more or less outside of its control?

3. The "tourism" aspects of the brand seem to have been targeted by the terrorists—how serious is this for the nation brand?

4. What would it take for tourism to come back?

Sources

Abawi, A., & Gubash, C. (2013,March 12). Egypt branded more dangerous for tourists than Yemen. *NBC News.* Retrieved from http://worldnews.nbcnews.com/_news/2013/03/12/17285608-egypt-branded-more-dangerous-for-tourists-than-yemen?lite

Kinninmont, J. (2013, July 4). Overthrow of Muslim Brotherhood leader "has international reverberations." *Special to CNN.* Retrieved from http://www.cnn.com/2013/07/04/opinion/egypt-brotherhood-kinninmont/index.html

Nelson, E. (2011, March 9). Egypt: the brand. *Maven Marketing Solutions.* Retrieved from http://www.mavenmarketingsolutions.com/egypt-the-brand/#sthash.ceGN9ilE.dpuf

SUGGESTED PROJECT

Personal Branding Exercise: To those who know you, you are a brand because you have a name and an identity and because they have an image and a personality impression of you. Throughout your life, you have been managing your brand, sometimes more consciously than others. Before gathering any data, answer the following questions:

1. What is your identity?

2. What would you like your image to be 1 year from now?

3. How would you like people to perceive your personality 1 year from now?

Now ask some of your friends or peers to write down the first three words that come to mind when they think of you. (Hint: To get the best data possible, you will probably want to ensure that they can do so anonymously. If you can get several of them together at once, you could do this by having everyone present drop three words on three different small pieces of paper into a hat.) Examine the results using the technique presented in Chapter 4's project exercise. Examine how this differs from how you would like to be perceived. Identify two activities you can undertake in the next month to reduce this mismatch. Set a plan to execute these two activities over the next month.

References

Aaker, D. A. (1991). *Managing brand equity.* New York: The Free Press.

Aaker, D. A. (1996). *Building strong brands.* New York: The Free Press.

Aaker, D. A. (2011). *Brand relevance: Making competition irrelevant.* San Francisco: Jossey-Bass.

Aaker, D. A., & Keller, K. L. (1990). Consumer evaluations of brand extensions. *Journal of Marketing, 54*(1), 27–41.

Aaker, J. L. (1997). Dimensions of brand personality. *Journal of Marketing Research, 34*(3), 347–356.

Aaker, J. L. (1999). The malleable self: The role of self-expression in persuasion. *Journal of Marketing Research, 36*(1), 45–57.

Adamson, A. P. (2006). *Brand simple.* New York: Palgrave Macmillan.

Alden, D. L., Steenkamp, J.-B. E. M., & Batra, R. (1999). Brand positioning through advertising in Asia, North America and Europe: The role of global consumer culture. *Journal of Marketing, 63*(1), 75–87.

Anholt, S. (2003). *Brand new justice: The upside of global branding.* Oxford, UK: Butterman and Heinemann.

Anholt, S. (2011). *Beyond the nation brand: The role of image and identity in international relations.* Retrieved from www.exchangediplomacy.com/wp-content/uploads/2011/10/1

Ansoff, H. I. (1965). *Corporate strategy.* New York: McGraw-Hill.

Badenhausen, Kurt (2012, October 22). Apple tops list of the world's most powerful brands. *Forbes.*

Bain, J. S. (1956). *Barriers to new competition.* Cambridge, MA: Harvard University Press.

Bajaj, V. (2012, August 30). Tata Motors finds success in Jaguar Land Rover. *The New York Times.*

Baker, J. (2012, December 1). Bookmarks: Angry Jackson fans attack Untouchable. *The Oregonian.*

Baker, S. (2013, January 6). Can social media sell soap? *The New York Times* [Sunday Review], p. 1.

Barber, B. R. (1995). *Jihad vs. McWorld.* New York: Ballantine Books.

Bartlett, C. A., & Lightfoot, R. W. (1993). *Phil Knight managing Nike's transformation* (Case No. 9-394-012). Cambridge, MA: Harvard Business School.

Batra, R., Ahuvia, A., & Bagozzi, R. P. (2012). Brand love. *Journal of Marketing, 76*(2), 1–16.

Batra, R., Ramaswamy, V., Alden, D. L., Steenkamp, J.-B. E. M., & Ramachander, S. (2000). Effects of brand local and nonlocal origin on consumer attitudes in developing countries. *Journal of Consumer Psychology, 9*(2), 83–95.

Batra, R., & Sinha, I. (2000). Consumer-level factors moderating the success of private label brands. *Journal of Retailing, 76*(2), 175–191.

Bauer, R. A. (1960). Consumer behavior as risk taking. In R. S. Hancock (Ed.), *Dynamic marketing for a changing world.* Chicago: American Marketing Association.

Beale, J. (1999, June 14). *Belgium bans Coca-Cola.* Retrieved from http://news.bbc.co.uk

Beamish, P. W., & Goerzen, A. (2000). *The global branding of Stella Artois* (Case No. 900A19-PDF-ENG). Cambridge, MA: Harvard Business School.

Belk, R. W. (1988). Possessions and the extended self. *Journal of Consumer Research, 2,* 139–168.

Best Practices. (2012, January 24). *Expanding a product portfolio without cannibalizing an established brand: Report summary.* (http://www.slideshare.net/bestpracticesllc/expanding-a-product-portfolio-without-cannibalizing-an-established-brand-report-summary)

Bitner, M. J. (1992). Servicescapes: The impact of physical surroundings on customers and employees. *Journal of Marketing, 56*(2), 57–71.

Blattberg, R. C., & Deighton, J. (1996). Manage marketing by the customer equity test. *Harvard Business Review, 74*(4), 136–144.

Bonawitz, D. (2001, May). *Honda: The power of dreams*. Presentation at the Workshop on Global Brands, McDonough School of Business, Georgetown University, Washington, DC.

Boulding, W., Staelin, R., Ehret, M., & Johnston, W. J. (2005). A customer relationship management roadmap: What is known, potential pitfalls, and where to go. *Journal of Marketing, 69*(4), 155–166.

Brady, S. (2010, September 13). UPS no longer cares what brown can do for you. *Brand Channel*. Retrieved from http://www.brandchannel.com/home/post/2010/09/13/UPS-New-Global-Campaign.aspx

Branson, R. (2009). *Virgin entrepreneur*. Retrieved from http://www.success.com/articles/712-richard-branson-virgin-entrepreneur

Brodesser-akner, C. (2008, November 8). Coke, Mercedes avoid gritty film cameos. *Advertising Age*. Retrieved from www.adage.com

Broniarczyk, S. M., & Alba, J. W. (1994). The importance of the brand in brand extension. *Journal of Marketing Research, 31*(2), 214–228.

Bruno, K. (2010, July 15). Old Spice mixes social media and web ads. *Advertising*. Retrieved from www.forbes.com

Brush, M. (2012, July 3). Why Burger King is no Big Mac. Retrieved from http://money.msn.com

Burrows, P., & Fixmer, A. (2012, May 10). Apple, the other cult in Hollywood. *Bloomberg Businessweek—Technology*. Retrieved from www.businessweek.com

Cammisa, J. (2013, May 27). Mercedes-Benz 190E 2.3-16 vs. BMW M3. *Motor Trend*. Retrieved from http://www.motortrend.com/classic/roadtests/13q1_mercedes_benz_190e_vs_bmw_m3/viewall.html#ixzz2bgrRpukw

Capon, N., with J. Mac Hulbert, J. (2007). *Managing marketing in the 21st century*. Bronxville, NY: Wessex Press.

Carducci, E., Horikawa, A., & Montgomery, D. (1994). *Levi Strauss Japan K.K.* (Case M-276). Stanford, CA: Stanford Graduate School of Business.

Castaldo, S., Perrini, F., Misani, N., & Tencati, A. (2008). The missing link between corporate social responsibility and consumer trust: The case of fair trade products." *Journal of Business Ethics, 84*(1), 1–15.

Chailan, C. (2008). Brands portfolios and competitive advantage: An empirical study. *Journal of Product & Brand Management, 17*(4), 254–264.

Chattopadhyay, A., Batra, R., & Özsomer, A. (2012). *The new emerging market multinationals*. New York: McGraw-Hill.

Cheng, R. (2012, June 14). 5 blunders that put Nokia in the hot seat. *CNET*. Retrieved from http://news.cnet.com

Chernev, A., Hamilton, R., & Gal, D. (2011). Competing for consumer identity: Limits to self-expression and the perils of lifestyle branding. *Journal of Marketing, 75*(3), 66–82.

Choi, C. (2012, March 23). Store-brand groceries now on premium shelves. *USA Today*.

Chow, J. (2011, January 14). At LV, this year's man is Chinese. *The Wall Street Journal: Life & Style*.

Claeys, C., Swinnen, A., & Vanden Abeele, P. (1995). Consumer's means-end chains for "think" and "feel" products. *International Journal of Research in Marketing, 12*(3), 193–208.

Cohen, J. B., & Houston, M. J. (1972). Cognitive consequences of brand loyalty. *Journal of Marketing Research, 9*(1), 97–99.

Collins, G. (1995, April 11). Ten years later, Coca-Cola laughs at "New Coke." *New York Times*.

Cunningham, S. M. (1967). The major dimensions of perceived risk. In D. F. Cox (Ed.), *Risk taking and information handling in consumer behavior*. pp. 82–108. Cambridge, MA: Harvard University Press.

De Pelsmacker, P., Driesen, L., & Rayp, G. (2006). Do consumers care about ethics? Willingness to pay for Fair-Trade coffee. *Journal of Consumer Affairs, 39*(2), 363–385.

Dimofte, C. W., Johansson, J. K., & Bagozzi, R. P. (2010). Global brands in the United States: How consumer ethnicity mediates the global brand effect. *Journal of International Marketing, 18*(3), 81–106.

Dimofte, C. W., Johansson, J. K., & Ronkainen, I. A. (2008). Cognitive and affective reactions of American consumers to global brands. *Journal of International Marketing, 16*(4), 115–137.

Dolan, R. J., & Fournier, S. M. (2002). *Launching the BMW Z3 roadster* (Case No. 597-002). Cambridge, MA: Harvard Business School.

Drivas, P. (2011, September 6). Glenn Beck's Obama "racist" comments cost him advertisers. *Huffington Post.* Retrieved from www.huffingtonpost.com

Dumaine, B. (1989, November 6). P&G Rewrites the Marketing Rules. *Fortune.* Retrieved from http://money.cnn.com

Duncan, T., & Moriarty, S. (1997). *Driving brand value.* New York: McGraw-Hill.

Edmondson, G. (2007, September 14). Skoda: Volkswagen's Hot Growth Engine. *Bloomberg Businessweek.* Retrieved from www.businessweek.com

Erdem, T., & Swait, J. (2001). Brand equity as a signaling phenomenon. *Journal of Consumer Psychology, 7*(2), 131–157.

Farber, D. (2012). The logic of Apple's premium-priced iPad mini. Retrieved from http://news.cnet.com

Fields, G. (1988). The Japanese market culture. *The Japan Times.*

Finland. (2010). *Mission for Finland Branding Report.* Retrieved from http://5000plus.net.au/assets/e255ea20503237ca10715157cfcd4e22207dc601/mission-for-finland-branding-report.pdf

Fischer, M., Voelckner, F., & Sattler, H. (2010). How important are brands? A cross-category, cross-country study. *Journal of Marketing Research, 47*(5), 823–839.

Fournier, S. (1998). Consumers and their brands: Developing relationship theory in consumer research. *Journal of Consumer Research, 24*(4), 343–373.

Fournier, S., Sensper, S., McAlexander, J., & Schouten, J. (2000). Building brand community on the Harley-Davidson Posse Ride. Harvard Business Publishing for Educators. Retrieved from http://cb.hbsp.harvard.edu/cb/web/product_detail.seam?E=28677&R=501009-MMC-ENG&conversationId=196263

Gerzema, J., & Lebar, E. (2008). *The brand bubble.* San Francisco: Jossey-Bass.

Glionna, J. M. (2009, May 3). How about, "South Korea: Way better than you think it is"? *Los Angeles Times.* Retrieved from http://articles.latimes.com/2009/may/03/world/fg-korea-brand3

Greyser, S. A. (2008, August 6). The three levels of branding at Beijing. *HBR Blog Network.*

Grossman, R. P. (1997). Co-branding in advertising. *Journal of Product and Brand Management, 6*(3), 191–201.

Gupta, S., Hanssens, D., Hardie, B., Kahn, W., Kumar, V., Lin, N., et al. (2006). Modeling customer lifetime value. *Journal of Service Research, 9*(2), 139–155.

Hamel, I. (2006, August 3). Fair Trade firm accused of foul play. *Swissinfo.* Retrieved from http://www.swissinfo.ch/eng/Fair_trade_firm_accused_of_foul_play.html?cid=5351232

Hansen, S. (2012, November 9). How Zara grew into the world's largest fashion retailer. *The New York Times Magazine.*

Hartmann, C. (2001). Endorsement branding: The endorser's promise endorses the product brands' promises. *Electrolux Corporate Communications Centre.*

Hayashi, J., & Fujimura, N. (2009, November 13). Suntory buys Orangina from Blackstone, Lion Capital. *Bloomberg.* Retrieved from www.bloomberg.com

Hays, C. L. (1999, April 10). Coca-Cola bid for Orangina rebuffed by French court. *The New York Times.*

Hill, S., & Lederer, C. (2001). *The infinite asset: Managing brands to build new value.* Cambridge, MA: Harvard Business School Press.

Hirsch, J. (2012, October 18). Toyota Prius is best-selling car in California; domestics lag. *LA Times.*

Hoch, S. J. (1996). How should national brands think about private labels? *Sloan Management Review, 37*(2), 89–102.

Hollis, N. (2008). *The global brand.* New York: Palgrave Macmillan.

Holt, D. B. (2004). *How brands become icons*. Boston: Harvard Business School Press.

Holt, D. B., Quelch, J. A., & Taylor, E. L. (2004). How global brands compete. *Harvard Business Review, 82*(9), 68–81.

Horyn, C. (2012, December 30). What's a store for? *New York Times Magazine*, p. MM30

Huber, J., & Holbrook, M. B. (1979). Using attribute ratings for product positioning: Some distinctions among compositional approaches. *Journal of Marketing Research, 16*(4), 507–516.

IPCN News. (2011). China to join top three global ad markets in 2012. Retrieved from http://www.ipcn .co.uk/news/entry/china_to_join_top_three_global_ad_markets_in_2012_warc

Insites Consulting. (2009). *Even better than the Real Thing: Understanding Generation Y's definition of "authenticity" for the Levi's brand. IS-2009-005*. Retrieved from www.insites.eu.

Joachimsthaler, E. (2007). *Hidden in plain sight. How to find and execute your company's next big growth strategy*. Boston: Harvard Business School Press.

Johansson, J. K. (2012). The promises of global brands: Market shares in major countries 2000–2009. In S. C. Jain & D. A. Griffith, *Handbook of research in international marketing* (2nd ed. pp. 20–47.). Northampton, MA: Edward Elgar Publishing.

Johansson, J. K., Dimofte, C. V., & Mazvancheryl, S. K. (2012). The performance of global brands in the 2008 financial crisis: A test of two brand value measures. *International Journal of Research in Marketing, 29*(3), 235–245.

Johansson, J. K., & Nonaka, I. (1996). *Relentless: The Japanese way of marketing*. New York: HarperBusiness.

Kapferer, J.-N. (2004). *The new strategic brand management*. London: Kogan Page.

Kapferer, J.-N. (2013, March). Why luxury should not delocalize: A critique of a growing tendency. *The European Business Review*.

Kapoor, J. (2010). *Twenty-four brand mantras*. Thousand Oaks, CA: Sage.

Kashani, K. (2003). *Make yourself heard: Ericsson's global brand campaign* (Case No. IMD040-PDF-ENG). Cambridge, MA: Harvard Business School.

Katz, E., & Lazarsfeld, P. (2005). *Personal influence: The part played by people in the flow of mass communications*. New York: Transaction Publishers.

Kelbie, P. (2004, September 11). Burberry checks out of baseball caps to deter hooligan fans. *The Independent*. Retrieved from www.independent.co.uk

Keller, K. L. (1999). Brand mantras: Rationale, criteria and examples. *Journal of Marketing Management, 15*(1–3), 43–51.

Keller, K. L. (2001). Building customer-based brand equity: A blueprint for creating strong brands. *MSI Working Paper*, Report no. 01-107.

Keller, K. L. (2008). *Brand planning*. Wilmington, DE: Shoulders of Giants.

Keller, K. L. (2013). *Strategic brand management* (4th ed.). Boston: Pearson.

Kelsey, E. (2010, July 29). Endangered species: East German trabants heading for extinction. *Spiegel Online*.

Kim, C. W., & Mauborgne, R. (2005). *Blue ocean strategy: How to create uncontested market space and make the competition irrelevant*. Boston: Harvard Business School Press.

Klein, J., & Dawar, N. (2004). Corporate social responsibility and consumers' attributions and brand evaluations in a product–harm crisis. *International Journal of Research in Marketing, 21*(3), 203–217.

Klein, N. (2000). *No logo: No space, no choice, no jobs*. London: Flamingo.

Klink, R. R., & Smith, D. C. (2001). Threats to the external validity of brand extension research. *Journal of Marketing Research, 38*(3), 326–335.

Kotler, P. (1973). Atmospherics as a marketing tool. *Journal of Retailing, 49*, 48–64.

Kotler, P., & Keller, K. L. (2012). *Marketing management* (14th ed.). Upper Saddle River, NJ: Prentice Hall.

Kowitt, B. (2009, December 15). Let's hear it for hipster beer. *CNN Money*. Retrieved from www.money .cnn.com

Krippendorff, K. (2010, June 17). Building a brand: Aflac takes a gamble on a long-term strategy. *FastCompany.com*. (http://www.kaihan.net/Kaihansfastcompanycompleteblogsfor2010.pdf)

Kumar, N., & Steenkamp, J.-B. E. M. (2007). *Private label strategy: How to meet the store brand challenge.* Boston: Harvard Business Review Press.

Kurien, A., & Nanji, E. (2009, August 19). Thums Up, the most successful campaign we created. *The Economic Times of India.*

Lau, M. (2012, April 30). "Coca-Cola apologises for contaminated drinks," *South China Morning Post.* Retrieved from

Lendon, B., & Simon, M. (2008, July 14). Foreign-owned Bud a wound to Americana. *CNN.* Retrieved from http://articles.cnn.com/

Leonard, C., & Fredrix, E. (2008, July 14). InBev snags Anheuser-Busch and its marketing clout. *USA Today.*

Levere, J. L. (2012, February 26). A campaign from Jaguar to show its wild side. *The New York Times.* Retrieved from www.nytimes.com

Levitt, T. (1983, May–June). The globalization of markets. *Harvard Business Review,* pp. 61, 92–102.

Lindemann, J. (2004). Brand valuation. In R. Clifton & J. Simmons, *Brands and branding* (pp. 27–45). New York: Bloomberg Press.

Linn, A. (2008, July 2). Starbucks to close 600 stores in the U.S. Retrieved from www.msnbc.msn.com

Linzmayer, O. W. (2004). *Apple confidential 2.0: The definitive history of the world's most colorful company.* San Francisco, CA: No Starch Press.

Lohr, S. (2011, August 11). Without its master of design, Apple will face many challenges. *The New York Times,* p. B1.

Lomax, W., Hammond, K., East, R., & Clemente, M. (1997). The measurement of cannibalization. *Journal of Product & Brand Management, 6*(1), 27–39.

Lubin, G. (2011). GOLDMAN: We could be due for another "Marlboro Friday." Retrieved from www.businessinsider.com

Mackey, J., & Sisodia, R. (2013). *Conscious capitalism: Liberating the heroic spirit of business.* Boston: Harvard Business Review Press.

Marketing Science Institute. (2013) June. *Beyond the product: Designing customer experiences.* Presented by Iñigo Gallo and Jolie Matthews with mediaX at Stanford University, Stanford, CA.

Marks, J. (2012, November 9). *Samsung Galaxy SIII blows iPhone sales out of the water.* Examiner.com

Marrs, M. (2012, February 14). The first step to building your personal brand. *Forbeswoman.* Retrieved from www.forbes.com

Martin, A. (2011, April 5). Once a great flop, now sold for billions. *The New York Times.*

McKee, S. (2009, July 10). The pros and cons of co-branding. *Bloomberg Businessweek.*

McLuhan, M. (1994). *Understanding media.* Cambridge, MA: The MIT Press.

Milberg, S. J., Park, C. W., & McCarthy, M. S. (1997). Managing negative feedback effects associated with brand extensions: The impact of alternative branding strategies. *Journal of Consumer Psychology, 6*(2), 119–140.

Mizik, N., & Jacobson, R. (2009). Valuing branded businesses. *Journal of Marketing, 73*(6), 137–153.

Mohammed, R. (n.d.). Versioning. *Pricing for Profit.* Retrieved from www.pricingforprofit.com/pricing-explained/versioning.php

Moilanen, T. (2008). *How to brand nations, cities, and destinations. A handbook of place branding.* Basingstoke, UK: Palgrave McMillan.

Mooney, P. (2012, May 24). Pan Am bags are a hit on Fab.com. *Examiner.* Retrieved from www.examiner.com

Morgan, T. (2010, April 2). TV works on the web, but TV advertising won't. *AdAge Digital.*

Morse, K. G. (2001, August 13). The other shoe drops. *SI Vault.* Retrieved from http://sportsillustrated.cnn.com/vault/article/magazine/MAG1023148/index.htm

Most trusted brands 2012. (2012, November 7). *The Economic Times, Brand Equity.*

Muniz, A. M., Jr., & O'Guinn, T. C. (2001). Brand community. *Journal of Consumer Research, 27*(4), 412–432.

Murphy, L. (2013). The fall of buzzmetrics & rise of the new social media analytics MR firm. Retrieved from www.greenbookblog.org.

Nathan, J. (2001). *Sony.* New York: Houghton-Mifflin.

Niemann, G. (2007). *Big brown: The untold story of UPS.* San Francisco: Jossey-Bass.

Normann, R. (1991). *Service management.* New York: Wiley.

Nudd, T. (2013, March 18). Ad of the day: Orangina. *Adweek.* Retrieved from http://www.adweek.com/news/advertising-branding/ad-day-orangina-148022

Okuda, H. (2001, May). *Sony global branding.* Presentation at the Workshop on Global Brands, McDonough School of Business, Georgetown University, Washington, DC.

Özsomer, A. (2012). The interplay between global and local brands: A closer look at perceived brand globalness and local iconness. *Journal of International Marketing, 20*(2), 72–95.

Özsomer, A., & Altaras, S. (2008). Global brand purchase likelihood: A critical synthesis and an integrated conceptual framework. *Journal of International Marketing, 16*(4), 1–28.

Papadopoulos, N. G., & Heslop, L. A. (1993). *Product-country images.* New York: International Business Press.

Park, C. W., Jun, S. Y., & Shocker, A. D. (1996). Composite branding alliances: An investigation of extension and feedback effects. *Journal of Marketing Research, 33,* 453–466.

Paumgarten, N. (2011, February 7). Interesting. *The New Yorker.*

Pechmann, C., & Stewart, D. W. (1990). The effects of comparative advertising on attention, memory, and purchase intentions. *Journal of Consumer Research, 17*(2), 180–191.

Peter, P. J., & Ryan, M. J. (1976). An investigation of perceived risk at the brand level. *Journal of Marketing Research, 13*(2), 184–188.

Peterson, R. A., & Jolibert, A. J. P. (1995). A meta-analysis of country-of-origin effects. *Journal of International Business Studies, 26*(4), 883–900.

Pfeiffer, A. (2011, February 21). Lost in traduction. *Le Figaro.* Retrieved from http://plus.lefigaro.fr

Plummer, J. T. (1984). How personality makes a difference. *Journal of Advertising Research, 24*(6), 27–31.

Podorowsky, G. (2001, May). *Sony Brand presentation.* Presentation at the Workshop on Global Brands, McDonough School of Business, Georgetown University, Washington, DC.

Porter, M. E. (1980). *Competitive strategy.* New York: The Free Press.

Porter, M. E. (1996, November–December). What is strategy? *Harvard Business Review*, pp. 61–78.

Poses, J., & Aaker, J. (2010). *The Pepsi Refresh Project: Social minded, social media on a new scale.* Stanford, CA: Stanford Graduate School of Business Case.

Prahalad, C. K. (2005). *The fortune at the bottom of the pyramid.* Upper Saddle River, NJ: Wharton School Publishing.

Procter & Gamble. (2011). *2011 Annual report: Innovating for everyday life.* Retrieved from www.pg.com/en_US/downloads/investors/annual_reports/2011/PG_2011_AnnualReport.pdf

Quelch, J. A. (1998). *Heineken N.V.: Global branding and advertising* (Case No. 596015-PDF-ENG). Cambridge, MA: Harvard Business School.

Quelch, J. A. (2006). *Lenovo: Building a global brand* (Case No. 507014-PDF-ENG). Cambridge, MA: Harvard Business School.

Quelch, J. A., & Harrington, A. (2008). *Samsung Electronics Co.: Global marketing operations* (Case No. 504051-PDF-ENG). Cambridge, MA: Harvard Business School.

Rao, A. R., Bergen, M. E., & Davis, S. (2000). How to fight a price war. *Harvard Business Review, 78*(2), 107–120.

Reardon, M. (2011, April 13). Why Cisco killed the Flip mini camcorder. *CNET.* Retrieved from http://news.cnet.com

Redding, E. (2012, February 28). Happy birthday Disneyland Paris: 20 years and counting at the resort that survived. *Daily Mail.* Retrieved from www.dailymail.co.uk

Reiss, C. (2010, July 18). Now look here, now learn from this . . . *Entrepreneur.com.* Retrieved from www.nbcnews.com/id/38282026/ns/business-small_business/t/now-look-here-now-learn/#.Ugr1VBaQy-8

Rego, L. L., Billett, M. T., & Morgan, N. A. (2009). Consumer-based brand equity and firm risk. *Journal of Marketing, 73*(6), 47–60.

Reichheld, F. F., & Sasser, W. E., Jr. (1990). Zero defections: quality comes to services. *Harvard Business Review, 68*(5), 105–111.

Reuters. (2007, June 27). *Visa to sponsor 2010 and 2014 World Cup*. Retrieved from www.reuters.com

Ries, A., & Trout, J. (2000). *Positioning: The battle for your mind*. New York: McGraw-Hill.

Ritzer, G. (1993). *The McDonaldization of society*. Thousand Oaks, CA: Pine Forge Press.

Roberts, K. (2005). *Lovemarks: The future beyond brands*. New York: Powerhouse Publishing.

Roedder-John, D., Loken, B., & Joiner, C. (1998). The negative impact of extensions: Can flagship products be diluted? *Journal of Marketing, 62*(1), 19–32.

Ryans, A. (2009). *Beating low cost competition: How premium brands can respond to cut-price rivals*. New York: Wiley.

Salter, J. (2008, August 24). Orangina advert "too sexy." *The Telegraph*. Retrieved from http://www.telegraph.co.uk/news/newstopics/howaboutthat/2612657/Orangina-advert-too-sexy.html

Saporito, B. (1985, December 23). Ganging up on Black and Decker. *Fortune*. Retrieved from www.money.cnn.com

Schmitt, B. H. (1999). *Experiential marketing*. New York: The Free Press.

Schmitt, B. H., with G. Van Zutphen. (2012). *Happy customers everywhere*. New York: Palgrave Macmillan.

Schuiling, I., & Kapferer, J.-N. (2004). Executive insights: Real differences between local and international brands: Strategic implications for international marketers. *Journal of International Marketing, 12*(4), 97–112.

Scott, D. M. (2010). *The new rules of marketing & PR* (2nd ed.). Hoboken, NJ: Wiley.

Sengupta, S. (2013, January 16). Facebook announces a way to search its trove of information. *The New York Times* [Business Day], pp. B1, B4.

Sheth, J., & Sisodia, R. (2002). *The rule of three*. New York: The Free Press.

Schwartz McDonald, S. (1990, February). *Brand equity: Working toward a disciplined methodology for measurement*. Presentation at the 2nd Annual Advertising Research Foundation Advertising and Promotion Workshop, New York.

Sen, S., & Bhattacharya, C. B. (2001). Does doing good always lead to doing better? Consumer reactions to corporate social responsibility. *Journal of Marketing Research, 38*(2), 225–243.

Sharp, B. (2010). *How brands grow*. Oxford, UK: Oxford University Press.

Sharp, B., & Romaniuk, J. (2007). There is a Pareto law—but not as you know it. *Report 42 for Corporate Sponsors*. Adelaide: Ehrenberg-Bass Institute for Marketing Science.

Siegel + Gale. (2012). *Global Brand Simplicity Index 2012*. Retrieved from www.siegelgale.com

Sloan, A. P. (1965). *My years with General Motors*. New York: MacFadden Books.

Sreejesh. S. (2012). Consumers' evaluation of co-brand extensions: The effects of concept congruity on the evaluation of co-branded products, analyzing the moderating role of task involvement. *International Management Review, 8*(1), 21–31.

Srinivasan, S. R., & Hanssens, D. M. (2009). Marketing and firm value: Metrics, methods, findings, and future directions. *Journal of Marketing Research, 46*(3), 293–312.

Srinivasan, S. R., Ramakrishnan, S., & Grasman, S. E. (2005). Identifying the effects of cannibalization on the product portfolio. *Marketing Intelligence & Planning, 23*(4), 359–371.

Steenkamp, J.-B. E. M., Batra, R., & Alden, D. L. (2003). How perceived brand globalness creates brand value. *Journal of International Business Studies, 34*(1), 53–65.

Strauss, S. D. (2012, July). A big risk for a big payoff; Corner office: Vizio's William Wang. *Success Magazine*. (http://www.success.com/article/corner-office-vizios-william-wang)

Sujan, M., & Bettman, J. R. (1989). The effects of brand positioning strategies on consumers' brand and category perceptions: Some insights from schema research. *Journal of Marketing Research, 26*(4), 454–467.

Tabuchi, H. (2012, April 14). How the tech parade passed Sony by. *The New York Times*, p. B1.

Tait, B. (2001, June). Do gaps in marketing theory make new brands fail? *Admap*. Retrieved from http://taitsubler.com/articles/

Tart, N. (2011, August 29). *25 fascinating stories behind your favorite brand names.* 14Clicks.com.

TerraChoice. (2007, November). The "six sins of greenwashing" study. *TerraChoice Environmental Marketing Inc.* Retrieved from www.terrachoice.com

Thompson, D. V., Hamilton, R. W., & Rust, R. (2005). Feature fatigue: When product capabilities become too much of a good thing. *Journal of Marketing Research, 42*(4), 431–442.

Toren, B. (2012, July 20). 8 apparel mistakes. *Fortune Magazine.* Retrieved from http://money.cnn.com

Truong, Y., McColl, R., & Kitchen, P. J. (2009). New luxury brand positioning and the emergence of *Masstige* brands. *Journal of Brand Management, 16,* 375–382.

Trusted brands 2013. (2013). *Reader's Digest.* Retrieved from www.rdtrustedbrands.com.

Tylee, J. (2003). Wolff Olins' D&AD award reflects shift in ad industry. *Campaign.* Retrieved from www .campaignlive.co.uk

Urban, G. L. (1975). Perceptor: A model for product positioning. *Management Science, 21,* 858–871.

Vanderbilt, T. (2010, January 15). Was the Yugo Really the Worst Car Ever? *Slate.com.* (http://www.slate .com/articles/life/transport/2010/01/was_the_yugo_really_the_worst_car_ever.html)

Vega, T. (2013, April 8). Sponsoring articles, not just ads. *The New York Times,* p. B1.

Verganti, R. (2009). *Design-driven innovation: Changing the rules of competition by radically innovating what things mean.* Boston: Harvard Business School Press.

Vergara, A. Y. (2012, July 6). Bulgari updates ancient coin collection—The only luxury brand with these relics. *Philippine Daily Inquirer.* Retrieved from http://lifestyle.inquirer.net/55883/bulgari-updates-ancient-coin-collection–the-only-luxury-brand-with-these-relics

Vivaldi Partners. (2013). *Social currency impact study. The top 25 list.* New York: Author.

Völckner, F., & Sattler, H. (2006). Drivers of brand extension success. *Journal of Marketing, 70*(2), 18–34.

Walker, R. (2003, November 30). The guts of a new machine. *The New York Times Magazine.*

Wang, H. H. (2012). Five things Starbucks did to get China right. *Forbes: Business.*

Warman, M. (2013, January 15). Dieter Rams: Apple has achieved something I never did. *The Daily Telegraph.* Retrieved from www.telegraph.co.uk

Weaver, C. (2012). A menu for success in Russia. *Financial Times, Management,* p. 1.

Weber, J. (2013). *How to create your personal brand in 6 easy steps.* Retrieved from www.pickthebrain.com

The Week. (2011, May 5). Retrieved from http://theweek.com/article/index/214924/james-bonds-record-shattering-product-placement-by-the-numbers

Whitla, P. (2009). Crowdsourcing and its application in marketing activities. *Contemporary Management Research, 5*(1), 15–28.

Wong, E. (2010, December 12). The most memorable product launches of 2010. *Forbes.com. (http:// www.forbes.com/sites/marketshare/2010/12/05/how-to-start-a-successful-ad-agency/)*

Wood, C. (2011). Honda to stay the course on design says U.S. boss. *AutoGuide.com.* Retrieved from www.autoguide.com

Wooten, D. B., & Reed, A., II. (2004). Playing it safe: Susceptibility to normative influence and protective self-presentation. *Journal of Consumer Research, 31*(3), 551–556.

Xing, W. (2009, January 19). *Lenovo reboots again for 2010.* Retrieved from www.chinadaily.com

Yalch, R. F. (1991). Memory in a jingle jungle: Music as a mnemonic device in communicating advertising slogans. *Journal of Applied Psychology, 76*(2), 268–275.

Yip, G. (2002). *Total Global Strategy II.* Englewood Cliffs, NJ: Prentice Hall.

Yip, G. (2007). Global strategy as a factor in Japanese success. *The International Executive, 38,* 145–167.

Zaltman, G. (2003). *How customers think.* Boston: Harvard Business School Press.

Zhang, S., & Schmitt, B. H. (2001). Creating local brands in multilingual international markets. *Journal of Marketing Research, 38*(3), 313–325.

Zmuda, N. (2010, February 8). Pass or fail, Pepsi's Refresh will be case for marketing textbooks. *AdAge Digital.* Retrieved from http://adage.com

Index

About the Authors

Johny K. Johansson Professor Johansson has published more than 70 academic articles and chapters in books. His main teaching and research focus is on global brands and marketing strategy. He has consulted with companies around the world, including Standard Oil of Indiana, General Electric and Xerox in the United States; Beiersdorf, Volvo, and Ford in Europe; and Honda, Mazda and Fuji Film in Japan. He has also conducted seminars at academic institutions, including Stanford, M.I.T., and Columbia University in the United States, INSEAD in France, Vienna's Neue Wirtschaftsuniversitat, and Hitotsubashi, Kobe and NagoyaUniversities in Japan. He is a Fellow of the Academy of International Business. In 2010 Professor Johansson received a Lifetime Award for Contributions to Global Marketing from the American Marketing Association. Professor Johansson is the author of *Global Marketing, In Your Face: How American Marketing Excess Fuels Anti-Americanism,* and co-author of *Relentless: The Japanese Way of Marketing.*

Kurt A. Carlson Professor Carlson's teaching and research involve the marketing management implications of consumer decision-making processes. His research has been published in several top journals in marketing, psychology, and management. From 2001 to 2009 he was on the faculty at Duke University. Professor Carlson has published extensively on the topic of the development of brand preferences and the influence of emerging brand preferences on the decision-making process. Though much of his research explores consumer decision making, he also studies how voters, jurors, and managers make decisions. He has consulted for the Wisconsin Center for Dairy Research and Wisconsin Milk Marketing Board. Dr. Carlson teaches courses on Analytical Problem Solving, Market Intelligence, Consumer Behavior, and Marketing Management. Professor Carlson is the Director of the Georgetown Institute for Consumer Research sponsored by KPMG and co-director of the McDonough School of Business Behavioral Research Lab.

⑤SAGE research**methods**

The essential online tool for researchers from the world's
leading methods publisher

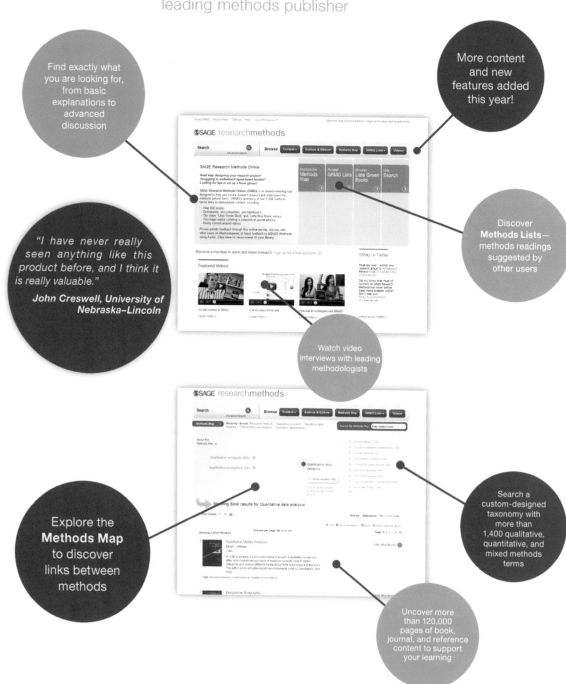

Find exactly what
you are looking for,
from basic
explanations to
advanced
discussion

More content
and new
features added
this year!

Discover
Methods Lists—
methods readings
suggested by
other users

*"I have never really
seen anything like this
product before, and I think it
is really valuable."*

**John Creswell, University of
Nebraska–Lincoln**

Watch video
interviews with leading
methodologists

Explore the
Methods Map
to discover
links between
methods

Search a
custom-designed
taxonomy with
more than
1,400 qualitative,
quantitative, and
mixed methods
terms

Uncover more
than 120,000
pages of book,
journal, and reference
content to support
your learning

Find out more at
www.sageresearchmethods.com